P9-CMK-870

ALSO BY MICHAEL CHABON AND AYELET WALDMAN

Kingdom of Olives and Ash

FIGHT
of the
CENTURY

Writers Reflect on 100 Years of Landmark ACLU Cases

EDITED BY

MICHAEL CHABON

& AYELET WALDMAN

AVID READER PRESS

New York London Toronto Sydney New Delhi

Avid Reader Press
An Imprint of Simon & Schuster, Inc.
1230 Avenue of the Americas
New York, NY 10020

Copyright credits continued on pages 303–305

First Avid Reader Press hardcover edition January 2020

Interior design by Kyle Kabel

Manufactured in the United States of America

1 3 5 7 9 10 8 6 4 2

Library of Congress Cataloging-in-Publication Data is available.

ISBN 978-1-5011-9040-7
ISBN 978-1-5011-9042-1 (ebook)

To the ACLU's clients, who for over 100 years have refused to accept injustice and have chosen to fight for civil liberties and civil rights

Contents

Introduction

MICHAEL CHABON AND AYELET WALDMAN

Every year the moon is struck, and its cratered face forever marred, by tens of thousands of asteroids and meteors. At least that many bodies rain down on Earth over the same period, and yet the Earth has very few craters and endures only a handful of relatively insignificant impact events every year. The difference, of course, is that unlike the moon, the Earth is blessed with and enveloped by an atmosphere that constantly shields it from attack. The Bill of Rights serves a similar protective function for individual Americans and their civil liberties, which, like the Earth, are and have always been under constant, relentless attack. From *Plessy v. Ferguson* in 1896 to *Trump v. Hawaii* in 2018, our federal and state governments—often abetted by the courts—have sought to curtail, constrain, and infringe on the rights defined and enshrined in James Madison's remarkable document. The protections of liberty and equality it guarantees have always been menaced by the overweening instruments of state and majoritarian power. But lately, as in some science-fiction thriller where the Earth is threatened by a monstrous, meteor-spewing aberration in space-time, the rate and intensity of those attacks seem to be increasing. Meanwhile, agents of the government are at work doing what they can to dilute and undermine both our protective atmosphere and people's belief in its integrity.

Things, we feel, have been getting worse. Liberty and equality are everywhere under attack. And that's why the work of the American Civil Liberties Union feels more precious to us than ever before. The ACLU lawyers and staff are the brave souls who suit up, blast off, and do what they can to divert and repel all those incoming meteors, or blow them right out of the sky. We admire them. We admire them the way you must admire people who devote themselves to doing, to the utmost of their ability, any thankless, impossible, and absolutely essential job.

Liberty and justice for all. We used to stand up with our classmates every morning and timelessly pledge liberty and justice for all, even and especially for those (as the Supreme Court, agreeing with the ACLU, ruled in *West Virginia State Board of Education v. Barnette*) whose consciences rebel at being compelled to pledge allegiance to a flag or to a country "under God." The Bill of Rights protects pledgers and nonpledgers alike, but of course it is only the nonpledgers—the contrarians, the cranks, the nonconformists, the radicals and fanatics, the outsiders and the ostracized, the powerless and unpopular and imprisoned—who ever really need its protections. They also tend to be the ones least likely to receive those protections—not without a fight, anyway. That's where the ACLU comes in.

The history of the ACLU is one of struggle, combat, of marginalized people and unpopular causes, of troublemakers and conscientious objectors, a history of battle and strife. But it is also the history of the very best our country has to offer to its citizens and, by way of example, to the rest of the world: the strong, golden strand of the Bill of Rights and the ideals it embodies, often frayed, occasionally snarled, stretched at times to the breaking point, but shining and unbroken down all the years since 1789. The ACLU holds the government, the courts, and the nation to their avowed and highest standard, insisting on the recognition of the protections the Constitution affords to every American, no matter how marginalized, no matter how unpopular the cause, even if the people it protects sometimes despise the freedom it represents.

As American Jews in our fifties, we both remember, powerfully, the moment we each first understood the austere and lonely fight of the ACLU, the thankless road to freedom on which it plies its trade. It was 1977, when the ACLU took on the case of the local branch of the American National Socialist Party, whose members wanted to hold a march along the main street of Skokie, a predominantly Jewish suburb outside Chicago. We remember wrestling with the difficult idea that the ACLU could be on the side of good (the First Amendment) and evil

(Nazis) at the same time. To understand the vital role that the ACLU plays in American society requires a nuanced understanding of the absolute value of freedom of speech, freedom of assembly, freedom from unwarranted search and seizure, of the right to due process and equal justice under the law, even—again, especially—when those rights protect people we find abhorrent or speech that offends us.

Nuance unfortunately seems to be in very short supply nowadays. In these pages, we have collected essays by some of our country's finest writers—not just because writers are and have long been among the principal beneficiaries and guardians of the First Amendment but also because they traffic, by temperament and trade, in nuance and its elucidation, in ambiguity and shades of gray. We turn to writers, here and in general, to help us understand and, even more, grasp both ends of ambiguities, to expand the scope of our vision to encompass the whole gray spectrum of human existence, in all its messy human detail.

Each of the writers in this book has chosen a seminal case in which the ACLU was involved, either as counsel or as amicus curiae—friend of the court—and made it the subject of an essay. Some have chosen to dig deep into the facts of the case and bring them vividly to life. Others have focused on their own personal experience with the civil liberty—and its abridgment—at issue by the case. Still others have crafted impassioned pleas on behalf of the rights being challenged or upheld in a particular Supreme Court case or have even, in at least one case, taken a reasoned position opposed to the ACLU's own. Regardless of approach each of the writers has, we hope you will agree, produced something thoughtful, challenging, enlightening, and as worthy of your time as the ACLU is worthy of your support.

Enjoy.

Foreword

DAVID COLE

"The decisions of the courts have nothing to do with justice." So proclaimed Morris Ernst, the ACLU's first general counsel, in 1935. You won't hear that from ACLU attorneys these days. The ACLU has spent the better part of its 100 years seeking justice from the courts—and often getting it. The cases that inspired the essays in this book are only a small selection of the ACLU's victories. Over the course of the ACLU's first century, the courts have recognized substantial safeguards for free speech and free press; protected religious minorities; declared segregation unconstitutional; guaranteed a woman's right to decide when and whether to have children; recognized claims to equal treatment by women, gay men, and lesbians; directed states to provide indigent criminal defendants an attorney at state expense; regulated police searches and interrogations; and insisted on the rights to judicial review of immigrants facing deportation and even foreign "enemy combatants" held at Guantánamo in the war on terror. In thousands of cases brought or supported by the ACLU, the courts have extended the protections of privacy, dignity, autonomy, and equality to an ever-widening group of our fellow human beings. We can expect—and must demand—justice from the courts.

Indeed, within days of the election of Donald Trump, the ACLU told the president-elect, "We'll see you in court," warning him that if he sought to implement the many unconstitutional promises he had made on the campaign trail, we would sue. He lived up to his promises, and so have we. In just the two and a half years since Trump took office, courts have repeatedly ruled against his administration's rights-offending policies. Courts have declared illegal a raft of anti-immigrant initiatives, including separating children from their parents in hopes of deterring refugees from coming to the United States; detaining asylum seekers whether or not they pose any risk of flight or danger; and denying asylum to those who do not enter at a border checkpoint, even though the asylum statute expressly provides relief to all who face persecution at home, regardless of whether they entered the country lawfully or unlawfully. Courts primarily ruled invalid Trump's effort to ban transgender individuals from the military. The Supreme Court blocked the Trump administration's effort to ask about citizenship on the census, a tactic that would have led immigrant families not to fill out the form, causing communities with large immigrant populations to lose their fair share of representation and federal funding. The courts have halted an executive order that would authorize employers to deny contraceptive insurance coverage to their female employees if the employer objects on moral or religious grounds to facilitating such access. They have issued a nationwide injunction against the administration's policy of barring young, undocumented women in federal custody access to abortion. They have stopped en masse deportation of young undocumented immigrants afforded temporary relief from deportation by President Barack Obama under the Deferred Action for Childhood Arrivals (DACA) program. They have stopped the administration from denying federal funds to cities and towns that adopt immigrant-friendly law enforcement policies. The Supreme Court rejected the Trump administration's argument that citizens have no Fourth Amendment right against the government's obtaining around-the-clock records of their whereabouts from their cell phone providers, ruling that the government must obtain a warrant based on probable cause of criminal wrongdoing to seek such information.

We don't always get justice from the courts, of course. After multiple federal courts struck down all three versions of Trump's ban on entry from several predominantly Muslim countries, the Supreme Court in 2018 upheld the third version of the ban by a 5–4 vote along partisan lines. In the same term, the Supreme Court ruled that immigration law permits extended detention of certain immigrants without even a hearing to determine whether they pose a flight risk or danger and that Ohio could strike voters from the rolls for failing to vote in two consecutive elections. And President Trump's two appointments to the Supreme Court are almost certain to make it a less sympathetic forum for civil rights and liberties issues. But thus far, the courts have held off many of the Trump administration's worst initiatives, upholding the rights of millions in the process.

Even a brief review of history demonstrates how far we have come. When the ACLU began in 1920, the Bill of Rights did not apply to state officials at all. It constrained only the federal government. Thus, state police arrests and searches did not violate the Fourth Amendment, no matter how abusive they were, and state legislatures did not violate the First Amendment, even if they directly prohibited unpopular speech. Even as to the federal government, the Bill of Rights offered only limited protections. Speech could be suppressed as long as it had a "bad tendency" to lead to criminal conduct. Under such terms, communists, anarchists, union leaders, and dissidents were targeted and penalized for their political beliefs. Newspapers were not protected from libel suits brought by government officials they had criticized in print. Despite the Fourteenth Amendment's equal protection clause, "separate but equal" was the law of the land. Women could be barred entry into the legal profession on the ground that the entire sex was too sensitive to handle the work. Criminal defendants had no right to the assistance of counsel, and if police gathered evidence illegally, they could use it against the defendant at trial. Practically the only constitutional right the Supreme Court recognized in the 1920s was the right of big businesses not to be subject to laws designed to protect workers and consumers from exploitation. No wonder Morris Ernst expressed such skepticism about the courts.

As the cases discussed in this book illustrate, much has changed in 100 years. While the process has been far from linear, rights have generally expanded, protecting more and more previously unprotected groups, recognizing as discrimination conduct once taken for granted, insisting on fair procedures where previously few rules applied, and expanding the freedoms of free speech and association, the core rights of a democracy. Indeed, the expansion of First Amendment rights has been so considerable that many of the recurring arguments today focus on whether the First Amendment is *too* protected (as Scott

Turow suggests in his essay on campaign finance legislation). It is easy to focus on how far we still have to go, but it is important not to lose sight of how far civil liberties and civil rights have come.

The ACLU has been at the forefront of many of these struggles, but it has by no means acted alone. We have long worked in collaboration with a wide range of individuals and groups from across the political spectrum in defense of liberty. We are nonpartisan and ecumenical; if you support liberty, we are your ally. In some of the cases discussed in this book, the ACLU was lead counsel, and sister organizations supported our work by filing friend-of-the-court, or amicus, briefs. In others, the ACLU appeared as amicus curiae, while others took the lead. Unions played a central part in the initial expansion of First Amendment rights, work that was later joined by civil rights activists and groups, so often the targets of repression for their political views. We have worked with religious groups across the spectrum to defend religious freedom, with libertarians from the left and the right to defend privacy, and with civil rights groups to extend the promise of equality to all. The defense and advance of liberty is a team effort.

It is an honor that so many immensely talented writers have contributed to this book. It is also, in a sense, fitting. Cases are, after all, stories. Although they are about real people and real events, not imagined ones, a lawyer's job is to weave a compelling narrative in the hope of persuading a court that an injustice has been done and that the court has the power to right the wrong—which it does by writing an opinion. The court is invited to provide, if not necessarily a happy ending, at least a just one—one that offers a measure of accountability. A lawsuit essentially asks the judge to finish the story. But, of course, the story is never really done, even after the Supreme Court rules. Just as the characters in novels and short stories generally go on at the story's close to "live happily ever after" or not, so, too, the conclusion of a lawsuit is generally at most the end of a chapter. The parties go on, as do the struggles to make their rights meaningful.

Every case, moreover, is but one part of a larger narrative. *Brown v. Board of Education* declared segregation unconstitutional, but the challenge of ending segregation and achieving integration continues to this day. *Roe v. Wade* protected a woman's right to decide whether to terminate a pregnancy in 1972, but the ACLU and others have been fighting ever since to preserve that protection in the face of repeated attacks. *Gideon v. Wainwright* ruled that poor criminal defendants have the right to the assistance of counsel, but providing meaningful representation to the poor remains elusive because public officials are unwilling to fund such services adequately. The Supreme Court in the 1970s answered Ruth Bader Ginsburg's call, in her capacity as codirector of the ACLU's Women's Rights Project, to recognize that treating people differently on the basis of sex violates the Fourteenth Amendment's equal protection clause. That legal recognition marked a major advance over earlier decisions upholding laws treating women differently because they were considered inherently the weaker sex. But to this day, women are paid less than men; suffer violence and harassment at the hands of male partners, bosses, family members, and acquaintances; and are the subject of discriminatory stereotypes that limit their access to full equality. The Fourth Amendment requires the police to get a warrant from a magistrate based on probable cause of criminal activity in order to search a home, but preserving privacy in the digital age requires constant rethinking and revision of the rules that govern surveillance, as computers, cell phones, and the Internet make feasible forms of mass spying unimaginable to George Orwell in *1984*, much less to the framers in 1789.

Cases, like novels, do not stand alone. They must be understood in context. Just as today's novels must be read against and in relation to the great novels of prior generations, so too cases are just part of a larger campaign for justice, one that occurs in multiple forums outside the Supreme Court, including Congress, the White House, state legislatures and courts, town councils, corporate boardrooms, university campuses, and religious communities. We often focus on an individual lawsuit because it provides a compelling story, but to understand the development of constitutional rights, one must look further. It is no coincidence, for example, that the Supreme Court's most significant expansion of equality rights came during the civil rights movement or that the Court first recognized sex discrimination as a constitutional violation in the midst of feminism's second wave in the 1960s and 1970s. To understand how the right of marriage equality was attained,

Andrew Sean Greer's essay on *United States v. Windsor* points out that one must look beyond the immediate arguments advanced in the Supreme Court to decades of struggle outside the federal courts to advance the basic notion that a human being deserves equal dignity and respect regardless of whether he or she loves someone of the same or a different sex.

All of the essays contained here reflect this insight. Not a single author limits his or her discussion to the legal arguments made in the courtroom. Every writer finds some different way into the subject matter, and that point of entry links the case to a broader context. Many authors find echoes in their personal experiences, whether as a student of color attending a segregated school in Huntsville, Alabama (Yaa Gyasi), a young black woman "loitering" on Easter Sunday in DeLisle, Mississippi (Jesmyn Ward), a gay man marching in New York's Saint Patrick's Day parade (Michael Cunningham), the husband in a mixed marriage driving through Virginia (Aleksandar Hemon), a college student who protested Alexander Haig (Elizabeth Strout), or an author who just likes to use the word *fuck* and appreciates that the Supreme Court has said that he can (Jonathan Lethem). The fact that so many authors understand the cases through their personal experience underscores how deeply these disputes affect us all and how intertwined individual rights and liberties are in the fabric of all of our lives.

One of the benefits of having talented writers, virtually all nonlawyers, write about legal cases is that they are likely to find new ways to describe and represent the issues at hand. I'm quite sure no one has described *Miranda* warnings ("You have the right to remain silent . . .") quite like Hector Tobar: "a civic poem in free verse." Michael Chabon's story of the creative tactics employed by the ACLU's Morris Ernst in challenging the seizure of James Joyce's *Ulysses* as obscene—including ensuring that the case was assigned to a judge "with literary pretensions"—is so engagingly rendered that the movie version feels inevitable. Anthony Doerr's account of the ACLU's successful challenge to an attempt to require the teaching of intelligent design, a form of creationism, in public school, not only captures the drama of the trial and the essence of the legal principles involved, but concludes with an empathetic evocation of the man behind the failed effort to impress intelligent design on the school's students in the first place, one that underscores how closely related we all are, even when we deeply disagree. George Saunders makes a complicated case about federal court jurisdiction over deportation cases into a compelling narrative of the rights of all humans to challenge their detention in a court of law, no matter what their country of origin.

And Moriel Rothman-Zecher concludes his essay on why he believes it was right for a black ACLU lawyer and civil rights activist, Eleanor Holmes Norton, and a Jewish ACLU lawyer, Allen Brown, to represent the leader of the Ku Klux Klan in *Brandenburg v. Ohio*, with an elegant defense of the ACLU's commitment to free speech in the most difficult cases:

> The ideologies of Brandenburg and the tiki torchers [of Charlottesville] are not as divergent from the core ideologies of the American political regime as many think they are. In truth, throughout American history, government suppression of speech and expression has been far more frequently and viciously directed against leftists and radicals, against black militants and Jewish communists, than it has against the various Brandenburgs of this nation. In that light, the Brandenburg case appears as a form of aikido, in which Norton, Brown, and the ACLU harnessed the force of American white supremacism itself as a means of ultimately defending those who would seek to undermine American white supremacism and its American cousins: bigotry, xenophobia, imperialism, and bellicosity. In other words, in challenging the government's right to punish Brandenburg for saying heinous things, a counterintuitive but profound sliver of freedom was wrested from this deeply unfree country. And for that, here in southwest Ohio, I am grateful.

A book about the ACLU would not be a book about the ACLU without some dissent. Discussing *Buckley v. Valeo* and *Citizens United,* Scott Turow, a longtime ACLU member, contributes a spirited critique of the ACLU's position on campaign finance regulation. In Turow's view, unregulated campaign expenditures threaten to undermine democracy itself, and the ACLU's position that the First Amendment restricts such regulation is deeply misguided. For the record, the ACLU's position is not that campaign finance regulation is necessarily unconstitutional, only that the government needs to point to a compelling justification and regulate narrowly, because limiting how much citizens can spend on speech of a particular content necessarily implicates the First Amendment. That said, reasonable people can and do disagree on this—within and beyond the ACLU. But on one thing we insist: we will defend Turow's right to disagree, and indeed proudly include him in our collection precisely because, above all, we cherish the right to dissent. We look forward to fighting for that right for the next 100 years.

FIGHT *of the* CENTURY

STROMBERG V. CALIFORNIA (1931)

In *Stromberg v. California*, the Supreme Court held that the state of California could not prohibit the display of red flags as "a sign, symbol or emblem of opposition to organized government." Writing for the seven-justice majority, Chief Justice Charles E. Hughes relied not on the First Amendment, but rather the Fourteenth Amendment, to rule the statute's ban unconstitutional. Nevertheless, the *Stromberg* decision laid the groundwork for future First Amendment rulings, including another significant ACLU victory, 1989's *Texas v. Johnson*, in which the Supreme Court held that flag burning constituted a form of constitutionally protected political expression.

No More Flags

VIET THANH NGUYEN

Flags are potent symbols. We fly them, we cherish them, we burn them. Some use flags as emblems of free speech and others use them to suppress free speech. Congress has occasionally tried to protect the American flag from being abused, and in 1919, California passed a law banning the public display of red flags. This would eventually lead to *Stromberg v. California*.

In the early twentieth century, the symbolism of red flags was obvious. The Soviet Union's flag was red, and when Americans saw red, they saw communism. Labor unions and the Socialist Party were strong in the United States, but they also faced opponents who saw unionization and socialism as gateways to communism. So when a nineteen-year-old camp teacher flew a red flag at a summer camp for the working class in California, the Better America Foundation (BAF)—whose name foreshadows "Make America Great Again"—took aim at her.

BAF was a "pro-business" organization that aimed to suppress radicalization and communism, opposed labor unions and minimum wage, and advocated for a six-day workweek. In summer 1929, it persuaded the local sheriff to search the Pioneer Summer Camp, a California youth camp for working-class children. They arrested Yetta Stromberg, a teacher and member of the Youth Communist League. Stromberg was charged in relation to a daily ceremony she did with the kids that involved raising a red flag and pledging allegiance to "the workers' red flag, and to the cause for which it stands, one aim throughout our lives, freedom for the working class." Stromberg was convicted, but took her case to the Supreme Court. In 1931, the Court ruled that California's red flag ban was too vague and could be used to disrupt the constitutionally protected rights of dissenters. California repealed the law in 1933.

Being a Vietnamese refugee, I am familiar with bitter controversies over flags, red or otherwise. I was born in the Republic of Vietnam, otherwise known as South Vietnam. Its flag was a field of yellow with three red horizontal stripes. When the South Vietnamese regime was defeated and Saigon fell on April 30, 1975, the victorious North Vietnamese army planted the blue, red, and yellow flag of the National Liberation Front on the roof of Independence Palace in Saigon. The National Liberation Front was the southern guerrilla and political movement that opposed the southern Vietnamese government and its American allies. Some of the NLF's leadership was covertly communist, however, and the NLF's nationalist flag would not fly for long. Soon the country would see only the flag of the Democratic Republic of Vietnam, the north, flying everywhere: a red flag with a yellow star in the center.

The defeated Vietnamese who fled from the south and came to the United States took their yellow flag with them. Here, the flag would come to symbolize everything about the Republic of Vietnam: a lost country from a lost time, a displaced and exiled nation whose citizens were steeped in bitterness, rage, sadness, and melancholy. As a child growing up in San Jose's Vietnamese refugee community, I saw the flag on every occasion the community gathered, carried by veterans who wore combat uniforms.

The anticommunism of Vietnamese refugees was completely aligned with the anticommunism that already ran deep in the United States, especially in California. Here lived the largest populations of Vietnamese refugees, who found sympathy from across the political spectrum for their political views. Conservative Republican support for Vietnamese anticommunism was not a surprise. But Democratic politicians also supported their Vietnamese constituents, and on August 5, 2006, the California legislature passed a bill declaring that the yellow flag of the south would be the Vietnamese Heritage and Freedom Flag of the Vietnamese community and would be displayed at official events in which a flag for Vietnam was called for. A red flag would once again be banned.

In the Vietnamese American community, no one dared to fly the red flag because the punishment from the community would have been immediate. Museums that had exhibited images of Ho Chi Minh and a Vietnamese American businessman who had put Ho Chi Minh's picture in his store window were protested and picketed by vocal Vietnamese activists, sometimes numbering in the hundreds. Free speech hit its limits in the Vietnamese American community around any words, images, or symbols, like the red flag, that invoked communism or could be seen as communist in any way. Even an art exhibit that featured a foot bath painted to resemble the yellow flag with red stripes was protested against by many in the community, who did not care that the foot bath was meant to represent one of the key industries of the Vietnamese American community: the pedicure and manicure shop. What the community saw was the desecration of a sacred flag.

On my campus at the University of Southern California, the red Vietnamese flag hung from the rafters of the international building, among all the other flags of the world's countries. Then, in 2009, an anticommunist Vietnamese activist came to campus and stapled the yellow flag around the red flag, and the flag controversy came directly to me.

A colleague and I called a meeting of the Vietnamese American community on campus, which was represented by two student associations: one for the children of refugees and the other for international students from Vietnam. The international students spoke about the need for forgiveness, reconciliation, moving on from the war-torn past. Their sentiments were noble, but perhaps these students could afford to be noble: they had won. The children of refugees spoke of their parents and all they had lost. They invoked defeat, shame, pain, and filial piety. They wanted the yellow flag to represent them—their families and their heritage.

The conflict over these red and yellow flags connects directly to *Stromberg v. California*. In the battle over free speech, the problem lies, as it always does, when both sides believe their speech is correct. In a democracy of plural public and private spaces, there should be enough room for all forms of speech, which is what the Supreme Court ruled in *Stromberg*. Stromberg could fly her flag, and the state of California and Better America Foundation could fly their flags. Neither the state nor a private group could create a singular space through ideology that ruled out all other forms of speech or symbolism.

For Vietnamese Americans, however, that is exactly what they have tried to do in the spaces that they dominate, like Orange County, where no one dares to fly the red flag. In other scenarios, anticommunist Vietnamese Americans have used the legal means at their disposal and created an alternate possibility of flying the yellow heritage flag in place of the red flag at official state functions. Or they have encouraged politicians, like Democrat Zoe Lofgren, to boycott public spaces where the red flag is flown; refusing to attend events commemorated by symbols we disagree with is also a form of free speech.

The irony, of course, is that Vietnamese Americans who are strongly anticommunist oppose the communist regime partly because of its suppression of free speech and dissenting views. And yet in many Vietnamese American communities, there is a bright red line—the one that signals even the most tentative reconciliation with or sympathy for the communist regime—that one cannot cross in public. Those who loudly proclaim the inherent goodness of free speech, and the evils of suppressing it, would do well to listen to their own words before preventing the words of others.

The politics of flag waving are inseparable from the actual and symbolic politics of free speech, which is intimately connected with free thinking. When it comes to flags, the most persuasive act of free thinking that I encountered during the debate between Vietnamese students came from one young Vietnamese American man. Perhaps, he said, we should fly both flags. And if we cannot agree to do that, we should not fly any flag at all.

POWELL V. ALABAMA (1932)
PATTERSON V. ALABAMA (1935)

In 1931, nine black American teenagers hopped on an Alabama train headed toward Chattanooga, Tennessee. Later called the Scottsboro Boys, their names were Haywood Patterson, Clarence Norris, Charlie Weems, Andy Wright, Roy Wright, Olen Montgomery, Ozie Powell, Willie Roberson, and Eugene Williams. When two white women falsely accused these black men of rape, all men were arrested and imprisoned.

What followed was a quintessential example of American injustice. The Scottsboro Boys were not allowed to speak with an attorney prior to trial, and a lynch mob encircled the jail that held them. When they finally met their two court-appointed lawyers, the Scottsboro Boys discovered them to be ill prepared for trial and completely unfamiliar with the case. One was actually an intoxicated volunteer from the trial's audience. Unnerved by the publicity and thousands of potentially violent onlookers, the trial judge rushed the cases through his docket. Over the course of two and a half days, a series of all-white juries sentenced all nine teenagers to death, despite the clear ineffectiveness of their counsel, the frenetic proceedings, and the complete lack of evidence that any rape had occurred, much less been committed by the Scottsboro Boys. The mere allegation of sexual relations with a white woman was sufficient to condemn them.

The Communist Party USA sponsored the appeal and provided counsel in what would become *Powell v. Alabama*. Recognizing the need for experienced counsel, the ACLU's Walter Pollak was retained to argue that the Scottsboro Boys' hasty trial and nominal legal counsel violated the Fourteenth Amendment's due process clause. The US Supreme Court agreed. Justice George Sutherland wrote that criminal defendants in capital cases are constitutionally entitled to legal counsel. However, mere presence of counsel is not enough. Due process demanded that court-appointed counsel be effective, well versed in the case, and prepared to protect the defendant's freedom. After this initial victory, two additional appeals were required, *Norris v. Alabama* and *Patterson v. Alabama*. In both, Pollak and the ACLU contested Alabama's systematic exclusion of black Americans from the jury pool based solely on their race. In a major victory, the Court agreed that such discrimination was unconstitutional.

This legal triumph, however, has a bittersweet ending. Charges were eventually dropped against four of the Scottsboro Boys, and they returned home after years of incarceration. The remaining five were convicted, despite one of the white women recanting her testimony and admitting the entire story of rape was a lie. Including pretrial detention, each served at least a decade in prison for a crime that never even existed.

Scottsboro, USA

A Brief History

JACQUELINE WOODSON

The youngest was thirteen. The oldest, twenty. Decades later when the Scottsboro Boys' musical came to Broadway, I began to cough as the actors smiled and danced their way through the play. I coughed as I turned to see the pleased faces of the white audience. I coughed as they clapped along and cheered. Coughed through the blackface on black faces. Through the minstrel show. I coughed so hard I had to leave the theater, and minutes later, I couldn't stop coughing. Returned later to cough from my seat through the standing ovation.

It's a response to stress, the coughing is. For as long as I can remember, my own body has told me to remember to breathe as it prevented me from doing so. Breathe. No don't. Breathe. No don't. Has told me, through the gagging spasms, that the moment I'm moving through is triggering. Call it genetic memory. Call it the curse of DNA. Call it America. Call it a country that makes black and breathing nearly impossible.

Please don't tell what train I'm on . . .

Call it a song by Elizabeth Cotten.

Call it cotton.

Before someone white decided to turn a black tragedy into music and dance for two hundred dollars a seat and no intermission, there were nine brown boys leaving Alabama. Olen, at seventeen, was nearly blind.

Think Blind Boys of Alabama.

Think Huck Finn.

Think Trayvon Martin.

Think the broken promise of forty acres and a mule, Jim Crow, the Great Depression, the big black brute, the white damsel in distress, the American dream—

Think strange fruit hanging from poplar trees.

Think Amos and Andy. Think Toms, Coons, Mulattos, Mammies and Bucks and—

The first movie we watched in my African Americans in Film course in college was *The Birth of a Nation.* Before *Cabin in the Sky* with the beautiful Lena Horne. Before Fredi Washington graced the screen in *Imitation of Life*, there was D. W. Griffith's gaze on America.

By then, four of the Scottsboro boys were already walking, two were suckling infants, and Ozie, Eugene, and Leroy hadn't yet been born.

In February 2008, my son was born. We named him Jackson Leroi.

Think twenty-two sophomores and freshmen. All of us knowing how black and blue we were at our small liberal arts PWI. With no BSU. Far away from any HBCU. It was the mid-1980s. We had Anita Baker, Luther Vandross, and a professor with an afro named Dr. Jackson getting us through. But by then, my hair was permanently straightened, and when I left my African Americans in Film class, there was my all-white cheerleading team. There was my all-white dorm and white boyfriend. There was my all-white major of English literature, my all-white minor—British Lit. A year later, there would be my all-black sorority. A year later, I would learn about nine black boys. And as the years bent into decades, I would call out their names.

The youngest one, brown skinned and baby-faced, was named Leroy. Andy, Clarence, and Charlie were the oldest. And between them there were Haywood, Olen, and Ozie.

And baby-faced Leroy was leaving home for the first time.

Olen, who was nearly blind. His dream—a pair of glasses.

This wasn't in the musical. The story of a boy so blind he had to leave home, steal a ride on a train with the hopes of a job. With the hopes of one day seeing.

* * *

How do we begin to tell this country's story without turning our own selves inside out?

In 1992, my college boyfriend died from the complications of AIDS. I was living on Cape Cod by then. By then, I had long cut off the damaged processed hair of my college days and grown it back as locs. When I remembered college, I remembered *The Birth of a Nation* and Dr. Jackson and the dividing line between the many white cheerleaders and the three black ones.

In an article that ran in *Life* magazine (1937), Eugene was described as a "sullen, shifty mulatto." What thirteen-year-old isn't sullen?

Mulatto: The term may derive from *mula* (current Portuguese word, from the Latin *mūlus*), meaning mule, the hybrid offspring of a horse and a donkey.

I know I know: Don't trust Wiki. Whatever.

Remember Leroy? Here's an excerpt of the letter he wrote to his mama: "I am all lonely and thinking of you. . . . I feel like I can eat some of your cooking Mom." Some sources say he was twelve. Some thirteen.

But the boys were from Scottsboro.

And this is America.

And the truth is never where it's supposed to be.

So shucks, y'all.

Let's all just keep smiling and dancing.

Smiling and dancing.

UNITED STATES V. ONE BOOK CALLED "ULYSSES" (1933)

United States v. One Book Called "Ulysses" marked an early case against government censorship. Arguing on behalf of Random House, ACLU cofounder Morris Ernst persuaded the District Court for the Southern District of New York that James Joyce's masterpiece was not obscene and therefore was importable under the Tariff Act of 1930. The Second Circuit affirmed the district court's decision in 1934. As a result, the book became widely published in the United States for the first time.

The outcome in the *Ulysses* test case did not involve the First Amendment, and, at least in the short term, its legal implications were negligible. Nevertheless, *Ulysses* laid the groundwork for future challenges to banned books and articulated a speech-protective standard for what constitutes obscenity, a standard that would later influence the Supreme Court.

The Dirtiest, Most Indecent, Obscene Thing Ever Written

MICHAEL CHABON

It was a setup: a stratagem worthy of wily Ulysses himself.

The conspirators were Bennett Cerf, publisher and cofounder of Random House, and Morris Ernst, a pioneer of the ACLU and its chief legal counsel. The target was United States antiobscenity law. The bait was a single copy of an English-language novel, printed in Dijon by Frenchmen who could not understand a word of it, bound in bright blue boards, and sold mail-order by the celebrated Paris bookshop Shakespeare & Company. When Cerf and Ernst first began to conspire in 1931, the novel, James Joyce's *Ulysses*, was the most notorious book in the world.

"It is," the editor of the London *Sunday Express* had written nine years earlier, sounding like H.P. Lovecraft describing *Necronomicon*:

> the most infamously obscene book in ancient or modern literature.... All the secret sewers of vice are canalized in its flood of unimaginable thoughts, images and pornographic words. And its unclean lunacies are larded with appalling and revolting blasphemies directed against the Christian religion and against the name of Christ—blasphemies hitherto associated with the most degraded orgies of Satanism and the Black Mass.

Regarded as a masterpiece by contemporary writers such as T.S. Eliot and Ernest Hemingway, celebrated for being as difficult to read as to obtain, *Ulysses* had been shocking the sensibilities of critics, censors, and readers from the moment it began to see print between 1918 and 1920, when four chapters were abortively serialized in the pages of a New York quarterly called *The Little Review*. Even sophisticated readers often found themselves recoiling in Lovecraftian dread from contact with its pages. "I can't get over the feeling," wrote Katherine Mansfield, "of wet linoleum and unemptied pails and far worse horrors in the house of [Joyce's] mind." Encyclopedic in its use of detail and allusion, orchestral in its multiplicity of voices and rhetorical strategies, virtuosic in its technique, *Ulysses* was a thoroughly modernist production, exhibiting—sometimes within a single chapter or a single paragraph—the vandalistic glee of futurism, the decentered subjectivity of cubism, the absurdist blasphemies and pranks of dadaism, and surrealism's penchant for finding the mythic in the ordinary and the primitive in the low dives and nighttowns of the city.

It was not the book's flamboyant modernism, however, that shocked and repulsed Mansfield and other early readers, among them Virginia Woolf, George Bernard Shaw, W.B. Yeats, and, of all people, D.H. Lawrence, who called its celebrated final chapter, "Penelope," "the dirtiest, most indecent, obscene thing ever written." Critics were not scandalized by the way Joyce represented his protagonists by means of discontinuous interwoven strands of interior monologue and sensory perception, nor by his narrowing of the massive novel's action to the span of a single June day in 1904. And when the upstanding bullies of the New York Society for the Suppression of Vice (NYSSV) had intervened in 1921 to bring federal charges against *The Little Review* after it published the novel's "Nausicaa" chapter—ensuring that *Ulysses* was thereafter effectively banned in the US—it was not because they objected to Joyce's depicting Homer's lissome Phaeacian nymph as a disabled working-class young Irishwoman or bold Odysseus as a timorous middle-aged Jewish seller of newspaper ads.

The source of the "horrors" that *Ulysses* aroused, in Mansfield, critics, and censors alike, lay in those "unemptied pails." *Ulysses* was the first modern novel of indisputable literary intent to explicitly depict its characters engaging in the universal bodily routines of human beings—shitting, fucking, farting, jerking off, etc.—and, perhaps even more shockingly, the first to affirm, often in the coarsest terms, that when they were not engaged in those activities, they spent a good deal of their time thinking about engaging in them.

In considering the case brought by the NYSSV against the publishers of *The Little Review* in 1921, the Supreme Court of New York had affirmed that while *Ulysses* might well be considered literature by certain types of dissolute, shiftless, intellectual aesthetes with anarchist politics and slovenly habits, it was also, patently and unquestionably, obscene. To publish, sell, or purchase it, or to import it into the United States, therefore, was a crime. All the offending numbers of *The Little Review* were burned, and over the next dozen years, here and in the United Kingdom (whose censors took their cue from the New York decision), hundreds, perhaps thousands of copies of the novel, whether imported from Paris or pirated locally, were consigned to what the British called "the King's Chimney."

Naturally, the relentless campaign to extirpate a book so pornographic that no one was allowed even to see or touch it, let alone read it, created a lively appetite for *Ulysses* among the reading public. With supply lines between Paris and the United States constantly threatened by the zealous activity of customs agents, opportunists stepped in, with their pirate presses, to satisfy that appetite. Foremost among the pirates of *Ulysses* was the legendary New York pornographer Samuel Roth. A semitragic, almost Dostoevskian figure, widely reviled, often imprisoned, a lifelong Orthodox Jew who wrote the notorious anti-Semitic screed *Jews Must Live*, Roth was a would-be modernist poet whose keen literary eye and canny sense of the marketplace were matched only by the unhappy mixture of bad luck and compulsive behavior that drove him to ply his trade in the sordid shadows of the New York publishing world.

Roth—who would go on to encounter success with a pirated edition of *Lady Chatterley's Lover* and a federal prison sentence in the mid-1950s, and whose 1957 Supreme Court case, *Roth* v. *United States*, would itself become a landmark in the history of First Amendment protection for obscene speech—brought out his unlicensed *Ulysses* starting in 1926. It was not, due to a technicality in US copyright law, truly a *pirated* edition, but it was printed without consent of or payment to the author. James Joyce and Sylvia Beach, the owner of Shakespeare & Company who had risked so much, personally and financially, to bring Joyce's masterpiece to the world, viewed its publication with alarm.

The New York publishing establishment, for its part, viewed the success of Roth's *Ulysses* with something closer to a covetous leer. Throughout the late 1920s, many of the most prominent publishing houses had flirted with or seriously explored the possibility of coming to terms with Joyce and of braving the prosecution that would likely if not inevitably follow publication of the most infamously obscene book in ancient or modern literature. But even publishers with the stomach for litigation were unwilling to stomach the noxious financial terms demanded by the resolute Beach, to whom Joyce had assigned control over the *Ulysses* rights—or perhaps it was simply that the gentlemen publishers of that time were too sexist to negotiate with a woman. Interest among the major houses faded away, and as the 1930s began, the US market remained wide open for exploitation by Roth, who was widely rumored to be preparing a second unlicensed edition. Joyce, contemplating from the photophobic gloom of his latest fugitive Paris apartment the prospect of never making a dime from the work that had cost him his eyesight, his health, and eight years of his life, felt his own financial resolve begin to weaken.

Two erudite, polished, and well-connected New York hustlers caught wind—or maybe it was simply an intuition, a canny surmise—of this wavering, and saw in it, as hustlers so often do in the face of weakness, an opportunity. One of these bon vivants was Bennett Cerf, then in his early thirties. Eight years earlier, Cerf had ditched a career in his Alsatian Jewish father's Harlem lithography business, using twenty-five thousand dollars inherited from his tobacco-heiress mother to buy himself a partnership in the celebrated New York publishing firm of Boni & Liveright. Eager, savvy, impulsive, and, like any good hustler, trusting implicitly in his own judgment, Cerf seized on his new partner Horace Liveright's financial straits to cut a deal and buy him out of the Modern Library, an imprint that Cerf astutely recognized as the hidden jewel of Boni & Liveright.

The books on the Modern Library's list of "modern classics" tended to have gone out of print or to have entered the public domain, which made them cheap to publishers and affordable to readers, even in the thick of the Great Depression. Building on the Modern Library's success, Cerf and Donald Klopfer, his boyhood friend and business partner, expanded into publishing new work by contemporary authors, chosen "at random," under the sobriquet of Random House. But if Random House were going to compete with the big houses, it needed a big hit. It needed to make a literary splash. It needed, Cerf decided, the dirtiest, most indecent, obscene thing ever written. He knew—publishers had known for years—that if you could somehow contrive to get around the obscenity problem, you could sell a million, or at least several hundred thousand, of the damn thing.

Pondering the question, trusting in his judgment but acutely conscious of the risk that must be courted, Cerf reached out in 1931 to that second erudite, polished, and well-connected New York hustler. An Alabama-born Jewish peddler's son, Morris Ernst had hustled his way through Horace Mann, Williams College, and night school at New York Law, idolized Louis Brandeis, oozed left-wing American patriotism of a kind all but forgotten today,* and had a table at 21.

Ernst dressed like a college professor, favoring bow ties and tweed jackets, but he was known, and much sought-after, as a gifted, skilled, and cagey courtroom attorney with a discerning eye for the kinds of cases that could change the law if you won them. He was thrilled to hear that Cerf intended to storm the grim edifice of Comstockery in which, for decades, a venerable legal standard known as the Hicklin test had kept art and literature imprisoned, jailing them indiscriminately along with naughty French postcards, racy English paeans to spanking and buggery, and guides to "marital hygiene." An admirer of Joyce and his work, a fierce First Amendment absolutist, and an experienced, battle-hardened defender of dirty books, Ernst could not resist the challenge that Cerf handed him, along with—once the two hustlers had finished working each other over—a 5 percent share in sales (if any) of the novel. Ernst, in return, agreed to forgo his standard fee. He was, like Cerf, and Joyce, and Beach, a taker of chances.

In the end, curiously, the strategy devised by Ernst and his associate Alexander Lindey entirely sidestepped the First Amendment.

* In the latter part of his career, however, this patriotism would congeal into a more conventional cold-warrior anti-Communism, fueling a prolonged, regrettable correspondence with J. Edgar Hoover.

Over the previous sixty years the Supreme Court had consistently upheld the constitutionality of the federal Comstock Act, which banned obscene speech. The New York State antipornography laws were broad, loose, and vaguely worded. And the standard used to determine whether speech was obscene, the Hicklin test, appeared to be invincible.

The Hicklin test, arising out of an 1868 British case, *Regina v. Hicklin*, defined and permitted the banning of obscene works when they tended "to deprave and corrupt those whose minds [were] open to such immoral influences, and into whose hands a publication of this sort [might] fall." (Enemies of obscenity have always unselfishly shown greater concern for the corruptibility of others than for their own.) The book at question in *Regina v. Hicklin* was not, strictly speaking, pornography but an anti-Catholic diatribe, *The Confessional Unmask'd*, a pamphlet adorned with a number of salacious passages purporting to be the first-person accounts of apostates, former nuns, etc., giving eyewitness to the "depravities" of the Church. The presence of these passages, ruled the court in *Hicklin*, was sufficient to render the whole pamphlet obscene. This was what made the Hicklin test so dangerous to a work like *Ulysses*: it could be applied piecemeal. The government had only to prove the obscenity of part of a book in order to ban it entirely. There was no obligation to consider context or the intentions of a work as a whole. A condemned book was hung, as it were, by its dirty parts.

There was one other problem with challenging obscenity law on the basis of the First Amendment: Cerf would actually have to publish the book first. He would have to license it from the author, advertise and solicit orders for it, typeset and print it, and ship it to booksellers. All that would cost money and labor and then, after he had spent tens of thousands of dollars, the court might very well rule against him, leaving *Ulysses* to the tender mercies of a bunch of vice squad bravos carrying cans of kerosene. But there was no other way to do it; to find out if speech was protected or not, one was obliged, first of all, to speak.

This was not Ernst's first obscenity trial—far from it—and his experience had led to an understanding that the smartest way to come at a judge, if you could find yourself a sympathetic one, was through the

Tariff Act of 1930. The Tariff Act, among many other provisions having nothing to do with suppressing the trade in pornography, empowered federal customs agents to seize obscene books as contraband, impound them, and—as ever—incinerate them.

A challenge to the Tariff Act, though it would not afford an opportunity to change the way the law looked at obscene speech from the perspective of the First Amendment, offered three evident advantages: first, the definition of obscenity under the act was clearer and less confusing than the definition that applied in a First Amendment case. Second, but no less appealing, taking on the Tariff Act would be a lot cheaper; Random House would not have to print a single copy. All one needed to do, to invite the scrutiny of the Customs Bureau, was purchase a copy of the book and have it shipped through a US port of entry. One copy was sufficient—if discovered, it would be seized, and the US attorney would then bring suit against it. Against *it*—that individual copy of *Ulysses*. The defendant in the case would not be Random House, or Bennett Cerf, or James Joyce. The defendant would be that lone, waylaid copy of the book—hence the name of the case, *United States v. One Book Called "Ulysses."*

This was the third and final advantage of going the Tariff Act route: the act contained a provision specifying that in the event of seizure, suit would be brought against the seized work itself. This practice, common in admiralty law and in forfeiture cases, derives from the courts' jurisdiction *in rem*, over things and property, and has brought us some of the most amusing case names in the history of American jurisprudence, among them *United States v. Forty Barrels & Twenty Kegs of Coca-Cola, United States v. 11 ¼ Dozen Packages of Articles Labeled in Part Mrs. Moffat's Shoo-Fly Powders for Drunkenness*, and, of course, *United States v. One Solid Gold Object in Form of a Rooster*.

So Cerf and Joyce came to terms on rights and royalties, and Cerf arranged for Joyce's assistant, Paul Léon, to purchase a copy of the book from Shakespeare & Company and send it, in the baggage of a willing confederate, to the Random House offices.

Ernst now made three further opening moves. Each formed a crucial part of his overall strategy for winning the case, which was to persuade a judge that *Ulysses* ought not to be evaluated solely on the basis of its "dirty parts" but in its entirety, as a work of literature, a "modern classic"—and therefore, by definition, not obscene.

To begin with, Ernst instructed Léon to amass a number of favorable press clippings and critical assessments of the novel, along with protests and petitions against Roth's edition drawn up by notable litterateurs, and affix them to the book itself, pasting and taping them into the covers and among the pages until it was swollen with encomiums, sympathetic analyses, and principled affirmations of Joyce's moral rights as an author. Doing this ensured that when the book was seized, on entering the Port of New York, all the plaudits and respectful critiques would be seized along with it and duly entered as evidence in the case, thereby obliging the judge to consider them. Following the same tack—establishing *Ulysses*'s importance and status as literature in the eyes of serious-minded readers—Ernst started a campaign to solicit the written opinions of librarians across the United States, so that these, too, could be entered into evidence.

Next, Ernst arranged for a second copy of *Ulysses* to be shipped to Random House, then applied for this copy to be exempted from seizure under the Tariff Act's "classics" exemption, which granted the Treasury Department the authority to refrain from seizing a book, even when deemed obscene, if it were also—as with Rabelais, say, or Casanova—widely considered a classic. Ernst was more than a little familiar with the classics exemption, having written it himself, with the connivance of a powerful friend in Washington, who saw that it was inserted into the Tariff Act. This handy bit of foresight, part of Ernst's long game on behalf of artistic freedom, paid off when the secretary of the treasury himself opined that while *Ulysses* was obscene beyond any doubt under the current definition, it was also, in his view, a modern classic. This highly placed literary judgment would also be entered into the record as part of the evidence Ernst presented in court.

On May 3, 1932, the first copy of *Ulysses*—the one stuffed with clippings and critical avowals of the book's importance and merit—arrived on schedule, aboard the *Bremen*, in the luggage of Ernst's confederate. Ernst had taken care to have his associate Lindey alert a lawyer who worked for customs to expect the shipment and prepare to seize it, but somehow the warning went amiss in the routine tumult of the *Bremen*'s arrival at the North German/Lloyd piers in Brooklyn. The hapless smuggler, bemused no doubt to find himself the object of no one's interest, waltzed right through inspection unmolested by federal agents, rode into Manhattan, and, perhaps somewhat sheepishly, delivered his unwanted contraband to the Random House offices.

Once again, as at so many points in the history of *United States v. Ulysses*, Ernst took matters into his own hands. Returning to the scene of the undiscovered crime, he found a likely-looking customs inspector and demanded, in strident tones, that one book called *Ulysses* be immediately impounded. It proved surprisingly difficult, however, to arouse the proper confiscatory spirit among the agents manning their posts that day. When it came to a question of the most obscene book in all literature, it appears that the officers of the United States Customs Service may, in fact, have been a little jaded. "Everybody brings that in," one of the customs men told Ernst, according to Cerf's memoirs. "We don't pay any attention to it." It was not until Ernst thought of letting them have a look at the book itself, freighted and festooned with newspaper and magazine clippings, angry petitions and stray bits of paper like the scrapbook of some mad theorist of anarchy, that he succeeded in persuading the agents of the book's being worthy of seizure.

This odd inertia on the part of law enforcement persisted as the book made its way up from the Brooklyn docks to the US attorney's office to the New York Supreme Court. It took the better part of 1933 for the chief of the Brooklyn customs office to turn the book over to the assistant US attorney, for the assistant US attorney to refer it to his superior, for the US attorney to decide to bring charges, and for a judge to be assigned who was willing and able to hear the case.

In the latter instance the delay was largely—but not entirely—due to skillful manipulation on the part of Ernst, as he maneuvered to ensure that the case landed on the docket of Judge John Woolsey, known to be an obscenity skeptic with literary pretensions. It's harder to explain the lotus-eaterish lethargy of the other principals. Perhaps the various officers of the law and of the court sensed that a change was occuring, that the drift of public opinion and private mores alike had begun to undermine the Hicklin test, the Societies for Suppression, and the whole dour edifice of Victorian Comstockery. Perhaps their hearts had gone out of the fight. Or maybe they just didn't feel like breaking their brains—it took assistant US attorney Samuel Coleman six weeks to read the thing—on a seven-hundred-page book that contained sentences like "Morose delectation Aquinas tunbelly calls this, *frate porcospino*." And then there is the curious fact that those who did manage to survive combat with the novel often emerged with the uneasy impression that the book was, in Coleman's words, "a literary masterpiece."

Coleman also came away from his six-week battle with *Ulysses* having no doubt that the book was, in certain passages—that last chapter!—obscene; but only in certain passages, and only as defined by the Tariff Act; not intrinsically or in effect, not by intent, and not when considered as a whole. The right judge, in the right frame of mind, might very well feel obliged to redefine obscenity in a way that excluded Joyce's literary masterpiece. It doesn't seem unlikely that when, at last, Coleman prevailed on his reluctant superior, US Attorney George Medalie, to bring suit, in the courtroom of Judge Woolsey, against *Ulysses*, he did so with the secret intention of helping to bring about this redefinition.

Judge Woolsey read *Ulysses*. He read it slowly and carefully, proceeding, like so many readers of the book before and since, in the company of Stuart Gilbert and the other sober hermeneutists and narrative picklocks whose explanatory guidebooks had sprung up, after 1922, to ease the reader's passage through Joyce's novel. These texts had been supplied to the judge, naturally, by Ernst, and naturally he was not just trying to be helpful. Like the sheaf of tributes and panegyrics he'd had Léon attach to the seized copy of *Ulysses*, the guidebooks helped to bolster Ernst's claim that Joyce was a genius and *Ulysses* a masterpiece dense with classical and learned allusion, as far from pornography as a book could possibly be. What use, after all, would a dirty book be to the Hicklin test's dull and corruptible minds, if you could not even understand what it was saying without the help of Gilbert and a raft of other professorial interpreters?

Ulysses is one of my favorite books—I adore it. And like generations of the book's admirers from the day Judge Woolsey issued his elegantly written ruling that *Ulysses* was not obscene, and therefore could legally be admitted to (and soon after published in) the United States (a decision afterward upheld by the US Court of Appeals for the Second Circuit), I have always been grateful to the judge for hissagacity, his principled reasoning, and his evident good taste in books. Every time I sit down to reread *Ulysses,* I begin with Judge Woolsey's ruling, included right up front in every US edition of the novel until the mid-1980s, and every time say a silent thank-you to that wise jurist for his integral role in bringing *Ulysses* to American readers like me.

Having looked into the story of *United States v. Ulysses*, however, I now see that my gratitude has been somewhat misplaced. With no disrespect to Judge Woolsey, whose charming acknowledgment that the book *does* have its dirty parts—"it must always be remembered that [Joyce's] locale was Celtic and his season Spring"—makes me smile every time, we owe the *Ulysses* decision less to the judge in the case than to counsel for the defense. What an incredible feat of lawyering! Morris Ernst exercised every bit of craft, persuasion, and influence he could bring to bear, from intervening in the writing of the Tariff Act, to buttressing the case with plaudits from highbrow critics and small-town librarians, to manipulating the court calendar and playing on the sympathy of his opposing counsel. Even the inclusion of Woolsey's ruling at the head of the edition Random House published in 1934 was a legal strategy conceived by Ernst as a hedge against future attempts to prosecute the book.

Knowing Woolsey, understanding both his sensitivity and discernment and his literary interests, Ernst played him like a violin. By presenting *Ulysses—packaging it* might be a more accurate characterization—in a dense apparatus of erudite debate and critical theorizing, Ernst had not just made it impossible for the judge to avoid considering an alleged dirty book as a work of literature, he had also issued a subtle challenge to Woolsey's amour propre as a literary man. The moment Woolsey accepted the book's status as literature, Ernst had the judge where he wanted him.

By definition, a work of literature could not be obscene, could not be pornographic, could not corrupt and deprave, could never be intended to arouse a reader, even if certain passages in said work dealt with sexual activity and bodily functions in plain, even vulgar terms. Otherwise, a reader like Judge Woolsey—and those two mysterious "friends" (in fact fellow members of the Century Association) whose opinions as "literary assessors" he said he had sought—would be forced to acknowledge having found edification and truth and beauty in a pornographic book, or else sexual arousal in a masterpiece—both of which conclusions, Ernst encouraged Woolsey to find, were absurd. (Though at least one subsequent reader, crawling into the lascivious thoughts and the warm bed of soft, round, fragrant Molly Bloom at the novel's end, has found the line less bright between edification and arousal.)

When we celebrate the American Civil Liberties Union that Morris Ernst helped to found, we tend—rightly, I'm sure—to focus on injustices confronted, rights upheld, principles established, victims vindicated. We revel in the Constitution and the Bill of Rights, thrill or shudder or shake our heads at the crimes, the outrages, the victories and defeats. The history of the ACLU is a history of great struggle, bitter and glorious. But it is also—it is first of all—a history of great lawyers, like Morris Ernst, who brought as much artistry and erudition and sly, masterful skill to defending one book, called *Ulysses*, as its author had brought to its creation.

EDWARDS V. CALIFORNIA (1941)

In 1937, California made knowingly transporting an indigent nonresident into the state a misdemeanor. The statute was a response to the Great Depression and the flood of poor migrants entering the state in search of work. In 1940, Fred Edwards was convicted of violating the law after he drove his indigent brother-in-law from Texas to California. The ACLU represented Edwards on appeal before the Supreme Court. It argued that freedom of movement was a fundamental constitutional right, one that was needed more than ever before in the economic wake of a depression that rendered millions of families indigent, and one that could not be denied by a state on the basis of poverty. The ACLU urged the Court to protect the rights of these transient unemployed in their search for economic opportunity.

The Court held that California's law violated the Constitution's commerce clause. The task of aiding poor citizens was the responsibility of the whole nation, and California could not shield itself from burdens common to all states by "shutting its gates to the outside world"; rather, the people of the United States had to "sink or swim together."

The Brother-in-Law

ANN PATCHETT

If a man leaves his home in Marysville, California, in December to drive to Spur, Texas, to pick up his brother-in-law and bring him back home with him to California, chances are good the trip has been undertaken at the behest of his wife. The year was 1939, so this was no casual trip. This was a haul. Marysville is a little town near the Sierra Nevada Mountains, not far from, and not dissimilar to, Paradise, before it burned in the California Camp Fire of 2019. He would have had to drive down the length of the state to pick up Route 66, probably in Barstow, and take it as far as Amarillo before turning south. The driver's name was Edwards. His brother-in-law was Frank Duncan. The fact that Edwards arrived in Texas to find that Duncan had very few possessions, little money, and no job couldn't have been much of a surprise. I imagine those were the very reasons he'd been sent to collect his brother-in-law in the first place. The stovepipe of northern Texas was in the heart of the Dust Bowl, and this was the height of the Depression. There were no crops and no prospects. One man had come to save the other.

You would think this would have been the story: the long drive to Texas and the long drive home—a trip divided into equal halves. In the first part, Edwards was alone in the car, maybe thinking about his wife, maybe wondering if they had enough to feed themselves, much less her brother. Then there was a brief intermission in Spur when Edwards saw the circumstances of Duncan's life for himself. He understood his trip was not just a matter of easing a burden. The situation was well past dire. There was, for both men, a feeling of shame, for Edwards that he was seeing his brother-in-law this way and for Duncan that he had had to ask. That was where the second half of the story began, the two men in the car together heading home to Marysville. I imagine they spent their time in the car talking about better days, both the future and the past.

But as it turned out, this wasn't the story at all. To transport an indigent into California was to break California law: "Every person, firm or corporation, or officer or agent thereof that brings or assists in bringing into the state any indigent person who is not a resident of the State, knowing him to be an indigent person, is guilty of a misdemeanor." It was known as the "anti-Okie" law, a law intended to hold back the poor at the state line because the poor had been flooding into California since the start of the Depression. One wonders who it was that reported Edwards's brother-in-law visiting in December. Who asked if he met the requirements of a sufficient amount of money and possessions, or if he had the job he needed in order to stay? At any rate, it was Edwards, the transporter, who was tried and convicted of the misdemeanor crime and given a sentence of six months in jail, suspended.

It is the novelist's job to assume that the people who wrote the law didn't understand Duncan's circumstances in Texas. They hadn't taken it upon themselves to imagine his life there. He lost his job on the farm where he worked when the farm went back to the bank, and in losing the job, he lost his place to live. There was no topsoil, no crops, no food. He had written to his sister in Marysville. The novelist must show the humanity in the moment when the two men meet again, one coming for the other. Edwards either didn't know before he left California that he would break a law saying that the poor may not be brought across state lines or decided he had no other choice.

The ACLU took on the task of fighting for Edwards's right to bring his brother-in-law back with him to California, and in 1941 the Supreme Court declared the law unconstitutional and vacated Edwards's conviction.

Everything I know about Edwards and Duncan, other than where they lived, when they made their trip, and the court case that followed, I imagined. I was able to imagine it because John Steinbeck was doing his job in 1939, the year he published *The Grapes of Wrath*. The Joad family left Sallisaw, Oklahoma, near the Arkansas border, and drove west to California on Route 66. Had they been real people, they might have passed Edwards on his way to Texas. Steinbeck explained the Joads in such a way that anyone picking up the book from the time it was first published until today would not only understand the plight of a poor family fleeing Oklahoma, they would feel it. It was impossible to stay. Nothing would grow on the land they were forced off of, their house was bulldozed, their children were starving. There was no other choice but to go in search of work in a place they knew they weren't welcome. Still, it was their dream of a better life, the very smallest request for a decent human existence, that is the most heartbreaking. Ma Joad says to Tom, "But I like to think how nice it's gonna be, maybe, in California. Never cold. An' fruit ever'place, little white houses in among the orange trees. I wonder—that is, if we all get jobs an' all work—maybe we can get one of them little white houses. An' the little fellas go out an' pick oranges right off the tree. They ain't gonna be able to stand it, they'll get to yellin' so." Steinbeck put the reader in the truck with the Joads. He put them in the fields and in the Weedpatch Camp in California, day after impossible day. This was how we came to understand that as awful as this choice was, there were no better choices.

The Grapes of Wrath won the National Book Award and the Pulitzer Prize in 1939. It became a best seller. In 1940, John Ford made it into a film starring Henry Fonda. In 1941, the Supreme Court of the United States ruled unanimously against the state of California in the case of *Edwards v. California*, striking down the law that prohibited the transport of indigents into the state. Do we have John Steinbeck to thank for that? May we thank the Joads? It couldn't have hurt. A voice rises up through experience, is made into art, and art then shapes the law. The story of the Joads allowed us to understand Frank Duncan and why he had to come to California.

The novelists of our age are doing their part to help us see the lives of people who struggle to leave places of violence and oppression and immigrate to what they hope will be a safer existence. Like the Joads, they understand the place they're going to may not be welcoming, but it's impossible for them to imagine how their lives could be worse. Recent stories of immigration that are as varied as experience itself include Dave Eggers's *What Is the What,* Mohsin Hamid's *Exit West,* Lisa Ko's *The Leavers,* Viet Thanh Nguyen's *The Refugees,* and Irina Reyn's *Mother Country*. Each book calls on the reader to climb up in the truck and ride along, and in doing so reminds us of one central fact: people must be aided and protected by the law.

In hindsight, the idea that it could have ever been illegal to drive your unemployed brother-in-law into California is so quaint it feels more like a misunderstanding than a misdemeanor. But circumstances can change in the time it takes the stock market to crash and the heartlands to dry up and blow away. We must work to create a society with liberty and justice for all. We will fail and fail and fail at this goal. Our failure is the history of the world. But our humanity is in the fact that we never cease to try.

WEST VIRGINIA STATE BOARD OF EDUCATION V. BARNETTE (1943) (*amicus*)

In *West Virginia State Board of Education v. Barnette*, the Supreme Court ruled that public schools could not force their pupils to observe patriotic "ritual[s]" like reciting the Pledge of Allegiance or saluting the American flag. The ACLU filed an amicus brief in support of the Barnettes, a family of Jehovah's Witnesses whose faith forbade making oaths to national symbols. Wrote Justice Robert Houghwout Jackson for a 6–3 majority, "If there is any fixed star in our constitutional constellation, it is that no official, high or petty, can prescribe what shall be orthodox in politics, nationalism, religion, or other matters of opinion or force citizens to confess by word or act their faith therein."

A mere three years before *Barnette*, the Court had upheld forced pledge policies. In an 8–1 decision, *Minersville School District v. Gobitis* affirmed a Pennsylvania public school's mandatory flag salute ceremony despite the objections of Jehovah's Witnesses enrolled in the district. The forced-pledge policy at issue in *Barnette* was enacted by West Virginia's Board of Education in the wake of the *Gobitis* ruling and borrowed language from Justice Felix Frankfurter's majority opinion, including the assertion that "national unity is the basis of national security." In *Barnette*, the Court rejected that reasoning, finding that the "relatively recent phenomenon" of nationalism could not and should not justify coerced or compelled patriotic gestures. Determining that compulsory demonstrations of patriotism in public school classrooms are a clear violation of the First Amendment, the Court affirmed the rights of students to remain seated for the pledge due to their religious beliefs, as a gesture of protest, or for any other reason.

Victory Formation

BRIT BENNETT

In August 2016, San Francisco 49ers quarterback Colin Kaepernick made headlines and, later, history when he chose to sit during the pregame national anthem. When asked later, he told NFL Media, "I am not going to stand up to show pride in a flag for a country that oppresses black people and people of color." A week later, Kaepernick, joined by teammate Eric Reid, knelt during the national anthem. The two players, concerned that their protest might be considered antimilitary or antipolice, chose to kneel instead of sit when Nate Boyer, a former NFL player and Green Beret, suggested it. "We chose to kneel because it's a respectful gesture," Reid later wrote in an op-ed in the *New York Times*. "I remember thinking our posture was like a flag flown at half-mast to mark a tragedy."

I used to wear an enamel pin on my backpack that featured the iconic image of Kaepernick, afro picked, kneeling. Sometimes I would forget it was there until I heard white people, standing in a line behind me, grumble about it. The suddenness of their anger always surprised me. Kneeling is, almost universally, considered a gesture of humility and respect. On the football field, players take a knee when someone gets injured. In different faiths, kneeling is a common posture of prayer. Servitude, even. And yet, kneeling during the anthem inspires rage because the issue, of course, is not the anthem or flag or military. The problem is black disobedience. A kneeling black body becomes dangerous because a disobedient black body is dangerous.

At the time, Kaepernick's protest seemed as if it might be just one controversial moment in a long NFL season. Few of us imagined then that Kaepernick's simple act would inspire hundreds of athletes to follow suit, across sports and nations; his protest created such a public firestorm that NFL team owners, worried it was crashing ratings, held crisis meetings, and the president of the United States capitalized on it as a polarizing issue that rallied his political base. Two years later, Colin Kaepernick is no longer what he has always been—a football player—and has instead transformed into something else: a hero or a traitor, a martyr or a pariah, depending on who you ask.

Several writers, including the *New Yorker*'s Jeffrey Toobin, have wisely connected Kaepernick's protest to a landmark 1943 Supreme Court case, *West Virginia v. Barnette*. The West Virginia Board of Education required public schools to include the salute to the flag as a mandatory school activity, and when children in a family of Jehovah's Witnesses, whose religion forbade them from pledging to symbols, refused to perform the salute, they were sent home, threatened with reform school, and their parents faced prosecutions for causing juvenile delinquency. In a 6–3 decision, the Court overruled its previous decision and held that forcing schoolchildren to salute the flag is unconstitutional. In an opinion written by Robert Houghwout Jackson, the Court found that reverence for a national symbol like the flag does not trump the constitutional right to free expression.

"Though the Flag Salute Cases are generally seen as involving freedom of religion," John W. Johnson writes in *Historic U.S. Cases: An Encyclopedia*, "that issue is virtually absent from Jackson's majority opinion." Instead, Jackson grounds his opinion as one of freedom of speech and expression. "Struggles to coerce uniformity of sentiment in support of some end thought essential to their time and country have been waged by many good, as well as by evil, men," Jackson wrote. "Those who begin coercive elimination of dissent soon find themselves exterminating dissenters."

Even further, Jackson argues that not only is it unconstitutional for the state to compel patriotic speech from its citizens but it is also ineffective. Forcing an NFL player to stand for the anthem, as President Trump has repeatedly suggested, cheapens the gesture altogether. "To believe that patriotism will not flourish if patriotic ceremonies are voluntary and spontaneous, instead of a compulsory routine, is to make an unflattering estimate of the appeal of our institutions to free minds," Jackson wrote. In other words, standing for the anthem actually means more as an expression of patriotism if players have the right to choose not to.

In February 2019, Kaepernick and Reid reached a confidential settlement with the NFL after alleging that team owners worked together to keep them off the field due to their protest. Days later, a news story went viral about a sixth grader in Lakeland, Florida, who faced misdemeanor charges after an altercation with a teacher began when he refused to recite the Pledge of Allegiance. Recently, during a literary festival in Vincennes, a French reader asked if I ever said the pledge in school and, if so, why I did not refuse. "You know those words are not true," she said, meaning, you as a black person know that there is not liberty and justice for all. I did know and yet I stood, every morning at 9:00 a.m., along with the rest of my class. Every so often, there were a few dissenters who remained seated. Always white kids, goths and punks, whose protest seemed to me then as just another way to be edgy. They could afford to broadcast all the ways in which they were different, but sometimes, when you were one of three black kids in a classroom, you just wanted to put your head down and get along. I grew up in a military town in a time of war. I still remember yellow ribbons on those black classroom doors.

The fact of it is, I wanted to tell the French reader, that I knew as a child what Kaepernick knew: kneeling, which is that dissent from my black body, is not safe. The same way I knew, standing, during a San Diego State football game, as the crowd cheered for military jets thundering overhead and service members marched onto the field to present the flag. And don't I sometimes find these symbols beautiful? Aren't I moved during Whitney Houston's National Anthem? Don't we keep a folded flag for my grandfather on the mantel? You can live this way, finding beauty within violence. But eventually it bowls you over, knocking you down to your knees.

KOREMATSU V. UNITED STATES (1944)

In *Korematsu v. United States,* the US Supreme Court held that discriminatory policies based on race were subject to high levels of judicial scrutiny and that the internment of Japanese Americans was constitutional because it was based not on racism but on national security and "military necessity." Two associated cases, *Hirabayashi v. United States* (1943) and *Yasui v. United States* (1943), follow nearly identical reasoning.

While *Korematsu* is often cited as one of the Court's worst decisions, the curious fact remains that *Korematsu* is arguably still good law. In numerous cases on racial discrimination, *Korematsu* was cited alongside *Brown v. Board of Education of Topeka* (1954) as binding precedent supporting heightened scrutiny. Even when the Court expressly renounced *Korematsu* in *Trump v. Hawaii* (2018), the repudiation's uncertain breadth and precedential value obscure whether *Korematsu* was overruled in its entirety or just in part.

The Nail

STEVEN OKAZAKI

Deru kugi wa utaeru. The nail that sticks up gets hammered down. Japanese Americans heard that proverb a lot in 1942, when their president ordered 140,000 of them forcibly removed from their homes by soldiers with guns and government guys in suits and herded (as in transported in livestock trucks and put into horse stalls) into "the camps."

The government designated them "assembly centers" and "relocation centers," which sounds like a church gathering followed by witness protection.

Most Japanese Americans called them "the camps," and they weren't talking about a place where they ran around in shorts and made lanyards. My Uncle Chico, who drove a semitrailer truck for a living and didn't tolerate bullshit, referred to them as "god damn concentration camps," which, minus the "god damn," is how the US government labeled them early on until they realized how bad it sounded.

They're usually referred to as "the internment camps," which seems accurate when you read the dictionary definition of *internment* as "the state of being confined as a prisoner, especially for political or military reasons." While that sounds plenty serious, a lot of Japanese Americans (I'll sometimes refer to them as JAs from now on) feel it's too soft. It makes what happened seem justifiable for a nation at war; it doesn't explain why they needed to incarcerate whole families; and it doesn't capture the injustice, humiliation, and devastating impact the experience had, and continues to have, on the JA community. Which is to say that *internment* doesn't reflect the racism of it all.

I think of them as the prison camps where my mother and father (who hadn't met yet), grandparents, aunts, uncles, and two cousins were sent because they had Japanese faces. Faces that made white people uncomfortable. Faces white people didn't trust to stand next to them in the grocery store, to be on their kid's baseball team, or sit next to in church. Faces they twisted into ugly caricatures with slanted eyes, buck teeth, bad haircuts, and big round glasses to make them feel okay about fucking them over, taking away their homes and businesses, and crushing the little bit of dignity they'd worked so hard to acquire. Since JAs hadn't committed any acts of espionage or sabotage, it could only have been because of their faces.

When FDR signed Executive Order 9066 and the mass incarceration of "all persons of Japanese ancestry" was implemented, virtually the whole country—liberals and conservatives, Republicans and Democrats, and every religious denomination except the Jehovah's Witnesses and the Quakers—either supported it or remained silent. California's attorney general, Earl Warren, later chief justice of the Supreme Court and revered civil liberties champion, vigorously pushed to strip "the Japs" of their rights and get them out of his state. He never apologized for it.

There was no one in the JA community to say, "Hey, this is wrong! Let's get organized and refuse to go," because immediately after the attack on Pearl Harbor, two months before the order was issued, the FBI picked up and imprisoned anyone who might say that: community leaders, teachers, priests, businessmen, judo instructors, and others. And if they *had* protested, the soldiers would have pointed guns at their heads, maybe beat the crap out of them, then thrown them into the special camp they built for troublemakers.

In Dorothea Lange's powerful photographs of the mass evacuation, you see JAs of all ages with numbers pinned to their coats, standing next to their belongings, waiting to board buses and trains. They look lost and bewildered, but not broken or hopeless, as if they still believe in their country, even as they enter the camps surrounded by barbed wire, with machine guns pointed at them, in the middle of nowhere.

The nail that sticks up.

Three Japanese Americans refused to go. Minoru "Min" Yasui, twenty-five years old, was born in Hood River, Oregon. He was passionate and superpatriotic. As a good American (and attorney and former Boy Scout), he believed it was his obligation to oppose the government's orders. He presented himself at a downtown Portland police station and demanded to be arrested. His case went all the way to the Supreme Court, which ruled unanimously that the government had the right to restrict the lives of citizens during wartime.

Gordon Hirabayashi, twenty-four years old, was born in Seattle, Washington. He was a college student and a registered conscientious objector supported by a community of Quaker friends. Stubbornly idealistic, he acted on principle and turned himself in to the FBI as an act of civil disobedience. He entered a plea of not guilty on "the basis that both the exclusion law and curfew were racially prejudiced and unconstitutional." In a decision on the same day as *Yasui v. United States*, the Supreme Court upheld his conviction.

Fred Korematsu, twenty-three years old, born in Oakland, California, was the most unlikely of resisters. When his parents and three brothers gave up their home and flower-growing business and reported for evacuation, Fred stayed behind with his Caucasian girlfriend. His response was essentially, "I didn't do anything wrong, so why should I have to go?" So he kept his head down and hid out, until the military police arrested him three weeks later in May 1942.

The national American Civil Liberties Union, which had close ties to President Roosevelt, refused to act. However, Ernest Besig, the director of the Northern California ACLU affiliate, broke from his national office, approached Fred, and asked him if he would be willing to be a test case to challenge the legality of the mass incarceration. Fred said yes, and an extraordinary attorney named Wayne M. Collins took his case.

Fred hadn't evaded the camps as a moral stand. He just didn't show up with his suitcase when he was told to. Why should he have?

He acted for himself and maybe for his girlfriend. He imagined himself an individual, with rights, the same rights as every other citizen. This was bold in 1942. People of color didn't do that. Fred Korematsu was a nail that stuck up.

So he was hammered down. He was tried and convicted, losing at every step of the way—at federal court in San Francisco, at the appeals court, and at the Supreme Court. He was sent to join his family at the Tanforan Assembly Center near San Francisco, and at the Topaz War Relocation Center in Utah. He had rocked the boat and brought unwanted notoriety to his family. In camp, he was shunned as a troublemaker who'd made all Japanese Americans look bad. After the war, as his family restarted their flower business, he drifted from the community, married, had two children, worked as a draftsman, and served as president of the local Lions Club.

Forty years after Fred's arrest, a law professor at the University of California, San Diego, Peter Irons, and a researcher, Aiko Herzig-Yoshinaga, discovered clear evidence that the US government attorney who had argued *Korematsu v. United States* before the Supreme Court in 1944 had deliberately lied, suppressed, and distorted evidence about the threat that Japanese Americans posed. With a team of young JA attorneys by his side, Fred Korematsu made national news when his conviction was vacated by the US District Court in San Francisco.

Fred didn't fit the image of a civil rights hero. He was shy, a bit awkward, and he mumbled. He wasn't comfortable talking about what happened. His life had been made harder because of it. But there was steadiness and confidence in the way he carried himself, always sharply dressed, clutching or smoking his pipe.

After forty years, he was embraced by a JA community that saw itself and Fred differently. He became comfortable speaking in public and inspired people with his straightforward honesty. He became a civil rights hero. His pursuit of justice resonated with the racial, ethnic, and social issues of the present. He spoke out against the targeting of Muslims and people of Middle Eastern and South Asian descent after 9/11 and against the detention without due process of prisoners at Guantánamo. An elementary school, middle school, and high school were named after him. In 1998, he was awarded the Presidential Medal of Freedom, the highest civilian honor in the United States.

The camps devastated the economic and social life of the Japanese American community. Ten years after the war, they still couldn't live, work, get their hair cut, or go bowling where they wanted. Seventy-five percent of JA men were self-employed, which means no one would employ them, except to mow their lawns or clean their houses. Twenty years after, the community began to thrive, build their own churches, establish their own baseball teams and bowling leagues, go to their own dentists and barbers, and raise families.

Then, gradually, the community stopped thriving. Before World War II, Japanese Americans represented the largest Asian population in America. Now we are among the smallest, the *only* Asian ethnic group that has shrunk instead of grown in the past twenty years. The community survives, but the trauma brought on by the camps, which broke down the family structure and undermined the psyche and aspirations of the JA people, both individually and as a community, is still being felt generations later.

Political hysteria and fear of immigrants continue to threaten our humanity. Asian Americans are confronted by the same ugly stereotypes or "poof"; they're invisible in the media. The other day, I heard a popular NPR host refer to China's economic rise as a "Chinese Pearl Harbor." Asian faces still make people uncomfortable. The big and little slights are a constant, often in the most progressive settings. People who don't see themselves as prejudiced express concern about Asians getting into the top universities.

Do we accept this kind of racism because it is so pervasive, or too minor to make a big deal about, or because we don't want to lose our job or personal relationships over it? It's painful and awkward whether we act on it or don't, but not acting is condoning it.

All Fred Korematsu wanted was to walk down the street with his girlfriend. My father just wanted to be seated at a restaurant. I want people to stop asking me where I'm from (Venice, California). And my fifteen-year-old daughter wants her life's choices to be determined by who she is and what she's capable of, not what box she checks off. We can make things better. Just make sure you bring plenty of nails.

HANNEGAN V. ESQUIRE (1946) (*amicus*)

In 1943, Frank Walker, the postmaster general of the United States, appalled by the pinup girl photos being circulated in *Esquire* and similar magazines, convened a hearing to seek public comment on whether these images were obscene. The committee in charge of deciding this question determined they were not. Undeterred in his quest to censor the magazine, the postmaster general terminated *Esquire*'s second-class mailing privileges. *Esquire* sued, arguing that at stake in the postmaster general's unilateral decision were fundamental questions—questions of the freedom to think for oneself, to consume media of one's choosing, and fundamentally to be free from arbitrary censorship. The Supreme Court found in the magazine's favor, ruling that the postmaster's personal tastes could not serve as the arbiter of obscenity. The Court wrote, ruling that "a requirement that literature or art conform to some norm prescribed by an official smacks of an ideology foreign to our system. . . . It would sanction withdrawal of the second-class rate tomorrow from another periodical whose social or economic views seemed harmful to another official." This degree of tyranny, the Court concluded, could not stand in a free society. The opinion stands as an emblem of the freedom of thought and media, and freedom from government censorship of content, that defines American First Amendment jurisprudence.

A Short Essay About Shorts

DANIEL HANDLER

In 1943, when it might strike you that there were better things to worry about, the United States postmaster general decided *Esquire* magazine was obscene. The ACLU disagreed, and after a media circus of a hearing, it prevailed. This case is one of many important ones in the cause of free expression, and the ACLU has gone many rounds with censorious scolds of every stripe. One article about the case is illustrated with a photograph of two old white guys gazing sternly at a pinup girl painting by Joaquin Alberto Vargas y Chávez, aka a "Vargas Girl." One of the men is the secretary of the "watchdog of New England's morals," and that's really all you need to know; such idiocy continues and the struggle continues. But what's really interesting about the case to me is what happened next, and what lesson it might convey. But first I'd like to go back to sixth grade, which is when I learned the lesson for the first time.

I learned about one thing in middle school, which as far as I can tell is pretty standard. It wasn't that there was nothing to learn in the 1980s in San Francisco, but I was in sixth grade, and almost everything felt like it was happening far away from my big, dilapidated public school in a quiet, foggy residential neighborhood. I was wrong, of course. Every crucial issue that comes to mind from that era and locale—AIDS, homelessness, drug addiction, domestic abuse, police violence, religious prosecution—was careening through the lives of my classmates and teachers, and it wasn't as if such struggles were at all distant from my own life. But ongoing issues of civil liberties did not feel present in the curriculum I was being fed (the transitive property, ancient Sumeria) or in my own preoccupations (*Dungeons and Dragons*, my freckly girlfriend). Until the heat wave.

A typical heat wave in San Francisco consists of a surprisingly warm afternoon, one full day of sunshine, and then another warm morning before the fog rolls back in and ends, a weather sequence known outside of San Francisco as "not worth mentioning." For us, it made for a nice break from the usual sullen gray sky. Some kids got some water balloons going. People shrieked, but it was middle school; somebody's always shrieking. Our principal got pretty shrieky herself, over the crackly intercom, and announced that henceforth, students would not be allowed to wear shorts. I remember that this seemed like a weird ruling—shorts?—but also that I didn't care much. I was a young teenager, self-conscious about my body, and besides, the heat wave was only going to last another day and a half.

I didn't think anything about it until a friend pointed out that our rights were being violated. She had a copy of our Student Rights and Responsibilities—a little pamphlet they'd given us on the first day of school. I hadn't kept mine, of course, because I didn't think rights and responsibilities had anything to do with me. They'd gone through them on the first day of school, and I'd vaguely followed along, but I was a geeky white Jewish kid who got straight A's. I was a good kid. I followed the rules.

Rule followers, though, tend to have an acute sense of injustice. When I saw that one of our rights was, "Students can dress how they choose," I was outraged in the instantaneous, remorseless way of the sixth grader. I helped everybody else get outraged too, and the next day we all wore shorts in protest. Faced with outrage from the administration, I was immediately ratted out as the ringleader and brought into the principal's office to argue my case. For many years, it was a badge of honor that I held off from crying until I was back outside in the hallway.

The argument went like you might imagine. The principal talked about water balloons and the mess they cause, puddles on the floor students could slip on, wet clothing making a mess of the classroom chairs. I just kept repeating that students can dress how they choose, that it was one of our rights. I remember she told me how hard it was to be a middle school principal, and that must have been the end of the argument. I left without getting in any official trouble, though I didn't feel very triumphant crying my way back to class, and everyone felt stupid the next day, when the fog rolled in and everyone was shivering in their shorts. Still, it felt like something of a victory, and we knew there'd be more heat waves in the future.

Our principal, however, was prepared. The next semester we had a new Rights and Responsibilities pamphlet, and the issue of our clothing was moved across the fold, from the right to dress how we chose to the responsibility to dress appropriately. For the next heat wave, my short-pants comrades and I had no bare leg to stand on.

This was, for me, the crucial lesson of middle school and one for the rest of life: that one can protest, fight, and win against injustice, but that those in power will just change the circumstances rather than concede the argument. The ACLU had to follow *Hannegan v. Esquire* all the way up to the Supreme Court because the postmaster, having failed to convince the right people that *Esquire* was obscene, revoked the magazine's second-class mail permit on the grounds that the magazine was morally improper, not for the public welfare. Having failed to be convincing, the postmaster elected to change the argument, starting up three more years of new arguments before a unanimous verdict, from the highest court in the land, finally scuttled this particular attempt at censorship—not that this signaled the end of old guys gazing sternly at something they didn't like and dreaming up strategies, one after the other, to keep other people from seeing it. They try and they keep trying. They're tireless and move quick. When we win the argument, they change the subject. When we prevail in court, they change the rules. It is not a fair fight because they keep fixing it, and there's no lasting victory, just small strikes, toeholds really, against shifting shiftiness. As the ACLU understands, it's our right, and our responsibility, to do this: to tussle like middle schoolers against our principals and in favor of our principles.

TERMINIELLO V. CITY OF CHICAGO (1949) (*amicus*)

Terminiello v. City of Chicago demonstrates that defending fundamental rights and liberties is not always pleasant or easy. Terminiello himself was a virulent racist, fascist, and anti-Semite. Yet the ACLU filed a brief on his behalf, just as it represented American Nazis in *National Socialist Party of America v. Skokie and* the KKK in *Capitol Square Review & Advisory Board v. Pinette*. Unflagging defense of liberty characterizes the ACLU's work, despite the strange circumstances and consequences this sometimes entails.

They Talk Like That

GERALDINE BROOKS

People talk like that. They talk like that. Let's deal with that.

—Jay-Z

On the facade of the Stadtkirche in the eastern German town of Wittenberg, a thirteenth-century bas-relief of a Judensau, or "Jew's pig," shows a rabbi with his hand up the rear end of a sow while members of his congregation suckle her teats. Since the entrance to the former Jewish ghetto lies just beyond, the medieval Jews of Wittenberg were constantly confronted and humiliated by this obscene image. Once common throughout medieval Europe, Wittenberg's Judensau is one of the last still in its original place. In 1988, to mark the fiftieth anniversary of Kristallnacht, the East German government commissioned a sculpture by the artist Wieland Schmiedel. It's a simple, eloquent attempt at interpretation and atonement. Set in the ground below the Judensau, it depicts paving stones, heaving, tilted out of place, as a noxious, black poison pulses powerfully from beneath.

When I visited Germany in 2009, I found the dialogue between these two works the most potent of all the numerous Holocaust memorials, museums, and historic sites we toured. The Judensau, on the facade of the very church where Martin Luther preached, was for me the loudest and grossest indictment of anti-Semitism—its entrenchment, acceptance, and official sanction not just under the Nazis but throughout centuries of immiseration. The Schmiedel work, with its understated Maya Lin-esque minimalism, both acknowledged this and addressed the probability that the vileness remains—maybe paved over for a while, but ready to bubble up and spill out into our own carefully curated idea of ourselves as a somehow more evolved and superior generation.

Terminiello v. City of Chicago, in which the ACLU was amicus, brought the Schmiedel work vividly to my mind. Arthur Terminiello, a Catholic priest from Birmingham, Alabama, was convicted of breach of the peace by the Chicago courts following a riotous night during which he whipped up a meeting of the Christian Veterans of America with anti-Semitic slurs and Left-baiting, while an even larger crowd of opponents protested violently outside the auditorium. Glass shattered as bricks flew through windows. Would-be audience members had the clothes torn off their backs as they tried to enter the auditorium. Police had to form a flying wedge to get Terminiello into the hall through the wall of bodies blocking the way and howling "Hitlers," and "damn fascists." Attempting to keep order, police dodged ice picks, rocks, and stink bombs.

Struggling to be heard over the roar of the protesters, Terminiello exhorted his "fellow Christians" against the "slimy scum" that he said were "going on to destroy America." Among these, he singled out "Zionist Jews" and leftists. "We have fifty seven varieties of pinks and reds and pastel shades in this country and all of it can be traced back to the New Deal" and "Queen Eleanor [who] is now one of the world's communists." Calling Franco "the savior of what was left of Europe" and excoriating unnamed "non-Christian" American servicemen, doctors, and nurses who, he alleged, had tortured and sterilized and infected Germans with syphilis—"Do you wonder they were persecuted in other countries in the world?"—he concluded by urging his followers not to be like the timid Apostles before the coming of the Holy Ghost: "We must not lock ourselves in an upper room for fear of the Jews." Chicago's court fined Terminiello one hundred dollars. He appealed to the Illinois Appellate Court and the Illinois Supreme Court, both of which affirmed his conviction. But the US Supreme Court overturned it.

As I read the Court's almost sixty-year-old opinion, it wasn't Terminiello who was on my mind. I found myself thinking instead about a night of flames and shouting in 2017 when a Terminiello-like provocateur, also given to wild and ugly defamations, also left-hating and anti-Semitic (although in this case the Semite victims of his slurs generally are Muslims), faced antifascist rioters at a speech he attempted to deliver on campus at Berkeley.

"A function of free speech under our system of government is to invite dispute," wrote Justice William O. Douglas for the majority in *Terminiello*. "The vitality of civil and political institutions in our society depends on free discussion," he wrote. This right "is therefore one of the chief distinctions that sets us apart from totalitarian regimes. Accordingly, it may indeed best serve its high purpose when it induces a condition of unrest, creates dissatisfaction with conditions as they are, or even stirs people to anger. Speech is often provocative and challenging. It may strike at prejudices and preconceptions and have profound unsettling effects as it presses for acceptance of an idea." Douglas goes on to assert that this kind of speech is protected "unless shown likely to produce a clear and present danger of a serious substantive evil that rises far above public inconvenience, annoyance, or unrest." There is, he writes, "no room under our Constitution for a more restrictive view. For the alternative would lead to standardization of ideas either by legislatures, courts, or dominant political or community groups."

About the same time as hate-speaking exhibitionists bee-lined to Berkeley, hoping to stir up more protests, the town of Wittenberg prepared to celebrate the anniversary of Martin Luther's Reformation. As it did so, the Internet lit up with petitions seeking removal of the Judensau. Put it in a museum if you must, said the petitions, but take it out of the public square.

But to put it in a museum is to remove it from its potent context. In a museum, we will no longer imagine the daily lives of the Jews who couldn't go to or come from their homes without passing beneath that hateful image. More dangerous, putting it in a museum consigns it safely to the past. It's as if to say that all this is over and done with, a relic of a barbarism that no longer exists. It's to assert that we're better than that, when the evidence to the contrary is everywhere around us, bubbling up from beneath, just barely paved over.

Yes, the image still causes pain. Today's alt-right hatemongers cause pain. Terminiello's words no doubt caused pain. But pain is better than the ineffable, unsustainable fantasy of the anesthetized opium dream.

Our pain, in the end, is what provokes us to seek healing.

BROWN V. BOARD OF EDUCATION OF TOPEKA (1954) (*amicus*)

Brown is perhaps the most famous case in American legal history. It was the culmination of the long fight of the National Association for the Advancement of Colored People (NAACP) for quality education for blacks and the advent of a longer struggle over what that means.

From the start of public education in the United States, children primarily attended schools segregated by race. Schools for white children received the bulk of state resources, leaving schools for black and other minority students to scrape by on whatever funding they could find. This was true in both the North and South, though the means and reasons differed.

Brown itself is predicated on this divide. Under the 1896 ruling of *Plessy v. Ferguson,* racial segregation was deemed constitutional so long as blacks' facilities were equal to those of whites. In *Brown,* the NAACP argued first that segregation is inherently unequal. Black schools lacked the connections, reputation, and institutional power of white schools. Categorically denying black students those benefits was unacceptable. Furthermore, the NAACP and its allies argued that segregation was a fundamentally subordinating experience for black and brown children, who were relegated to ill-equipped schools. The

ACLU joined this argument with a powerful amicus brief, encouraging the Court to abandon *Plessy* and hold states accountable to their black citizen-students.

Chief Justice Earl Warren, writing for the majority, ruled that segregated schools were a violation of the Fourteenth Amendment's equal protection clause of the Constitution. The ruling required schools with statutory segregation to integrate their student bodies. It is here that *Brown* stumbles. The Court ordered integration to begin not immediately, but with "all deliberate speed," which became a license for resistance and retrenchment. What's more, *Brown* was narrowly tailored to segregation in schools, leaving the other abuses of Jim Crow untouched.

Rocket City

YAA GYASI

In 1961, President John F. Kennedy delivered a speech in which he declared his commitment to landing a man on the moon before the end of that decade. "There is no strife, no prejudice, no national conflict in outer space as yet. . . . Its conquest deserves the best of all mankind, and its opportunity for peaceful cooperation may never come again," he said. "We choose to go to the moon. We choose to go to the moon in this decade and do the other things, not because they are easy, but because they are hard, because that goal will serve to organize and measure the best of our energies and skills, because that challenge is one that we are willing to accept, one we are unwilling to postpone, and one we intend to win."

It was Kennedy's first year in office, his first year presiding over a country gripped by racism, a country that was forged in strife, prejudice, and conflict. That year saw the Freedom Rides, the bus burnings and passenger beatings of black people hoping to desegregate transportation. The next year, President Kennedy would send the National Guard and federal troops to the University of Mississippi when riots broke out after James Meredith, the first black student to be admitted to the school, attempted registration. Two people died and dozens were injured. The year after that, 200,000 Americans would march on Washington. But on that day, the day of his famous moon speech, JFK was able to offer a vision of a new world, unsullied, as blank and as innocent as a newborn baby. NASA had received its mandate, and the journey to the moon began.

* * *

On January 27, 1967, the command module of the Apollo 1 spacecraft caught fire during a launch rehearsal test, killing astronauts Virgil "Gus" Grissom, Ed White, and Roger Chaffee. Several things had gone wrong on the morning of the test, from a foul odor in the breathing oxygen of the crew's suits to a faulty communication system. "How are we going to get to the moon if we can't talk between two or three buildings?" Grissom asked. Hours later, the word, "Fire!" A stray spark, a pure oxygen environment, a hatch door that wouldn't open. The three men became the first and last casualties of the Apollo moon landing program.

Many of the schools in my hometown of Huntsville, Alabama, "The Rocket City," home of the Marshall Space Flight Center, are named in commemoration of the people and spacecrafts that have perished over the sixty years of NASA's space flight programs. There's Challenger Middle School, where my younger brother went for a time. There's Chaffee Elementary, which is still open, and Ed White Middle, which has since closed. My high school, Virgil I. Grissom High, opened its doors in 1969. Today, sixty-five years after *Brown v. Board of Education of Topeka* ruled that separate educational facilities are inherently unequal, the Rocket City is still trying to get out from under a federal desegregation order that was issued the year after Grissom High opened.

I never gave much thought to space travel when I was a child. Though my imagination was big and wild, it had always been tethered to Earth. By the time my parents announced we were headed to Huntsville, my family had already moved three times, across continents and states. Earth had enough upheaval and uncertainty all its own. Why go searching for more? My parents told my brother and me that depending on which house they chose, we'd be headed to school at either Mountain Gap or Challenger. I remember hoping they'd choose the Mountain Gap house because who would want to go to a school with *challenge* in its name? A school named after a shuttle that exploded a mere seventy-three seconds after liftoff? I wanted to stay grounded.

Mountain Gap Elementary School was one mile from the house my family rented on Running Meade Trail. On mornings when neither of my parents could drive me to school, I walked, past the Publix and the gas station and Aldridge Creek, and sometimes the only other black person I would see on my way there was the crossing guard, with her yellow jacket and her white gloves. She always waved me through traffic with a smile, her stop sign held high. She knew who my brother was without me ever having to tell her. In fact, nearly everyone in that neighborhood recognized my family by sight by the simple fact that we were among the handful of black families that lived in southeast Huntsville, the white part of town. "You're that black professor's kid," a stranger once said to me. I'd lived there long enough not to wonder how he knew. Years later, when I asked my parents whether it ever bothered them, being the only black family for miles around, remembering how much those stares and comments had bothered me, they shrugged it off. "The schools were better," they said.

It is impossible to talk about schools in Alabama, indeed schools all across America, without also talking about race. This was true in 1963, when Dr. Sonnie Wellington Hereford III filed the lawsuit against the Huntsville Public School system that enabled his son, Sonnie Hereford IV, and four other black students in Huntsville to become the first children to integrate public schools in Alabama, and it is still true today. Today, south Huntsville is white, and north Huntsville is black. The school zones reflect this, and the quality of the schools within these zones reflects the history of racism in America. "The schools were better," my parents said, but what they didn't say, what they didn't have to say, was that the schools were better because they were whiter—that nothing in America, not even its public schools, escapes the taint of white supremacy. My parents, African immigrants unattuned to the nuances of race in their new country, had come to the United States to further my father's education as well as to provide greater opportunities for their children. They made a choice unavailable to many African Americans, a choice they should never have been required to make.

When the *Brown v. Board of Education* ruling was handed down on May 17, 1954, the Court asked that public schools move toward desegregation "with all deliberate speed," but as many journalists and scholars have pointed out, "deliberate speed" meant different things to different states. If the word *deliberate* is to be taken at its dictionary definition, then it can in fact be interpreted as the opposite of speedy, a calculated and unhurried way of processing something before acting on it. And in a state once governed by a man who declared, "Segregation now, segregation tomorrow, segregation forever," it comes as little surprise that desegregation wasn't a matter of great urgency.

Many school districts across the country are still under federal desegregation orders from the 1960s and 1970s, and "[inactivity] is not unusual among longstanding segregation cases." Perhaps the Huntsville City School Board was expecting more of that same inactivity in 2014 when it submitted a modification of school zones that would have further entrenched segregation for Huntsville's black students. Instead, it was met with US District Judge Madeline Hughes Haikala, who decided to review the case's fifty-year history, bringing *Sonnie Wellington Hereford, IV v. Huntsville Board of Education* back to light. In her memorandum opinion, Judge Haikala compares a few of the schools in Huntsville, including Grissom, where my brothers and I went to school, and Butler High School, just eight miles away.

The figures in the opinion are damning. They show that in 2011, Grissom, a school where 8 percent of the student population was African American, had a graduation rate of 88 percent. By contrast, Butler, a school with an African American population of 71 percent and a white population of 13 percent, had a graduation rate of 31 percent. Only 22 percent of Butler students were reading at or above grade level as compared to 78 percent of Grissom students. Dr. Casey Wardynski, the superintendent of the public school system for Huntsville City Schools at that time, said, "My feeling about Butler was it was barely a school."

While my many childhood moves never took me to outer space, they did make me the kind of person given to imagining life as an unending sequence of roads not taken, roads blocked or cut off or rerouted. Had my family gone down one road, we might have stayed in Ghana. I might have grown up surrounded by all of the aunts and uncles, cousins and grandparents I never got the chance to know. Had my family lived eight miles up the road in Huntsville, crossing that invisible line that divides races and determines school outcomes, I may never have read at grade level. The life that I know now, a life full of literature and writing, may never have come to pass.

In her 2014 memorandum opinion, Judge Haikala counters the Huntsville City School Board's claim to have done everything within its power to end segregation in its schools. She writes that "[children] have no control over where they live now, but giving them a strong education is the surest way to ensure that they will have choices about where they will live and what they will do when they become adults." This couldn't have been truer in my case. I cannot trace the line of my life without passing through my world-class education, my four years spent at Virgil I. Grissom High School, which, in the year that I graduated, had been listed among the top 5 percent of *Newsweek*'s rankings of all high schools in America. My graduating class sent two students to Princeton, one to Harvard, one to Yale. Some of these classmates were, like my own family, first- and second-generation immigrants, transplants who had moved to Huntsville to work at NASA or the University of Alabama in Huntsville or the Redstone Arsenal. Some were Alabama born and bred, Huntsville natives for generations upon generations, proud, white Alabamians for whom a decent education was a birthright. All of us Grissom students were the beneficiaries of a great gift beyond our choosing or control.

It took eight years, and six manned Apollo missions for the United States to accomplish President John F. Kennedy's goal of landing a man on the moon. That "one small step for man, one giant leap for mankind," was indeed triumphant, and the lead-up to Neil Armstrong's first step comprised countless steps, countless staff hours, countless triumphs and disappointments.

I imagine that Grissom, White, and Chaffee would have wanted to be the first three to touch Tranquility Base. Had Grissom lived, it may well have been his voice we heard from Earth. The school that was named in his honor was recently rebuilt in an entirely new location, upgraded and expanded to include things like a café and a media center and a robotics lab and a 3D printer for students interested in a class called "advanced manufacturing," all of which were unheard of when my friends and I were students there. The demographics at Grissom have also begun to shift. Thanks in part to renewed attention to the desegregation order, Grissom now has a black population of 17 percent and a white population of 63 percent. It's a beautiful school, one that makes it easy to imagine a world of possibility and promise for the children who walk through its doors. And if one day, Americans are able to look at the work of desegregation and racial justice with as much urgency as we once looked upon the race to the moon, then perhaps the work that *Brown v. Board of Education* began could finally be seen as a challenge we are willing to accept, a challenge we are unwilling to postpone. Perhaps the doors of public schools all across the country might further widen, their promises might expand, to include all of America's children.

GIDEON V. WAINWRIGHT (1963)

(*amicus*)

Prior to *Gideon v. Wainwright*, indigent criminal defendants possessed only a tenuous right to counsel. In *Betts v. Brady* (1942), the Supreme Court had ruled that states weren't obligated to provide indigent defendants with representation unless some special circumstance was present, such as illiteracy or a mental disability. *Powell v. Alabama* (1932) had established an exception to this rule and mandated that all defendants in capital cases receive effective legal counsel. Under these rules, some states created proto-public defenders to represent indigent criminal defendants. Others contracted indigent cases out to private attorneys, and still others (like Florida) did nothing at all. *Gideon* eliminated this last option and demanded states create some institutional mechanism for indigent criminal representation.

While subsequent case law has mostly expanded and affirmed this principle, *Gideon*'s promise remains unfulfilled. Overburdening and inadequate resourcing plague many public defenders, undermining their ability to protect indigent defendants. Correcting this injustice remains a priority for the ACLU, and it continues the fight to ensure all criminal defendants receive quality representation.

One Will Be Provided for You

SERGIO DE LA PAVA

I guess technically I'm not yet on Rikers Island, but it sure feels that way. Where I am is outside a trailer just before the bridge to that island, and the correction officer inside it wants to know things. Who I am, of course, but also which of the more than ten thousand inmates I wish to visit and, less intuitively, where precisely on that island he is located. My reward is a placard for my car that entitles me to drive across that bridge onto the island proper.

Rikers Island is a jail, really a complex of ten separate jails. So it's more like a penal colony, probably the most notorious one in the world. An actual island, but one that quadrupled in size through inmate labor and landfill. The mayor of New York recently announced that one of his goals is closing Rikers. This feels like when physicists warn that one day, the sun will burn itself out.

My next step is a control room of sorts. I fill out a card that then gets time-stamped; in a place where time signifies so greatly, even the duration spent getting me to my ultimate destination must be measured. The way to a specific facility is by bus. I sit in one, and it's a Sunday morning and I'm wearing a suit. The driver looks at me while something palpably builds in the air until he asks if I'm a private attorney. I answer that I'm a public defender, and the situation immediately deflates.

There didn't have to be public defenders. If you define a public defender as an attorney whose practice consists entirely of representing indigent criminal defendants who would otherwise not be represented by counsel, then the United States has only about fifteen thousand of them. By comparison, there are currently about forty-five thousand professional writers. And while there may be significant variance jurisdiction by jurisdiction in the work of a public defender, everyone agrees on the foundational document of American indigent defense: a relatively brief and unanimous decision handed down on March 8, 1963, by the US Supreme Court.

Clarence Earl Gideon didn't invent or discover anything. His contribution to America's conception of legal justice resides firmly in the realm where common sense meets personal injury. If no one is in a better position to identify injustice than its recent victim, Gideon was perfectly perched. Charged in Florida with the after-hours burglary of a pool hall, he correctly intuited that he could benefit from the services of an attorney at his imminent jury trial, a trial that had as a possible, if not probable, ending the imposition of a significant prison sentence. Better yet, he converted this belief into a formal request of the trial judge. He requested that the judge assign an attorney to his case so that he, Gideon, would not have to conduct the trial himself.

Especially for a nonlawyer, this request was a nice piece of preservation. Preserving the record, the written account of a court proceeding, is the legal practice of alerting a lower court of a potential or actual legal error in a case in the hopes that it will avoid or correct it. Failure to do so in a timely manner or with sufficient specificity can allow a subsequent higher court to pointedly ignore the issue altogether, never deciding on the merits whether or not reversible error was made. No one would ever argue that Gideon failed to preserve his issue for appellate review and that review would ultimately extend to the highest possible level.

But a more accurate depiction of Gideon's legal acumen would follow with his statement that "the United States Supreme Court says I am entitled to be represented by counsel." This was untrue. In fact, the Court was on record saying something quite like the opposite. Not to be outdone, the ruling judge seemed to have no greater grasp of the issue when it denied Gideon's request and asserted that under Florida law, "the only time the court can appoint counsel to represent a defendant is when that person is charged with a capital offense." This was also untrue. The only time appointment of counsel was mandated was in capital cases, but it was not true that the court lacked the ability to appoint an attorney to assist Gideon in his upcoming felony trial. He could have, but he didn't, and he didn't because they never did. In other words, it was 1961 in a country somehow self-renowned for its respect for human rights and no one really knew what they were doing.

The facility I'm in has the best area for meeting with clients, a small room with a circular table and two colored plastic chairs without edges. Client walks in and manages a smile. We're good, he and I. We met almost two years ago. I'm now the world's foremost expert on Client's prearrest social media presence; I know it far better than he does. His wife kept me posted on her pregnancy, then too graphically on the resulting childbirth. She has made it clear to me more than once that she has little interest in the specifics of her husband's case beyond the fact that it must not end in a trial. His father can't decide if I'm grossly incompetent or actively engaged in disloyal malfeasance in cahoots with the prosecutor. In the final analysis, he concludes that I am the dumbest person alive because I consistently fail to be wowed by his analyses of the US Constitution and how it relates to his son's case.

But that's his family. Client and I are good. We're like friends. Only we're not friends, it's much stranger than that. I'm his attorney. I have a client facing a quarter-century in prison who has paid me not a cent and whom I made no explicit decision to represent. It's kind of weird is what I'm saying.

When the US Supreme Court heard argument on *Gideon v. Wainwright*, it was a pretty one-sided affair. The Court had assigned Abe Fortas to represent Gideon. Fortas had a wealth of experience; he would soon thereafter become one of the justices of the Court. But what he really had was a clear edge on the merits. For example, there was the question of the parties' respective amicus curiae.

Amici are friends of the court who have an interest in the proceeding but are not actually party to it. If permitted, they file a brief in support of a party's position. Florida had appealed to the other forty-nine states to ask for that kind of legal friendship. Their pitch was something like inviolable majesty of the states, or whatever. It didn't work. A clear majority of these states already provided counsel for their criminally accused poor. Ultimately, twenty-three states did sign on to an amicus brief, but in opposition to Florida and in favor of the proposition that Gideon had been entitled to an attorney. Only Alabama and North Carolina joined as amicus on the side of Florida.

Of all amici, the American Civil Liberties Union had the greatest impact. Unsurprisingly, it did so in support of Gideon's argument. Its lawyers provided a detailed overview of how the existing Supreme Court rule was adversely affecting state court defendants and their appellate litigation. They argued, essentially, for the dignity and importance of the legal profession and did so effectively enough that they were granted the uncommon-for-amici opportunity to participate in the oral argument.

The argument ostensibly centered on legal principles like federalism, states' rights, stare decisis, and the relationship between the Sixth and Fourteenth Amendments. But, really, it was about fundamental fairness and what the American conception of it would be as it relates to its criminal justice system. A criminal trial is a complicated sui generis affair—a special blend of art, technique, and legal knowledge with your basic terrifying stakes. For those reasons, even wide swaths of the legal profession opt out entirely. Forcing a layperson to conduct a criminal trial while under the extreme pressure of losing his or her own liberty seemed, let's say, constitutionally unfair.

The questioning that day seemed to implicitly acknowledge this fact to such an extent that a lot of the drama was drained from the proceeding. And for those who really had their hearts set on more criminal trials conducted by impoverished people whose formal education ended at age fourteen, it wasn't too difficult to identify a lowlight. Asked if Gideon would've been allowed to represent someone else in court, Bruce Jacob, Florida's attorney, incredibly asserted that he would. Immediately reminded by two justices that this would constitute the unlicensed practice of law and that the local bar association might object, his response spoke volumes: "I'm sorry, your honor, that was a stupid answer."

* * *

Client and I are having an odd interaction. One of us believes a trial is the most dignified weapon against mass incarceration, certainly the most exciting. That person has scrutinized every element and angle of the case and identified a clear, admittedly narrow, path to victory. Narrow or not, that same person has the early symptoms of trial fever and is an egomaniac and also just feels that guilty pleas, so many guilty pleas, are just too damn dispiriting. But the other person is Client and the decision whether or not to proceed to trial is solely his.

It's not what he's explicitly saying, it's what I'm sensing within him. Sitting there together on Rikers, he outwardly agrees with everything I'm saying about the majesty of a trial and how the sole burden is on the prosecution to not just prove their case but to prove it beyond a reasonable doubt to the unanimous satisfaction of a jury of his peers and the right to counsel and to due process and to confront the witnesses and all that. If I say it, he knows it's true. It's just not true true. Client suspects I'm too invested or maybe uninvested to admit it: that a trial is just a mechanism by which criminal defendants are given even more incarceration than if they just pled guilty. In the communities where a lot of my clients live, there is ample anecdotal support for this belief.

To review, Client and I are like friends, but with one crucial imbalance: no matter what unfolds from here on out, I am never going to be sentenced on the case that links us. I'm free to theorize about the evolution of the right to counsel and the strange relationships it has birthed. Client wants to know when he's getting out.

The Court's decision in *Gideon v. Wainwright*, 372 US 335 (1963), surprised no close observers but still managed to be seismic. Its reasoning was not extensive, but it was unimpeachable. The Sixth Amendment clearly guaranteed anyone accused of a crime the right to "the Assistance of Counsel for his defence." It was well settled that the Fourteenth Amendment made obligatory upon the states any provision of the Bill of Rights that was "fundamental and essential to a fair trial." Was the right to counsel that kind of fundamental? Yes, and according to the Court, this was an "obvious truth." Obvious because "reason and reflection require us to recognize that in our adversary system of criminal justice, any person haled into court, who is too poor to hire a lawyer, cannot be assured a fair trial unless counsel is provided for him." That certainty, undeniably warranted, maybe masked the inherent oddness of the Court's ruling. For the first time ever, and never since, the Court had deemed that a specific human being helping another, not a general procedure or concept, was constitutionally essential.

We are in a trial courtroom and all the preliminaries are out of the way. Only one question remains unanswered. Does Client really want the court staff to bring a panel of potential jurors in to commence his trial, or will there be a disposition? The System is always ready for a disposition, it's never too late to create another long-term prisoner of war and decades of toxic mass incarceration have done nothing but streamline the process.

The judge is one of the better ones. But even she feels the need to bring up the trial tax. The tax is a powerful prosecution weapon. At its core, it's a warning. It warns the individual debating whether to exercise their prized constitutional right to a trial that should it not work out, should he finish second, then he can expect a heavier sentence than the one currently on offer. Defenders of the tax will say that it is a necessary product of heavy volume, very usually not mentioning that the volume itself is the miscarried product of a kind of social sickness that took hold in the seventies and metastasized into a global-leading 700 percent increase in our incarceration rate.

The tax is also illegitimate for other reasons. What sentence is appropriate given certain criminal conduct and the history of the actor is almost always entirely ascertainable months before a trial. And except in rare instances, there is no legitimate cause to enhance that sentence simply because a trial, the alleged foundation of our system, has taken place. Whatever its legitimacy, Client pleads guilty to avoid the tax even though, given the lack of actual harm, the promised sentence is way too severe for my taste. Then, in what feels like an extra little defeat, Client turns to me in great sincerity, shakes his head, and apologizes for not going to trial.

The aftermath of the court's decision was immediate: states scrambled to comply, but the specifics were up to them. Some created government public defender offices (see New Jersey), others entered into contracts with nonprofit entities like mine in New York. *Gideon v. Wainwright* didn't create public defenders. Brilliant legal innovator Clara Shortridge Foltz had brought the concept to Los Angeles half a century before. But by dragging the concept from contingency to necessity the Court gave it something invaluable: endurance.

It remains a lovely concept. But we know what happens to those. This one has managed to simultaneously evolve and devolve. For example, the Court has subsequently made clear that what's constitutionally required is the "effective" assistance of counsel, and not just before and at trial but also on direct appeal. But theory and practice don't always meet, and too often, states do the bare minimum to comply while intentionally denying the resources that would make for a robust right to counsel for the poor. Like so much else from that Court around that time—hell, like everything American—it was primarily aspirational, these newly enunciated principles, a statement of who we wish we were. And as with any such statement, reality likes to fight back.

Still, done right, there's a purity to what we do. The true public defender exists outside the marketplace in an arena of pure legal combat. She pursues something intellectually based but also deeply and intimately interpersonal. The job is equal parts thinking and feeling, scholarship and friendship, with the slightest failure in either threatening dire consequences. How many activities like that even exist, let alone enjoy the imprimatur of constitutional force?

Also there's this. The world is full of misperceptions, may be nothing more than a giant one. An example is the common stereotype of the public defender as a kind of harried subcompetent. Harried, yes, but don't let pop culture kid you. When we talk about public defenders, we're mainly talking about ironclad experts. Because the volume is crushing, true, repetition also builds skill and knowledge. Pair that with the fact that the average public defender just seems really smart, not surprising when you consider the intellectual underpinnings of the work, and you start to realize that if you're ever arrested in a big city, you're almost certainly better off with a public defender, or at least a former one, than whatever pretender you might otherwise scare up.

It all makes for something so organically intense it probably can't be adequately explained to a civilian. I've tried and failed. But, in my defense, deep down, I probably just want it to remain private; so few things anymore have such genuine authenticity.

At Client's sentencing, I calculate how old he'll be when he gets out. He will one day be released from prolonged stasis into a vastly different world. I also can't help calculating how old I'll be and projecting what my life will be then. I decide it will be whatever it will be.

I do more math. I have represented more than ten thousand clients, a city's worth of troubled souls. Chance linked us, but once linked it felt like fate. Our connections traceable to Gideon but forged individually each time.

I wish for all of them the best thing you can wish for a soul. The result we strove for together but only sometimes achieved.

I wish them freedom.

ESCOBEDO V. ILLINOIS (1964)

In *Escobedo v. Illinois,* the ACLU of Illinois brought suit on behalf of a man convicted of murder largely based on a statement he made alone while subjected to police questioning. Although the lower courts dealt with the case primarily in terms of settled Fifth Amendment tests of voluntariness, the Supreme Court, in an opinion written by Justice Arthur Goldberg, chose instead for the first time to extend Sixth Amendment "assistance of counsel" protections to an accused person under police interrogation. This 5–4 split decision built on *Gideon v. Wainwright* (1963) to make such statements inadmissible due to denial of attorney assistance, a principle that was later advanced by *Miranda v. Arizona* (1966).

Legal Counsel at the Moment Most Crucial

DAVE EGGERS

On the night of January 19, 1960, Manuel Valtierra was murdered in Chicago. The police suspected that his brother-in-law, Danny Escobedo, might have pulled the trigger, given that Escobedo's sister, Grace, claimed that Valtierra had abused her. Escobedo was arrested a few hours after the shooting and was brought in for questioning. He said nothing substantial to the police and was released that day. On January 30, Benedict DiGerlando, also a suspect in the killing, told the police that Escobedo had fired the fatal shots, and Escobedo was brought in again on January 30.

Once at the precinct, Escobedo told the police that he wanted his lawyer, Warren Wolfson, present during any interrogation. The police refused. Escobedo's mother called Wolfson, notifying him of Escobedo's arrest. Wolfson arrived at the precinct and made his presence known to the sergeant on duty. The sergeant refused to allow him to see Escobedo. At one point, Wolfson caught sight of Escobedo as he was being interrogated, but police still did not grant him the right to speak to his client until, they said, they "were done" with him. Meanwhile, during the interrogation, Escobedo repeatedly asked to have his counsel present, but police told him that Wolfson did not want to see him. During their interrogation of Escobedo, detectives extracted what they claimed was a confession, and at trial, Escobedo was convicted of murder.

Escobedo appealed this conviction, and the case wound its way to the Supreme Court, with Bernard Weisberg arguing for the ACLU with Walter T. Fisher. The Court decided, 5–4, in Escobedo's favor, noting that the Constitution guarantees a defendant the right to a lawyer, and thwarting that right during interrogation defeats the entire purpose of that right. "The guiding hand of counsel," the Court wrote, was most crucial at this most delicate part of the criminal justice process. In the end, the conviction was overturned and the precedent in *Escobedo v. Illinois,* decided in 1964, established the right of any suspect to have a lawyer present during police questioning. In their ruling, made in the thick of the Cold War, the Court also noted that "the Soviet criminal code does not permit a lawyer to be present during an investigation. The Soviet trial has thus been aptly described as 'an appeal from the pretrial investigation.'"

Escobedo v. Illinois brought necessary progress that improved the criminal justice system. A few years later, *Miranda v. Arizona* established what we now know as our Miranda rights, which must be read to anyone being arrested prior to questioning and which include the right to remain silent and the right to an attorney. *Miranda* built on, and in a way supplanted, *Escobedo*. Thereafter, not only did a suspect have a right to an attorney during interrogation, but police had to inform the suspect of these rights during the arrest. All of this was positive and long overdue.

And yet.

And yet we still have widespread, even epidemic, problems with forced confessions. According to the Innocence Project, one out of every four defendants whose convictions were later overturned using DNA evidence were originally convicted through false or forced confessions. And the problem is diabolical. Even when innocent suspects know their rights, they often agree to answer questions without an attorney present *because they know they are innocent*. They want to be helpful. They feel they have nothing to hide. And they don't want to appear guilty by hiring a lawyer.

And thus they answer questions and are frequently tricked or pressured into a confession. Sometimes they're interrogated so long—on average, interrogations last sixteen hours—that they'll say anything to leave the room and go to sleep. Sometimes detectives simply lie to them, claiming evidence they actually don't have, or they fabricate witnesses who implicate them in the crime. And then there are the instances of force, or the threat of force. And the instances of the suspect being too young or otherwise mentally unable to understand the nature of an interrogation and the gravity of what might be self-incrimination.

Culturally, we have to change our thinking about interrogations. Every police procedural on television and film glamorizes these interrogations and implicitly approves of what are undeniable human abuses and violations of the Constitution. Suspects are kept chained to chairs, are denied food and water, are kept under hot lights, and are pitted against friends and family. They are deceived and intimidated. They are told that their conviction is assured, and their punishment will be far worse unless they confess. And all the while, audiences are expected to approve because the detectives, certain of the suspect's guilt, simply need to get to the desired result, conviction, with a minimum of interference. This makes for good and satisfying entertainment but represents a fundamental misunderstanding of the rights of suspects in a free society.

As a nation, we still, nearly sixty years after *Escobedo v. Illinois*, look askance at anyone who asks for an attorney before speaking with police. We still see this as some kind of admission of guilt. Why would an innocent person need a lawyer? we ask. This attitude must change. Waiting until an attorney is present must be seen as an act of wisdom—an acknowledgment of the wisdom of the Sixth and Fourteenth Amendments—rather than evidence of guilt.

And after we achieve that, we have more changes ahead: all interrogations must be electronically recorded to be valid; interrogations must be limited to a reasonable amount of time (a study by the Center on Wrongful Convictions and the University of California-Irvine found that 84 percent of false confessions occurred after interrogations of more than six hours); and interrogators should be prohibited from lying to suspects—presenting false evidence, false witnesses, and false scenarios involving leniency if the suspect confesses.

We have a ways to go to make the system better and to prevent the towering moral offense of wrongful conviction. But *Escobedo* was a landmark case that no doubt prevented thousands of innocent men and women from being railroaded into self-incrimination. "We have learned the lesson of history, ancient and modern," Justice

Goldberg wrote in the majority opinion, "that a system of criminal law enforcement which comes to depend on the 'confession' will, in the long run, be less reliable and more subject to abuse than a system which depends on extrinsic evidence independently secured through skillful investigation."

NEW YORK TIMES CO. V. SULLIVAN (1964) (*amicus*)

New York Times Co. v. Sullivan emerged during a tense chapter in American history. By 1960, Dr. Martin Luther King Jr. had galvanized America into grappling with its racism, past and present. Attempting to tamp down this threat to the status quo, Southern officials and law enforcement filed perjury charges against Dr. King.

To back King, civil rights supporters purchased a full page of the *New York Times*'s March 29 issue. Their ad primarily solicited donations to fund King's legal defense, but also detailed some of Southern law enforcement's excesses, such as the penchant for using dogs, fire hoses, and tear gas on nonviolent black protesters.

L. B. Sullivan was the Montgomery safety commissioner at the time, whose duties included supervising law enforcement. Although he was not named in the ad, Sullivan claimed the ad defamed him by inaccurately reporting that he criticized the police, which in turn impugned his competence as the police's watchdog.

After several unfortunate decisions in Alabama state courts, the *Times*'s appeal reached the Supreme Court. The ACLU filed a thorough amicus brief on behalf of the *Times* and was pleased to see Justice William Brennan protect freedom of the press against de facto censorship. At its core, *Sullivan* creates a two-tiered system of libel law. To prove libel, private citizens must simply show that the statements were false and damaging to their interests. Conversely, public figures must prove that the statements were false and damaging, and that the speaker knew the statements were false. This higher standard forms the bedrock of freedom of the press and government accountability.

How the First Amendment Finally Got Its Wings

TIMOTHY EGAN

In Alabama, in the midst of the blood, fear, and trauma of the civil rights battles, a police commissioner by the name of L. B. Sullivan took a legal whack at one of the foundational pillars of a free society. In 1960, he sued the *New York Times* for running a full-page advertisement from people who urged both restraint by the authorities and respect for Martin Luther King Jr.'s campaign to give African Americans the full rights of citizenship. The ad was headlined, "Heed Their Rising Voices."

The cops behind what was called "an unprecedented wave of terror" against black college students were not named in the ad; Sullivan, in particular, went unmentioned. But the mere insinuation that an elected official from Montgomery County might have done something heavy-handed was enough for Sullivan to sue. His reputation, he claimed, was severely damaged.

He won a local jury verdict of $500,000, no small sum in those days, and the Alabama Supreme Court upheld the result. It was part of a pattern across the South: the enforcers of Jim Crow racism using the courts to stifle and frighten voices of opposition. Now, the *Times* had been put on notice.

Well before there was a president who labeled the press "Enemy of the People" and urged lawmakers to make it harder for watchdogs of the powerful to do their jobs, one of the biggest threats to free expression was the law—specifically, libel law, and how the courts viewed it. The American founders specifically prohibited Congress from making any law "abridging the freedom of speech, or of the press." They couldn't have been blunter in the first and the broadest of the liberties given to the people in the Bill of Rights. This was a reaction to the tyranny of the British, who had shut down colonial newspapers at whim and had stringent laws protecting public figures from criticism.

But how the First Amendment protections came to be interpreted was another matter. Over the past two centuries, through the years of a partisan hack press, to the yellow journalism phase, to the more modern attempts at professional objectivity of the twentieth century, courts had given more sway to people who said they were defamed to go after the press.

Times v. Sullivan changed everything. In a unanimous decision in 1964, the Supreme Court overturned the earlier state court verdict against the paper and opened the way for robust and free-ranging reporting and discussion of public officials. It was a deliberate—critics said overreaching—decision by the court to free journalists. Justice William Brennan, in his written opinion, said use of the courts to shut down criticism was clearly at odds with the essence of the First Amendment.

The Court made it very hard for public figures to win a libel case. It established a tough new standard: the plaintiff had to prove that a newspaper, or any other press outlet, knew that what it was reporting was false, defined as "actual malice," or "reckless disregard" for the truth. So in *Sullivan*, some of the things claimed in the ad had in fact been false. But the paper didn't know it at the time, staffers said. The Court held that "erroneous statement is inevitable in free debate, and it must be protected if the freedoms of expression are to have 'breathing space.'" All of this was applied to public figures, not average citizens, for whom the standard of proof is lower. The Court cited the view of Justice William O. Douglas from one of his lectures. "Where public matters are involved," he wrote, "the doubts should be resolved in favor of freedom of expression rather than against it."

The decision had a ripple effect, touching just about every aspect of free speech, from comments at town hall meetings to satirists working their trade in now-defunct magazines like *National Lampoon*.

A lone blogger, laboring in a kitchen cubby to shed light on a nefarious public figure, has the same protection of *Times v. Sullivan*. If, say, a small-town sheriff didn't like the things that a country editor or a local radio station was saying about him, he would have to surpass the new legal standards to win a case.

Scholars say the case was one of the most important free speech decisions of the twentieth century. "There are few Supreme Court decisions that are so closely intertwined with the values that define America and epitomize our rights of self-expression and rights to create, express ourselves and critique our leaders," wrote Roy S. Gutterman, a free speech expert, in an essay in *Forbes Opinion*.

The Watergate reporting that brought down President Nixon might never have happened had the *Washington Post* not had the freedom given them barely a decade earlier in *Times v. Sullivan*. Nixon's attorney general, John N. Mitchell, had famously threatened the *Post*'s owner, Katharine Graham, in a call to reporter Carl Bernstein. "All that crap you're putting in the paper?" said Mitchell, as both Graham and Bernstein later recalled in their books. "It's all been denied. Katie Graham's going to get her tit caught in a big fat wringer if that's published." It was published. And Mitchell later served nineteen months in prison for multiple Watergate crimes.

In the Watergate era, journalism was a settled profession, with rules of conduct followed by most practitioners. Now, who's to say who's a journalist? Is the conspiracy theorist Alex Jones, a man who has questioned the slaughter of children by a gunman? In 2018, Jones was sued for defamation by several parents of children killed in the 2012 mass shooting at Sandy Hook Elementary School. After Jones posted videos alleging that the massacre was faked as an attempt to promote gun control, the parents said they had been harassed and forced to move.

Jones claimed that he was no different from Woodward and Bernstein. But it seems a stretch to say that the smearing of innocents by a man whose stock-in-trade is bogus conspiracy theories is what the justices were trying to protect when they decided the case. The parents also do not appear to be public figures, which may be one reason that case proceeded past its initial phase. People with no experience in the public eye only have to prove that what was said about them was false and that they suffered as a result.

The Court did not intend for their 1964 decision to protect the powerful; their goal was to make it harder for the powerful to harass individuals. Because of *Times v. Sullivan,* the United States is a fortress of free speech. It's much easier to win a libel case in Britain, which puts the burden of proof on those being sued. English law has stifled some of the most brisk public debates—and, yes, mockery—that are common in the United States. But there's no guarantee the judiciary will always be a friend of the press. In cases regarding national security and sources leaking official secrets, the courts have been leaning the other way. More troubling, Justice Clarence Thomas recently called for a reconsideration of *Times v. Sullivan,* reversing a half-century of press protection by the High Court. "We should reconsider our jurisprudence in this area," he wrote, criticizing the landmark case as "legal alchemy."

In his disdain of the landscape that developed after *Times v. Sullivan,* Thomas was echoing Donald Trump, though his view doesn't appear to have the backing of a majority of the Court today. As president, Trump is no longer suing comedians for making fun of him. But he has repeatedly called for making it more difficult for people to criticize him.

"I would love to see our libel laws get toughened up so you can take people and sue them," he says. No other leader of the free world has been such an open foe of a free press. At rallies, the president often points to reporters, setting them up for jeers, derisive chants, and occasional assaults from his supporters.

Libel laws can't be changed by legislative whim or an executive order from a president in a temper tantrum. For now, the protections of free speech are settled law, based on the ringing affirmation written into the Constitution, and boosted by cases like *Times v. Sullivan.* For now.

LAMONT V. POSTMASTER GENERAL (1965) (*amicus*)

In *Lamont,* the Court struck down a statute that required recipients of materials deemed to be "Communist political propaganda," like periodicals and magazines, to submit a request in writing on a special reply card in order to have that mail delivered to them. Corliss Lamont, a professor of philosophy, former chair of the Friends of the Soviet Union, and a member of the board of directors of the ACLU, filed suit. The Supreme Court's decision in Lamont's favor was unanimous. In an influential concurrence, Justice William Brennan wrote, "The dissemination of ideas can accomplish nothing if otherwise willing addressees are not free to receive and consider them. It would be a barren marketplace of ideas that had only sellers and no buyers."

Your Mail Belongs to Us

YIYUN LI

I grew up in a Soviet-style apartment block in Beijing in the 1970s, and our ground-floor unit was right next to the green mailbox for the building. Twice a day, the postman put letters and newspapers in the box with a dangling door, and the moment I learned how to read, I started to peruse the newspapers before the legal subscribers arrived and checked out the postcards and letters coming into the unlocked box.

The postcards, drab colored with the official post office signs, were sent not by people on holiday, but by those who wanted to show the world that they hid nothing in their correspondence. And one'd be better off, in my country and at that time, not to have any secret.

Letters arrived, of course. The envelopes offered limited information: names of recipients and senders, the value of the stamps, penmanship that was a good indication of the educational level of the senders. I paid extra attention to the stamps: an eight fen stamp meant the letter was sent from out of town; a four fen, however, meant the letter was sent from the same town, which was of great interest to me. It did not happen often that a person would send a letter to another person living in the same town. There was no telephone, but there was plenty of time for anyone to drop by at another person's place. I had a detective's mind then, treating those letters with four fen stamps with suspicion. (Later, I would understand that those letters were often written from a young person to his or her lover. When I came to that understanding, I liked to pinch the envelopes to feel the thickness of the letters.)

A sealed letter was an impediment for me to get to know a few things about our neighbors, but I was a law-abiding child. The only letters I stole and read were to my parents and my grandfather, who lived with us. An open envelope was too much of a seduction.

Then one day a letter came to my father, written in a foreign language instead of Chinese characters, with a stamp of a foreign woman's face, sent from England, as my father explained to us. He worked as a nuclear physicist, but his own interest was in quantum physics. The story was that he spent his spare time thinking through a problem in the field and writing to a foreign physics journal. His letter got into print. The English scientist disagreed with my father's approach and sent a letter to discuss their difference.

My father was wise enough to use our home address for his correspondence with the journal. But a letter from abroad was a sight for all the neighbors, and there was, as the old saying went, no wall in the world that does not have a crack for a sniff of air to go through. My father was summoned by his work unit to explain the letter. He got a warning of some sort. Soon after, he applied to transfer to a research institute of quantum physics that had nothing to do with nuclear weapons. For a while, the transfer seemed certain, and he seemed cheerful, but all of a sudden, everything changed and he was assigned to a place called the Institute of Marxist Dialectical Materialism. It was one of the many reasons that my father was not a happy man for the rest of his life. Instead of doing research he loved, his job there was closer to a clerk's.

An epistle from abroad spelled danger, but that did not happen only in communist China. In the United States, as mandated by Postal Service and Federal Employees Salary Act of 1962:

> Mail matter, except sealed letters, which originates or which is printed or otherwise prepared in a foreign country and which is determined by the Secretary of the Treasury pursuant to rules and regulations to be promulgated by him to be "communist political propaganda," shall be detained by the Postmaster General upon its arrival for delivery in the United States, or upon its subsequent deposit in the United States domestic mails, and the addressee shall be notified that such matter has been received and will be delivered only upon the addressee's request, except that such detention

> shall not be required in the case of any matter which is furnished pursuant to subscription or which is otherwise ascertained by the Postmaster General to be desired by the addressee.

In 1963, the post office retained a copy of *Peking Review*, addressed to Dr. Corliss Lamont, a director of the ACLU for twenty-two years. (*Peking Review*, established in 1958 by the Chinese government and published in five languages, was a tool for the Chinese government to communicate with the rest of the world in the Cold War era. History, on both sides of the Iron Curtain, was not isolated.)

Lamont did not respond to the notice of detention sent to him but instead instituted this suit to enjoin enforcement of the statute, alleging that it infringed his rights under the First and Fifth Amendments. The Post Office thereupon notified Lamont that it considered his institution of the suit to be an expression of his desire to receive "communist political propaganda" and therefore none of his mail would be detained. Lamont amended his complaint to challenge on constitutional grounds the placement of his name on the list of those desiring to receive "communist political propaganda."

In 1965, Lamont won a suit against the US postmaster general for violating his First Amendment rights by opening and withholding his mail. The Supreme Court held the Postal Service and Federal Employees Salary Act of 1962 to be unconstitutional:

> The Act sets administrative officials astride the flow of mail to inspect it, appraise it, write the addressee about it, and await a response before dispatching the mail. . . . We rest on the narrow ground that the addressee in order to receive his mail must request in writing that it be delivered. This amounts in our judgment to an unconstitutional abridgment of the addressee's First Amendment rights. The addressee carries an affirmative obligation which we do not think the Government may impose on him. This requirement is almost certain to have a deterrent effect, especially as respects those who have sensitive positions. Their livelihood may be dependent on a security clearance. Public officials, like schoolteachers who have no tenure, might think they would invite disaster if they read

> what the Federal Government says contains the seeds of treason. Apart from them, any addressee is likely to feel some inhibition in sending for literature which federal officials have condemned as "communist political propaganda."

The Cold War ended. The Iron Curtain, lifted, was placed into the museum. We have long moved onto digital forms with our communication. But are we better off now? When I travel back to China, I cannot get access to my Gmail, Google, and the *New York Times* website, all of them blocked in China. But more than that, I cannot get a cell phone number in China as an American citizen because all cell phone numbers in China are directly logged in along with citizens' ID numbers. It is not a secret that all things that happen digitally in China are supervised and censored by the government. But the danger, one must assume, is not far from us in America either. The US Border Control is increasingly using questionable authority to search the cell phones of passengers arriving in America. In May 2018, US District Judge Denise Casper in Boston ruled that a lawsuit by eleven travelers had raised a plausible claim that such border searches violate the US Constitution's Fourth Amendment protections against unreasonable searches and seizures. One can, however, see the possibility of such scenarios migrating from the US border into everyday American life. Would it be far-fetched to imagine—as an immigrant, with the history of the internment of Japanese Americans always close to my thoughts—that should the political atmosphere continue as it is under the current administration, that one day we would be required to unlock our cell phones to show that, in our texts and emails, we have not expressed any thoughts of disloyalty?

GRISWOLD V. CONNECTICUT (1965)

(*amicus*)

In November 1961, Estelle Griswold, executive director of the Planned Parenthood League of Connecticut, and Dr. C. Lee Buxton, a gynecologist at the Yale School of Medicine, opened a birth control clinic in New Haven, Connecticut. Within ten days, the state closed the clinic and arrested the pair under a Connecticut law enacted in 1879 that forbade the use of "any drug, medicinal article, or instrument for the purpose of preventing contraception." They were found guilty of prescribing contraceptives and fined one hundred dollars each.

The pair appealed their conviction, and in 1965 the Supreme Court heard their case. The ACLU filed a friend of the court brief on behalf of Griswold and Buxton, arguing that the contraceptive law violated a constitutional right to privacy. The Supreme Court agreed with the ACLU's argument, and held, for the first time, that the Constitution guarantees people a marital right to privacy, and declared the Connecticut law unconstitutional as it applied to married couples.

The landmark right to privacy established in *Griswold* would be cited in a number of other important cases concerning the right to control one's personal life, including *Roe v. Wade* (1973), *Lawrence v. Texas* (2003), and *Obergefell v. Hodges* (2015).

Protection

MEG WOLITZER

Mary McCarthy's 1963 novel *The Group*, which takes place in the 1930s, includes a scene in which recent Vassar graduate Dottie Renfrew loses her virginity to a divorced painter, Dick Brown. Afterward, he instructs her, "Get yourself a pessary," and when she misunderstands, he clarifies that she should go to a "lady doctor" and obtain "a female contraceptive, a plug."

Philip Roth's first-person 1959 novella, *Goodbye, Columbus*, details the sexual relationship between Neil Klugman, twenty-three and a clerk at the Newark Public Library, and Brenda Patimkin, a privileged and beautiful student at Radcliffe.

> "Brenda, I want to ask you something. . . . I know this is out of the blue, though really it's not. . . . I want you to buy a diaphragm. To go to a doctor and get one."
>
> . . .
>
> "You just want me to own one, is that it? Like a walking stick, or a pith helmet—"
>
> "Brenda, I want you to own one for . . . for the sake of pleasure."
>
> "Pleasure? Whose?"
>
> "Mine," I said.

As a novelist, I looked to these works to get a sense of the prevailing culture in the years leading up to the 1965 Supreme Court case, *Griswold v. Connecticut*. The case concerned one of the Comstock laws that hailed from the Grant administration, calling for the "Suppression of Trade in, and Circulation of, Objects of Literature and Articles of Immoral Use." Clearly, readers of fiction in the late fifties and early sixties were sophisticated about sex and contraception, which peppered the literary landscape, but Connecticut during that era was still, at least legally, on contraceptive lockdown.

Privacy is the foundation of *Griswold*. But while *Griswold* is a consequential ruling, to me it has always had a sepia tinge about it, an antiquated, peculiar, butter-churn quality. People were having sex and using contraception, in novels and in real life, and yet here, still, was this old, anachronistic law, which needed to be changed.

Estelle Griswold had traveled abroad with her State Department husband, and after seeing the conditions under which people in other countries lived, she had become passionate about various human rights concerns. By 1954 she began work as the executive director of the Planned Parenthood League of Connecticut and became involved in the mission to change Connecticut's laws. Her partner in the mission, Dr. C. Lee Buxton, knew well the urgency of access to contraception. In addition to his patients who were sexually active and didn't want to bear children, he had treated many women who would have died if they conceived, and others who had experienced multiple miscarriages and would do so again if they became pregnant.

Buxton's lawyers had filed five cases for him along with a group of his anonymous patients in an attempt to challenge the law, but all were unsuccessful. Though the Supreme Court agreed to hear his appeal in one of the cases, it was ultimately dismissed, even though one of the dissenting opinions argued that the issue was "ripe," which meant ready for litigation.

The word *ripe* jumped out at me. A question of ripeness or unripeness seems such fitting imagery in this story of women and their wombs. Buxton joined up with Griswold, and together they announced the opening of a birth control clinic in 1961. Nine days later they were arrested, as they knew they would be, and when the case went before the Connecticut Supreme Court, the judges ruled against them. It was only on appeal in 1965 that Griswold and Buxton, led by their lawyer, Catherine Roraback, were victorious; the Supreme Court declared the original anti-contraception law unconstitutional on the grounds of the right to marital privacy. It would be seven more years before the law applied to all couples, not just married ones.

I am drawn to the word *privacy*, which seems to suggest that corner of our lives that no one can see except the person or people we want to see it. That's a novelist's corner, of course, and he or she has the ability to illuminate and analyze all kinds of private material. Mary McCarthy and Philip Roth looked at the private bedroom moments of men and women in their fiction. While there is also an oppressiveness in these scenes, with the men pressuring the women to get themselves birth control so the men wouldn't have to pull out or wear a condom, that is perhaps for another essay. What these scenes mostly illustrate in a *Griswold* context is how sex in that era was folded deeply into people's lives, as ordinary as anything, and that it was necessary for the law to catch up with reality.

The feminist writer Katha Pollitt, who happens to have been a recipient of the Catherine Roraback Award, "given to individuals and organizations that have demonstrated leadership, courage and activism in the struggle to protect privacy rights, the legal right to obtain an abortion, and access to reproductive health for all," reflected on the importance of *Griswold*. "When society gets ahead of the law," she said to me, "eventually the law comes around. The law is very important. With abortion, in the fifties they started to crack down on practitioners; before that they usually let it go unless someone died. The reason it's so important to have the law on your side is that it can protect you from backlash such as we are experiencing now."

Most recently, Griswold made an appearance during the Kavanaugh hearings. Unlike previous judges during their confirmation hearings, Kavanaugh would not say he agreed with *Griswold* and would not say the Constitution offered protection for people's rights to make decisions about their own family planning. If this courtroom scene were a scene in a novel, it would be effectively chilling, and the smug, rageful character being questioned would most likely reappear later in the book, having wielded his power in a terrible way. But it isn't a novel; it is our lives, our bodies, our privacy that need protection. The time is ripe.

MIRANDA V. ARIZONA (1966) (*amicus*)

Miranda v. Arizona was the culmination of a series of Supreme Court cases going back over thirty years, pitting the Constitution's promise of the protection against self-incrimination against a favorite tool of law enforcement: the confession. In *Brown v. Mississippi* (1936), the Court held that after being beaten, whipped, and strung up by his neck from a tree in a mock lynching, the defendant's "confession" could not stand. From there, the Court continued to address the problem of coercion, honing in on a definition of what constituted a freely given confession: suspects could not be held for long periods of time without food, police could not lie about the possibility of leniency, and so on. Finally, with *Miranda*, the Warren Court declared that police custody was in and of itself inherently coercive, and that the Constitution not only guaranteed the right to refrain from self-incrimination, but demanded that individuals be informed of that right and given the opportunity to exercise it. Few other cases in jurisprudential history have had the impact of *Miranda* on cultural understanding or have contained such a specific interpretation of the Bill of Rights as the now *ubiquitous* phrase, "You have the right to remain silent."

Representing Ernesto Arturo Miranda, the ACLU shepherded his case from Phoenix, Arizona, to the nation's highest court, arguing that all individuals were not only entitled to the protections of the Fifth and Sixth Amendments, but entitled to be made aware of those protections.

Ernesto's Prayer

HECTOR TOBAR

To those who met him during his long odyssey through the criminal justice system, Ernesto Miranda was a pitiful, small-time criminal from central casting. Tattooed, lecherous, a hard drinker, and a drifter, he'd been in trouble since childhood. His first felony conviction came in the eighth grade, for car theft. The next year, he was arrested for burglary, then attempted rape. In the army, he got thrown in the stockade on a Peeping Tom charge.

History does not tell us much about the demons that persecuted him. More than likely, his parents were poor and had some experience in farmwork. He was born in Mesa, Arizona, in 1941, when Mesa was a rural town surrounded by citrus groves and cotton fields past the edge of preboom Phoenix. We know his mother died when he was six. In the publicly available photographs of him (all mug shots), "Ernie," or "Ernest" can look handsome and wholesome, or menacing and thuggish. Many of the lawyers and police officers who met him believed he suffered from a mental illness.

His name is now a verb. To "Mirandize," as defined in most American dictionaries, is to apprise criminal suspects of their rights against self-incrimination and their right to have a lawyer present during any interrogation. Thanks to Ernesto Miranda (and also thanks to the overzealous Phoenix Police Department and a host of civil rights attorneys), the protections of the Fifth Amendment became a civic poem in free verse, a recitation of constitutional rights embraced by American popular culture.

"You have a right to remain silent. Anything you say can be held against you in a court of law . . ."

On television and in movies, the Miranda moment is a short, celebratory speech, usually intoned in the final act, when a police officer or detective, having ferreted out and hounded the bad guy for most of the plot, finally catches him. With righteous anger in his voice, the good-guy cop delivers a pithy reminder of the protections afforded in the Bill of Rights.

"You have a right to an attorney. If you cannot afford an attorney, one will be appointed for you."

The series of events that led to Ernesto Miranda's arrest and fame began when an eighteen-year-old woman set off for home after her night job at a movie theater in central Phoenix. It was 1963, and Phoenix in many ways still resembled a segregated southern town. Cul-de-sacs and freeways did not yet fill the Salt River Valley, and irrigated cropland still surrounded the city, which had a large, marginalized population of Mexican Americans and Mexican immigrants.

A man kidnapped and raped the young woman. (Her name was never released to the public.) When she reported the crime to police, she could give only a vague description of the car her abductor was driving. She thought it might be a Chevrolet, but she wasn't sure. About a week later, her cousin spotted a Packard circling suspiciously in the same neighborhood and jotted down a partial license plate. The police searched records and found a Packard belonging to a woman who lived with Miranda, an ex-con with an extensive criminal background, including prior sex crimes.

The police knocked on Miranda's door and suggested he come into the station to answer questions; they said they wanted to spare him the embarrassment of interrogating him in front of his common-law wife (and the mother of his child). Not long after he arrived at the station, the officers asked him to stand in a police station lineup. Two witnesses said he resembled the perpetrator of both the rape and a second crime, a robbery. But they couldn't be sure.

The detectives lied to Miranda; they told him he had "flunked" the lineup and took him to an interrogation room. According to Miranda, the detectives told him some of the charges would be dropped if he confessed; otherwise, they would "throw the book at him." The detectives also promised to get him help for his mental health issues, Miranda said later. He agreed to write out his confession. The police had not informed him of his right to remain silent or to have an attorney present at his questioning.

Besides the confession, prosecutors presented no other evidence of Miranda's guilt at his rape trial. He was convicted.

While Miranda's appeals were working their way through the Arizona courts, the US Supreme Court delivered two landmark rulings on the rights of people accused of crimes: *Gideon v. Wainwright* (1963), which established that the government must provide lawyers to indigent defendants, and *Escobedo v. Illinois* (1964), which held that suspects have a right to representation during police interrogation.

In Escobedo the court found that the right to have an attorney at trial was, in effect, rendered meaningless when police tricked suspects into providing the evidence that would lead a jury to convict them. Robert J. Corcoran of the Phoenix office of the American Civil Liberties Union saw in Miranda's case an opportunity for the Supreme Court to broaden the rights established in Escobedo. He reached out to John J. Flynn, a criminal defense attorney widely regarded to be Arizona's best trial lawyer. Flynn represented Miranda pro bono and sought out the assistance of his firm's top appellate lawyer, John P. Frank.

More than one hundred defendants submitted similar appeals to the High Court. Of those, the justices chose four to hear, including Miranda's. Flynn made oral arguments before the Supreme Court in *Miranda v. Arizona* on February 28, 1966. He characterized Miranda as a man poorly equipped to understand his rights when the police arrested him. At that moment, "under the facts and circumstances in *Miranda* of a man of limited education, of a man who certainly is mentally abnormal, [and] who is certainly an indigent . . . the police, at the very least, had an obligation to extend to this man not only his clear Fifth Amendment right, but to accord to him the right of counsel."

On June 13, the court ruled 5–4 in Miranda's favor. Writing for the majority, Chief Justice Earl Warren said that the Fifth Amendment's protections against self-incrimination extended beyond the courtroom, reaching into police stations and to street-corner traffic stops. His ruling contained language that would later be adopted into the Miranda warning. A suspect, Warren wrote, "must be warned prior to any questioning that he has the right to remain silent, that anything he says can be used against him in a court of law, that he has the right to the presence of an attorney, and that if he cannot afford an attorney one will be appointed for him prior to any questioning if he so desires."

That summer, at the direction of the attorney general of California, California's assistant attorney general, Doris H. Maier, and Nevada County's district attorney, Harold Berliner, drafted a version of the warning for police to use in their state. Berliner also happened to be a printer; he produced hundreds of thousands of vinyl cards of the new warning and sold them to law enforcement agencies across the country.

One of those cards ended up in the hands of Jack Webb, the television producer, as he was writing the first episodes of the relaunch of the series *Dragnet*, a police procedural based on real-life Los Angeles Police Department cases. In the name of verisimilitude, Webb had his hero, the fictional Sergeant Joe Friday, recite the Miranda warning twenty-five times during *Dragnet*'s inaugural season. In the first episode, broadcast on January 12, 1967, Friday and his partner roll out to a vacant lot in East Hollywood and find a young man under the effect of LSD. "Alright son, you're under arrest," Friday says. "It's our duty to inform you of your Constitutional rights. You have the right to remain silent . . ."

Miranda's conviction was overturned, but he remained behind bars because Maricopa County immediately refiled the charges against him. In February 1967, his second trial began, this time without his confession entered as evidence. But his common-law wife had turned against him while he was in prison; among other things, the couple had fought a bitter custody battle. She told police that Miranda had confessed the rape to her during a jailhouse visit after his 1963 arrest. He'd even suggested he might marry his alleged victim, she said. Her testimony helped convict him.

Hollywood, meanwhile, was falling deeper in love with the Miranda warning. One evening, Miranda joined his fellow inmates at the Arizona State Penitentiary as they watched a television cop show. When the fictional police officer ordered his partner to read a suspected car thief his "Miranda rights," the cell block broke into applause.

After Miranda was paroled from prison in 1972, he obtained some Miranda rights cards from the police and signed and sold them for $1.50 each. He returned to prison briefly, on a charge of illegal possession of a firearm. In January 1976, a man stabbed him to death during a fight in a bar in a seedy corner of Phoenix.

Miranda's killer escaped, but the police arrested his accomplice—and read him his Miranda rights, a final irony that has proven irresistible to everyone who's written about Ernesto Miranda's life ever since.

The very ubiquity of the Miranda warning has allowed it to endure despite shifting political and legal winds. In 2000, *Dickerson v. United States* was widely seen as an opportunity for a conservative-leaning Supreme Court to roll back *Miranda*; instead, the Court voted 7–2 to reaffirm it. Chief Justice William Rehnquist, a conservative Nixon appointee, wrote the majority opinion: "*Miranda* has become embedded in routine police practice to the point where the warnings have become part of our national culture."

The civil rights attorneys who fought for Ernesto Miranda's rights helped change the way an entire country thinks about its relationship to authority. Today, the Miranda warning is repeated about 10 million times each year on the streets and in the police stations of the United States and on film and television around the world. In Russia, crime dramas often end with police reading suspects their Miranda rights, even though there is no such requirement in Russian law.

The 2012 movie *21 Jump Street* ends with two police officers making an arrest, following a spectacular car chase and shoot-out. The officers, played by Jonah Hill and Channing Tatum, Mirandize their wounded arrestee in a shouted, joyful chorus. They end with the question Maier and Berliner drafted into their warning in 1966, followed by an insult, and more.

"Do you understand these rights as they've been read to you? Fuck you! Yes! Yes! Yes! We did it! It feels so good!"

In American drama, the words Ernesto Miranda never heard in that Phoenix interrogation room are the moment when reason triumphs over chaos and violence. On the real-life streets of the United States, they are a court-ordered interlude of reflection. We are a nation of laws, the words say, and those laws protect you now and at all other times. You have rights, the words say, even when there are cuffs on your wrists or when a police detective is glaring at you as if you were the villain in a movie.

LOVING V. VIRGINIA (1967)

In the early hours of July 11, 1958, a sheriff and two deputies burst into Mildred and Richard Loving's bedroom in Central Point, Virginia. The sheriff had received an anonymous tip that Mildred Loving and Richard Loving were living together as husband and wife, a crime in Virginia. While it is commonly believed that Mildred was of mixed black and Native American descent, she identified as Native American. Richard was white. With his flashlight trained on their startled faces, the sheriff demanded to know who the woman in Richard Loving's bed was, to which Mildred replied, "I'm his wife." When Richard Loving tried to prove the fact of the marriage by pointing to the framed marriage license hanging on their bedroom wall, the sheriff told them, "That's no good here." The Lovings were arrested and charged with violating Virginia's anti-miscegenation law.

Anti-miscegenation laws, which had existed in the United States since the colonial era, prohibited interracial marriage. At the time of the Lovings' arrest, sixteen states still had anti-miscegenation laws on the books, including Virginia's Racial Integrity Act of 1924. Under this statute, it was illegal for a white person to "intermarry with a colored person" in Virginia or to evade the prohibition by marrying a member of a different race in another state and returning to Virginia as husband and wife.

On January 6, 1958, the Lovings pled guilty to violating Virginia's ban on interracial marriage and were sentenced to one year in jail. However, the judge suspended this sentence for twenty-five years on the condition that the Lovings leave Virginia and never return. After their convictions, the Lovings moved to Washington, DC. However, when they were arrested yet again during a trip to visit family in Virginia, a frustrated Mildred wrote to Attorney General Robert Kennedy. He referred them to the ACLU, which filed a motion in Virginia to have the Lovings' convictions vacated and sentences set aside on the grounds that Virginia's anti-miscegenation law violated the Fourteenth Amendment.

After numerous appeals, the Lovings' case arrived before the Supreme Court. In a landmark decision, the court unanimously found anti-miscegenation statutes to be unconstitutional, rejecting Virginia's argument that the law's equal application to the races protected the law from the Fourteenth Amendment's "proscription of all invidious racial classifications." The Court held that anti-miscegenation laws violated both the equal protection clause and the due process clause of the Fourteenth Amendment because they were intended to "maintain White Supremacy," and thus served no legitimate state interest. The Court also held that marriage, as one of the "basic civil rights of man," is a fundamental right that "resides with the individual and cannot be infringed by the State."

The Court's decision in *Loving v. Virginia* was a victory in the fight to eliminate Jim Crow laws. More recently, the decision was crucial in the struggle for marriage equality, laying the foundation for *Obergefell v. Hodges* (2015) in which the Supreme Court found bans on same-sex marriage to be unconstitutional.

Loving

ALEKSANDAR HEMON

I come from a place where a notion of "mixed marriage" has existed for a while. That place is Bosnia and Herzegovina, mainly known for the worst of the wars of Yugoslavia, where I was born and lived before it all came apart and I ended up in Chicago, Illinois. "Mixed marriage" (*miješani brak*) referred to a marriage between two people of different ethnicities, and I happened to be a product of one of those. There were no laws against "mixed marriage" when I was growing up, and the concept was not particularly frowned on, at least not in Sarajevo, my hometown. On the contrary, these marriages were cherished as evidence that the ideology of brotherhood and unity successfully bonded the myriad ethnicities of the socialist Yugoslavia—Bosnia and Herzegovina being its most diverse part—and helped people overcome their ethnic differences. Some say that up to 40 percent of marriages in Sarajevo before the war were interethnic, which was deemed to be a mark of its cosmopolitan openness.

When I was young, I hated the term *mixed marriage*. For one thing, I'd rail, unless you're marrying yourself, every marriage is inescapably mixed. Indeed, the whole point of getting voluntarily attached to other people is to mix with someone who is not you—however you may define or perceive yourself. Moreover, *mixed marriage* implied that what was being mixed was not two people but some larger categories—ethnicity, race—to which the people congenitally belonged. While two people may have felt that, by way of love, they reached a degree of connection that rendered boundaries and differences between them irrelevant, or at least less important, their involuntary belonging to their respective categories superseded all their desires and agency. The label "mixed marriage" was culturally available to convince them that no human connection could ever transcend those essential differences. "Mixed marriage" suggested that people were deprived of emotional agency because their feelings were inherently nationalized. No one could ever fully own their love.

In retrospect, the mixed marriages of the multiethnic socialist Yugoslavia look positively quaint, for with the advent of the basest nationalism that would destroy the country, the concept acquired a more sinister value. In nationalist imagination, as practiced in the Balkans (and now in the Trumpist United States), the nation is defined by some mystical, transcendental, historical essence, shared by its members and acquired at birth. That essence is the locus of difference and the source of inherent superiority over some other nation (ethnicity, race); that essence, which is both metaphysical and biological, must be kept pure lest the nation be weakened by foreign contamination. Individual people contain the essence; it is what connects them to the other members of the nation, so that mixing with others (who are arranged as individuals around their own, different national essence) severs the connection with their national kin. The ideological victory of the Balkan nationalists therefore resulted in cultural and political devaluation of mixed marriage to the point that outside a few urban centers that contain relatively mixed ethnicities, it is effectively prohibited due to local segregationist policies that, among other things, might prevent children of different ethnicities from attending the same school. With all that, there are no segregation laws as such in Bosnia and Herzegovina, nor are mixed marriages illegal. They're just considered unnatural by the nationalists and actively discouraged by their rhetoric and blatant discrimination.

All this is to say that my understanding of *Loving v. Virginia* is at least partly determined by a historical experience acquired thousands of miles away from the American history and reality in which I now live. Mildred and Richard Loving's marriage was deemed to be mixed and therefore subject to anti-miscegenation law of the Commonwealth of Virginia. What deep connection they might have felt between them was invalid because, as the local court wrote in its ruling on the motion to vacate in the case of *Loving v. Virgini*a, "Almighty God created the races white, black, yellow, malay and red, and he placed them on separate continents. And but for the interference with his arrangement there would be no cause for such marriages. The fact that he separated the races shows that he did not intend for the races to mix." The monstrous logic of Judge Leon M. Bazile, the author of the ruling, is painfully familiar to a Bosnian like me, as is its natural and transcendental essentialism; the presumed eternal quality of the "arrangement"; and the alleged danger of mixing that could be redressed only by vigilant segregation—up to and including ethnic/racial cleansing and genocide. The absurd cruelty of such logic ought to have been self-evident, but it wasn't until the Supreme Court ruled against the Commonwealth of Virginia, holding that "the freedom to marry, or not marry, a person of another race resides with the individual and cannot be infringed by the State."

For more than twelve years, I've been married to an African American woman; we have two children together. One of the many things that bonds me to Teri, my life partner, is the way our personal and family histories overlap in our hatred of bigotry. Her maternal grandfather was a lawyer who was friends with Justice Thurgood Marshall; his children registered voters in the South in the 1950s. Her paternal grandfather, who in the 1930s had an integrated dental office in segregated Pensacola, Florida, was known to stand up to white men with a shotgun in his hands. Race and American racism are our life, our bedtime and morning conversations. Hence we appreciate the fact that a generation ago in large parts of this damaged country, our marriage would have been illegal and our daughters illicit. When we drive through the territories of the former eastern Confederacy (including Virginia, to see my in-laws in Pensacola), we tell our girls that a generation ago, their mother and father would have risked arrest and imprisonment just for sleeping together. The last time Teri and I drove down to Florida with our girls, we talked to them about *Loving v. Virginia*—about the meaning it has in the history of our family and of this country. They're still young, only beginning to learn about the terrible, complex history of America, but they could admire Mildred and Richard's love and the courage that came with it, just as they could see the exquisite value of loving so soundly defeating bigotry.

Soon, we hope, they will be able to understand the importance of the work the ACLU did in undoing American racist laws, the work without which our lives would be much different. And with that, they might be able to learn that laws can and must change to reflect the indelible realities of human life and love.

TINKER V. DES MOINES INDEPENDENT COMMUNITY SCHOOL DISTRICT (1969)

February 2019 marked the fiftieth anniversary of this landmark First Amendment case, whose holding established that students and teachers do not shed their constitutional rights to free speech at "the schoolhouse gate." *Tinker* has its origins in the intensely divisive national debate surrounding US involvement in the Vietnam War. The teenaged students who became the petitioners in this case, two siblings and their friend, first sought counsel from the Iowa Civil Liberties Union after their school suspended them for wearing black armbands to school to demonstrate their support for a Christmas truce. Initial negotiations with the school district failed, and the ACLU agreed to take the case on behalf of the students and their parents. Thirty-year-old attorney Dan Johnston, at the time just a year out of law school, argued and won this case before the Supreme Court.

The Black Armband

ELIZABETH STROUT

The year was 1981; I was twenty-five years old and a law student. That spring, Alexander Haig, the secretary of state of the United States, came to speak to the graduating class of my university. I decided to protest. I had never gone to a protest before. I had essentially missed the sixties, living in isolated areas of this country, but here was a man I found to be dangerous, and so I decided to wear a black armband and stand with a number of other students outside the entrance to the dome where he was speaking. At the last minute, I was sent to the back entrance—on my own—by the person organizing us. Perhaps he thought I was disposable, not angry enough? Anyway, off I went alone to the back door.

The back door is where Haig entered. A black car pulled up and a man got out; suddenly there was Alexander Haig, walking into the back door. I yelled something—I can't remember what—and stuck my arm with the black armband on it up into the air. And this is what I think I saw: he glanced at me and a tiny smile came to his mouth, and I thought, *Oh my God, this makes him feel more important!*

Doesn't matter.

What matters is that I had the right to wear that black armband; I had the right to stand there with it on and protest this man. If I was nervous as a twenty-five-year-old adult, then just imagine what courage it took for a thirteen-year-old schoolchild to do the same sixteen years earlier in Des Moines, Iowa.

Mary Beth Tinker was the daughter of civil rights activists. Her father was a Methodist pastor, and her parents had been instrumental in getting the swimming pool in Des Moines desegregated, and they had traveled to the Deep South where they took part in many aspects of the civil rights movement. They came home and told their children about these things—about, as Mary Beth Tinker says in an ACLU podcast in 2009, "little old ladies being shot at in the night."

At the age of thirteen, Mary Beth Tinker decided, along with her brother, John Tinker, aged fifteen, and a friend, Christopher Eckhardt, aged sixteen, to wear black armbands to school to protest the Vietnam War. The school sent them home. In fact, the school, having heard of their plans, had already put into place a policy that anyone wearing a black armband would be suspended from school until they returned without the armband. The school believed that the very existence of these black armbands was disruptive. It is interesting to note that at this time, there were other things students wore in that school; for example, some students wore the Iron Cross, a symbol of the swastika. These were not considered by the school to be disruptive. But the black armbands were. So the students wearing them went home. Eventually they came back to school and dressed in black for many weeks as a sign of protest. The school could do nothing about this.

But Mary Tinker's father and Christopher Eckhardt's father decided, on behalf of these children, to sue the school district on the grounds that the students had a First Amendment right to wear black armbands. The US District Court dismissed the complaint and therefore upheld the school's position, as did the court of appeals. The case was argued in front of the US Supreme Court in 1968, and a decision came down in favor of the right to wear armbands in 1969.

The school's policy claimed that the wearing of these armbands would incite disruptions within the student body, causing problems of discipline. Oddly (to me), the district court's decision relied on an earlier decision by the Fifth Circuit Court of Appeals, *Burnside v. Byars* (1966), that had held that wearing symbols like these armbands was constitutionally protected except for when such a thing "materially and substantially interferes with the requirements of appropriate discipline in the operation of the school." Using this standard, the district court upheld the decision of the school district, saying the school district had the right to make the decision that the armbands would cause a discipline problem and the court would not interfere. The court of appeals upheld this decision.

When the case reached the Supreme Court, it spoke to the district court's decision, saying, "But in our system, undifferentiated fear or apprehension of disturbance is not enough to overcome the right to freedom of expression." Justice Abe Fortas, who wrote the opinion, also said:

> It does not concern aggressive, disruptive action or even group demonstrations. Our problem involves direct, primary First Amendment rights akin to "pure speech."

The "Tinker Test," as set forth in the *Tinker* opinion, asks: Did the speech or expression of the student "materially and substantially interfere with the requirements of appropriate discipline in the operation of the school?"

Justice Fortas continued:

> The school officials banned and sought to punish petitioners for a silent, passive expression of opinion, unaccompanied by any disorder or disturbance on the part of petitioners. There is here no evidence whatever of petitioners' interference, actual or nascent, with the schools' work or of collision with the rights of other students to be secure and to be let alone.

The constitutional rights of students in schools was not a new issue for our Supreme Court. In 1943, at the height of World War II, Justice Robert Jackson, who later was the lead prosecutor in the Nuremberg trials, wrote a decision that upheld the right of students to not salute the flag (*West Virginia v. Barnette*, 1943). Given that war was ripping across the world and the country was feeling great patriotism, this was an extraordinary and brave decision.

But what is somehow especially moving to me in the *Tinker* decision is Justice Fortas's use of a quotation by Justice William Brennan in an earlier case. Speaking for the Court in *Keyishian v. Board of Regents* two years earlier, Justice Brennan wrote:

> The vigilant protection of constitutional freedoms is nowhere more vital than in the community of American schools. . . . The classroom is peculiarly the "marketplace of ideas." The Nation's future depends upon leaders trained through wide exposure to that robust exchange of ideas which discovers truth "out of a multitude of tongues, [rather] than through any kind of authoritative selection."

Look at that. In the defense of students and their rights—in American schools—the Supreme Court wrote that "this nation's future depends" on the protection of a student's right to free expression. The fundamental intelligence involved in this thinking is conspicuously striking.

Because of *Tinker v. Des Moines*, these students now had the constitutional right to wear armbands. These are hugely important decisions of our right to free speech and the First Amendment. Attempts have been made to override them, but none of them have yet been successful.

When I look back to the day I raised my arm in the face of Alexander Haig, I did not think about the fact that my right to do so was based on courageous decisions by our Supreme Court. I just did it because I knew, as an American, I could do this. My actions seem more important to me now than they did back then. There was a youthful confidence to me that day: we had the right to do this. But times have changed, and we must now worry about the erosion of these rights. One can only hope—ferociously—that the Supreme Court will continue to have these open-minded (and open-hearted) beliefs as our country goes forward.

We can hope.

GREGORY V. CITY OF CHICAGO (1969)

Gregory v. City of Chicago is unusual in that its holding does not matter. What makes it a significant First Amendment case is Justice Hugo Black's concurrence discussing the heckler's veto: when a speaker's opponents threaten violence against the speaker, causing the government to silence the speaker in order to avoid that violence. It is therefore a form of government censorship. In an early articulation of the concept, the Court ruled in *Terminiello v. City of Chicago* (1949) it was impermissible to arrest a speaker simply because that person's message stirred up discontent. The concern is that the government will pick favorites, allowing pro-government figures to speak while silencing critics under the pretext of avoiding unrest. *Gregory* therefore sits squarely within the ACLU's ongoing battle against government censorship, especially when attacks on free speech arrive cloaked in benign concern for the speaker's well-being.

Crowd Work

ADRIAN NICOLE LEBLANC

Case law moves slowly. That movement requires extraordinary persistence—not only countless hours of effort on the part of advocates but also a refusal to give up in the face of repeated failure. The entertainment business provides excellent training: for performers, persistence is the practice and rejection the norm. Indeed, the need for persistence is perhaps even more the case for stand-up comedians than for legal activists. Bits tend to take shape very slowly. Their refinement occurs through repeated interaction with audiences, who are rich in instruction—their sighs, their contempt, their silence, their adulation, their impatience, their excitement and boorishness. Crowd work is a reciprocal tutelage, which, ideally, holds things in common with the practice of democracy. How to speak as oneself and hold the attention of others? And persuade the group of facts they don't see? Finding one's voice, the right moment to pause, or the phrase to elicit a certain quality of laughter can take comedians months, sometimes years.

In 1962, NAACP leader Medgar Evers invited stand-up comedian Dick Gregory to Mississippi to speak at voter registration rallies. Gregory, a well-known performer, was the first black comic to cross over to white audiences. The previous year, a gig at Hugh Hefner's Playboy Club in Chicago had led to an appearance on *The Jack Paar Show* and after his performance, Gregory was invited to sit beside the white host for a talk. That particular chair signaled industry anointment, and the TV visibility bumped Gregory's club rates to Sinatra level. Some in Gregory's position might have hesitated before accepting an invitation like Evers's to headline a political rally—but not Gregory. For him, the struggle for justice was imperative, and he admired integrity more than earning power. According to Gregory's son, Christian, "Medgar Evers was a God to my Dad." The march on the streets of Mississippi transformed Gregory permanently into an activist.

By the early 1960s, wherever Gregory went, the press (and FBI) usually followed. Not only did his presence bring more attention to the issues, but that press attention potentially decreased the likelihood that bystanders or police would attack the civil rights protesters. In addition, Gregory was eminently quotable, quick to illuminate complex issues with a concise comment and a biting wit.

Soon Gregory was dedicating as much time to the civil rights movement as he was to his comedy career. The press constantly asked him why he risked it. "The answer was as clear then as it is now," he wrote in a 2001 memoir, *Callus on My Soul,* one of his twelve books. "Yes, I was losing money, but the stakes were just too high to turn back." By the summer of 1965, Gregory was commuting from San Francisco's storied club, the hungry i, where he performed regularly, to downtown Chicago, where he was marching in some of the daily protests to demand improvements in the city's overcrowded, underfunded black schools. The protests began that June in response to Mayor Richard Daley's reappointment of Benjamin Willis, whose policies supported de facto segregation, as superintendent of schools. Instead of moving black students into the empty classrooms of new schools in white neighborhoods, or renovating black schools, or building new schools for black children on the South Side, Willis provided aluminum trailers to hold the overflow of black students—many on the grounds of those same decrepit black schools. The trailers became known as Willis Wagons.

The summer of 1965 was a long, hot one. For sixty days, protesters had been demonstrating in downtown Chicago—in front of the office building of the chair of the school committee, in front of Buckingham Fountain, in front of city hall. But Mayor Daley wasn't showing up at city hall much that summer, so on August 1, a hundred activists took their bodies on the road. They walked the five miles to his house in Bridgeport. The police warned them that they would be arrested for breach of the peace if they were caught singing in this white residential neighborhood. After the march, the *Chicago Defender* quoted

Gregory, who brought a useful sense of comedic timing wherever he went: "As for the singing, when we get ready to get ourselves arrested we'll let the police know," he said.

The following afternoon, accompanied by one hundred police officers, Dick Gregory and sixty-four others began the five miles from downtown once again. This time, both the protesters and the police had attorneys advising them. According to police testimony, the protesters were greeted by approximately thirty-five people on a Bridgeport corner, holding signs. The taverns had been closed. Other white residents came out of their homes to jeer as the demonstrators peacefully circled the four blocks of Daley's neighborhood. Additional officers were stationed at the intersections and along each of the four blocks in their loop. Nevertheless, with each lap, the hostile white crowd grew—to one hundred, then one hundred fifty, then double that.

The court record quoted Gregory preparing his fellow marchers for their own form of heckling. "Don't stop and don't answer any one back," he told them. "Don't worry about anything that is going to be said to you. Just keep marching. If anyone hits you or anything, try to remember what they look like, but above all means, do not hit them back. Keep the line straight, and keep it tight." At one point, a group of white bystanders pointed their sprinklers at the demonstrators; others tried to join the march, but the police ushered them back onto their lawns. Gregory told an officer, "They have as much a right to demonstrate as we do." According to a Sergeant Golden, at 9:00 p.m., new onlookers suddenly seemed to pour in from everywhere, and the streets and sidewalks swelled with more whites. Newspaper accounts estimated between fifteen hundred and two thousand people. Whatever their number, the white mob was angry. Many were shouting. Some held signs supporting the Ku Klux Klan. Some were singing the Alabama Trooper song. Others threw eggs and rocks. People in cars blasted their horns. Police believed the situation was verging on a riot. By 9:30, police asked Gregory to let them escort his group out, explaining that they could not ensure their safety. Three civil rights demonstrators took the escort, but Gregory and the others stayed. The police arrested them for disorderly conduct.

As a First Amendment case, *Gregory v. Chicago* is cut-and-dried. As to the question of how much a hostile audience influences the exercise of a constitutional right, the Supreme Court's decision was unanimous: the government had no right to restrict the speech of the demonstrators due to the anticipated potential violence of the mob. The canonical significance of *Gregory v. Chicago* resides in Justice Black's concurrence elaborating on the heckler's veto, which draws not from the lay meaning of *heckler* but from the silencing power of counterprotesters. Some of the related issues would be taken up a decade later in *Skokie*, refining the assertion that the government cannot allow opponents to stop the speech of those they oppose, even in anticipation of violence this may incite, whether they are Nazis, or civil rights activists, or Klansmen—as Justice Black had once been himself. Today the heckler's veto remains relevant including in cases of demonstrations against speeches by, for example, Ann Coulter and Milo Yiannopoulos.

But whatever advances *Gregory v. Chicago* signified for First Amendment case law, it was a footnote in the unstoppable life of Dick Gregory. There aren't many other people who could have easily been lead plaintiffs in any number of civil rights cases, and fewer still who were famous show business talents who turned their gifts full time toward activism. Gregory went on to protest the Vietnam War, apartheid, world hunger, on behalf of Native American fishing rights, the Equal Rights Amendment, and for the rights of black people on numerous fronts. He ran for mayor of Chicago and for the presidency, and launched a successful health food business after working as a nutritionist for Muhammad Ali. There were years during which Gregory spoke at three hundred colleges. "He evolved into an incredibly honed person who really used himself to live his cause," said Gretchen Law, a playwright who wrote *Turn Me Loose*, a 2018 play about him. "And his cause really was combating racism in all of its psychoses and all of its horror. He became so clear about that."

John Bracey Jr., the recently retired chair of the W. E. B. Du Bois Department of Afro-American Studies at the University of Massachusetts, Amherst, met Dick Gregory that summer of 1965 in Chicago. Bracey was a young activist working for Lawrence Landry, who was by then the head of the Coordinating Council of Community

Organizations, which organized the protests. "When we see the movies, we see the high points. We don't see the postraumatic stress. A lotta people in SNCC [the Student Nonviolent Coordinating Committee] had breakdowns," Bracey told me. "Dick Gregory managed to sustain himself at the front of what he wanted to do. That's remarkable. Every ten years you look up, Dick's still out there! He hasn't taken a break!"

Bracey ran into Gregory at Landry's memorial and recognized the spirit of the young fighter in the old man who stood before him. Gregory was "warm and friendly, insightful, and kept you calm," he said. "I don't think it was practiced," he added. "It was his way of relating to the world."

"It feels like he lived five lives, and was just a comedian at the beginning and the end," Neal Brennan, the co-creator of *Chappelle's Show*, observed.

Today, Gregory's name is no longer well known. For years, Edward Schmitt, Gregory's biographer, has been pondering this troubling disappearance from mainstream consciousness. "He was a household name, and the press certainly did cover him through the sixties," he told me. The FBI has a file on Gregory that runs over eight hundred pages. We have as much to learn from the life of Dick Gregory as Gregory did from every audience.

Was the focus of Gregory's persistence the problem? Jack Healey, a former priest who went on to be the head of Amnesty International in the United States, once told Schmitt about a conversation he had with journalist Dan Rather on an airplane. "I'm kind of tired of Dick Gregory," Rather had said. Of course, injustice isn't quickly addressed, and continued activism can seem tiresome, especially to those who remain unaffected by those inequities.

Perhaps the mainstream press lost interest in Dick Gregory because he continued to show up in places where the need was as persistent as he was—in black communities where so many of the promises of civil rights, enshrined in law, have yet to be honored. The Chicago public schools remain segregated and underfunded, a majority of their students living in poverty.

Ten days after his arrest in Chicago for that demonstration in front of Mayor Daley's house, Gregory flew to California, where the Watts neighborhood in Los Angeles was imploding. Thirty-four people would die in the riots, a level of civil unrest Los Angeles wouldn't experience again until Rodney King in 1991. Gregory was shot in the leg there while attempting to stop a fight. Soon afterward, he appeared on the *Merv Griffin Show*.

That day's panel included a young, ebullient Richard Pryor and an angry, young Phil Spector. After arrogantly deflecting Merv's friendly questions, Spector turned his misogyny onto Eartha Kitt, a famous black entertainer. Today this would likely be the story whose regurgitated anecdotal meaning would trend on the Internet. But talk shows allowed for substantive conversation then and Kitt easily took care of Spector herself. The segment ended with an eager Merv Griffin engaging with Gregory about the activity on some American streets. Gregory pointed out that police violence had ignited every riot to date. He listed the factors that often lead to the expression of despair and rage that had just occurred in Watts—unemployment, overcrowding, underserved schools, and police brutality. Griffin noted the improvements in legislation that resulted from the Movement, but expressed skepticism about the way in which activists seemed to insist that "the only way to get things done is to disobey the law."

Dick Gregory's reply that day holds as much weight as any Supreme Court case: "Read the Constitution," he suggested, "and see how many times it mentions law and obeying the law. The one thing the Constitution talks about, which the Negro do not have, and when we get that we will have no more problem with the law, is justice. Until you give me justice, you can't talk to me about disobeying the law. Once you have proper justice, the law takes care of itself."

STREET V. NEW YORK (1969)

After the shooting of civil rights icon James Meredith, Sidney Street, a fifty-one-year-old African American New York City bus driver with no previous criminal record, set his American flag on fire on a public street. A crowd gathered, and a police officer demanded that Street explain what was going on. Street replied, "If they let that happen to Meredith, we don't need an American flag." Street was arrested and eventually convicted of violating a state statute making it a crime to publicly "cast contempt upon [the US flag] either by words or act."

After New York's appellate and high courts affirmed his conviction, the US Supreme Court overturned it in a 5–4 decision, ruling that the part of the law prohibiting contemptuous "words" against the flag violated the right to freedom of speech protected by the First Amendment. The Court wrote, "Freedom to differ is not limited to things that do not matter much. That would be a mere shadow of freedom. The test of its substance is the right to differ as to things that touch the heart of the existing order."

Because the part of the law against words was unconstitutional and because it was not possible to know from the general verdict at trial whether Street's words had played a role in his conviction, the Court overturned the guilty verdict. It would take the Supreme Court another twenty years to return to the question of whether the First Amendment protected even the act of burning the flag.

The Right to Offend

RABIH ALAMEDDINE

In the days of the mighty King Nimrod, there lived a young man named Abraham, son of Azar, an idol maker. Out of wood, Azar sculpted beautiful gods that the people loved and worshipped. Azar would send his son to market with the idols, but Abraham never sold any. He called out, "Who'll buy my idols? They're cheap and worthless. Will you buy one? It won't hurt you." When a passerby stopped to look at the beauty of the craftsmanship, Abraham slapped the idol. "Talk," he said. "Tell this honest man to buy you. Do something." There would be no sale.

Of course, his father was upset. He was losing money and had a nonbeliever for a son. He told Abraham to believe in the gods or leave the house. Abraham left.

Abraham walked into a temple while all the townsfolk were in their homes preparing for an evening of worshipping their beloved gods. Abraham held out food for the gods. "Eat. Aren't you hungry? Why don't you talk to me?" Again he slapped their faces, one by one. Slap, move to the next, slap. Then he took an ax and chopped the gods to pieces, some as small as toothpicks. He chopped up all but the largest and put the ax in this idol's hand.

When the people came to worship their gods, they found them in a splintery pile around the chief idol. They bemoaned their fate and that of their gods. "Who would do this?" they cried in unison, a chorus of wails.

"Surely it was someone," Abraham exclaimed. "The big one stands there with a guilty ax in his hand. Perhaps he was envious of the rest and chopped them up. Should we ask him?"

"You know they don't speak," the priest said.

"Then why do you worship them?"

"Heresy," the people cried in unison, and took him to see his king.

About four years ago, I was on a cartoonist panel at the Lahore Literary Festival in Pakistan. I wasn't sure why I, a novelist, was asked to pontificate on political cartoons and graphic novels. That was part of the overall charm of Lahore: not much made sense, so you went with the flow. There were two other panelists, one arguably Pakistan's most famous political cartoonist, and the second a graphic journalist who, in my opinion, was nothing short of a genius. The audience hall was overfilled, more than seven hundred people, mostly young adults, university students, some high school kids. The conversation was lively, and as was to be expected, halfway through, the moderator asked how the panelists felt about the Danish cartoons depicting the prophet Muhammad. The other panelists, while defending free speech and the right of the Danish newspapers to publish the cartoons, argued that it was not a good idea to offend religions and that the newspapers should not have done so. Those two panelists knew more about the subject than I ever could, but that did not stop me from keeping up a running uninformed commentary. I mentioned that my problem with the cartoons was that they were not funny. I talked about how insults and offenses are ways for humans to figure out boundaries. Like children, we have to test the rules, have to figure out how strict those rules are.

During the Q&A, it became obvious that the majority of the audience preferred that no one offend their religion. The moderator asked the panelists if they had any last thoughts to close the session. Well, I did.

I said that had the prophet Muhammad not wished to offend, we would not have had Islam.

Many Christians will tell you: proclaiming truth always offends.

Jesus caused trouble wherever he went. He was so offensive that he was crucified for it. He violently insulted the beliefs of the time.

He made a whip out of cords and drove everyone from the Temple. He overturned the tables of the moneychangers and the seats of those who were selling doves.

What did he have against doves? I ask you.

Muhammad destroyed the idols surrounding the Kaaba, 360 of them that various Arab tribes worshipped. He showed no respect to the pagan religions of his time.

Moses not only offended; he challenged an empire.

Would a plague of frogs be considered a sign of disrespect?

Martin Luther King Jr. said, "Freedom is never voluntarily given by the oppressor; it must be demanded by the oppressed."

And usually demanded with no little offense.

Sidney Street was an African American veteran of World War II and a Bronze Star recipient. On June 6, 1966, when he heard that civil rights activist James Meredith had been shot by a sniper during his march through Mississippi, Street went to the intersection of Lafayette Avenue and Saint James Place, one block from his apartment in Brooklyn, and burned an American flag. He was arrested for it. The New York City Criminal Court charged Street with malicious mischief for willfully and unlawfully defiling, casting contempt on, and burning an American flag. The Supreme Court overturned the conviction.

The details of the burning are what I find fascinating. Sidney Street placed a piece of paper on the sidewalk. The flag he set on fire was properly and exquisitely folded. He held the burning flag in hand as long as he could, then laid it on the paper so that it would not be soiled by the sidewalk.

When I was fifteen, I made a list of all the ways in which I could kill my parents. I separated the murderous possibilities into two categories: on the left were those where it would be obvious that I killed them, and on the right were those I would almost certainly have gotten away with.

Even at that confused age, I knew that I loved my parents dearly, at least most of the time. I also knew that I couldn't survive without them. After all, they paid for everything, and the food in our house was really good. That did not mean that I should let them get away with always telling me what to do.

When I told my father about the list, he said, "That's lovely. I do hope you pick the right method."

I always wondered whether there was a law against throwing tea into a harbor; in other words, was the beginning of the American Revolution illegal or simply offensive?

Someone who knows much more than me explained that it was probably both. The colonists boarded the ships and stole the tea: illegal. They threw the chests of tea into Boston Harbor: definitely offensive.

E. M. Cioran wrote, "Once man loses his faculty of indifference he becomes a potential murderer."

Abraham stood defiantly before his king, the one and only Nimrod, who grew nervous, since it was his first encounter with a free soul. "You are not my god," Abraham told Nimrod. That was blasphemy. The young man grew in stature when he defied the hunter-king.

"Who is this mighty God you speak of?" asked the frightened Nimrod.

Abraham was resolute. "He it is who gives life and death," he answered, his gaze unwavering.

The king said, "But I too give life and death. I can pardon a man sentenced to die and execute an innocent child."

Abraham said, "That is not the way of God. But can you do this? Each morning God makes the sun rise in the east. Can you make it rise in the west?"

Nimrod grew mighty angry. He did not have the wit to suggest that maybe Abraham's god should try to make the sun rise in the west for a change. Oh no. Nimrod had his minions build a great big fire and ordered Abraham thrown into it. The men came to carry Abraham, but he told them he could walk.

After suitable burning time had elapsed, the servants opened the oven door expecting to see nothing except charred remains, but there our prophet was, as glorious as ever; the young Abraham was singing, lying indolently on a bed of red roses, red like the color of fresh blood. Thousands upon thousands of crimson rose petals. The attending courtiers ran away in terror as if they had seen a jinni or an angel.

Abraham, unblemished and untouched, walked out of the furnace, smirked as he passed Nimrod, and went home.

But not before the great prophet Abraham said, “I spit on your god and fart on everything you hold dear. I will destroy your religion and install mine. Once everything is set up, make sure to start being civil. Don’t you dare do what I did or my new god will smite you!”

BRANDENBURG V. OHIO (1969)

Prior to the ruling in *Brandenburg v. Ohio*, courts had examined speech for "clear and present dangers" and "bad tendencies." The former allowed the government to censor antidraft speech on the basis that it created the danger of draft riots. The bad tendency test operated similarly and allowed criminal sanctions against speech that tended to incite or cause illegal activity. Together, these rulings carved deep exceptions into the First Amendment, allowing the federal and state governments to both censor and censure any speech they believed might threaten society's tranquility. Often this meant smothering unpopular political speech under the guise of keeping the peace.

The *Brandenburg* decision overruled both tests and created the "imminent lawless action" test. Though itself replete with failings, imminent lawless action is far less prone to governmental abuse and remains the standard in First Amendment Law.

On Jews, Blacks, the KKK, Ohio, and Freedom of Speech

MORIEL ROTHMAN-ZECHER

The first time I met an aspiring white supremacist was during a class trip to a county career center in southwest Ohio. He was tall, and had buzzed hair, and told my friend Niquelle and me that he loved the movie *American History X*. He wanted to be like Edward Norton's character, he told us, "but before the part where he turned all pussy." Norton's character is an American neo-Nazi who is sent to prison—where he undergoes his aforementioned conversion—after forcing a black man to place his mouth around a curb and then executing him by stomping on the back of his skull. I remember looking over at Niquelle, who is black. I remember feeling my breath catch in my chest, upon which my Star of David necklace dangled, outside my shirt.

Growing up in southwest Ohio, I was aware of the way in which I could become more or less invisible—more or less white—based on whether I tucked my necklace in or wore it out. (A soggy sort of superpower: Jewboy to the rescue?) I often wore it out in new places, perhaps with an edge of defiance, seeking some sort of confrontation. But then when it came, like on that day—

I didn't say a word.

I asked Niquelle about this incident recently, and she told me she also remembered the day and the guy vividly, but couldn't recall the context: "Did he just look at us and let out this terrible thought? Did someone say something that made him angry?" We both remembered being whisked away by the teacher or staff person who was leading the tour, and then that was that.

Later, for a period of a few weeks, a group of kids at our high school started cracking jokes that centered around "curb stomping."

I remember one guy grabbing my shoulder right after making one such joke. *Don't be so sensitive, dude.*

This was 2004. Exactly four decades earlier, a bit farther south in Ohio, a full-fledged white supremacist made a speech that would fundamentally change what can legally be said in these United States of America. The date was Sunday, June 28, 1964. A journalist and cameraman from the Cincinnati-based TV station, WLWT Channel 5, made their way to a Hamilton County farm just outside the city, where they had been invited by a local Ku Klux Klan leader named Clarence Brandenburg to cover his group's rally.

Three weeks earlier, on June 5, 1964, in my hometown of Yellow Springs, Ohio, a barber named Lewis Gegner decided to sell his shop and leave town rather than desegregate his business, after facing a years-long nonviolent campaign that culminated with the arrest of 108 activists. The Ku Klux Klan would later invite him to speak at a rally in Dayton, Ohio, in recognition of his "steadfastness."

That same month, on June 22, in nearby Oxford, Ohio, Freedom Summer volunteers learned that three of their colleagues had gone missing while investigating a KKK church bombing in Mississippi the night before: a black civil rights activist named James Earl Chaney and two Jewish activists named Michael Schwerner and Andrew Goodman. According to historian Taylor Branch, a Mississippi sheriff responded to their disappearance by saying, "If they're missing, they just hid somewhere trying to get a lot of publicity, I figure."

Their bodies were found on August 4. According to an article by civil rights leader Marian Wright Edelman, James Earl Chaney had been chained to a tree, tortured, and castrated before being shot thrice. Michael Schwerner cradled Chaney's body in his arms, before being shot in the heart. Andrew Goodman tried to run and was shot. An autopsy showed that he had red clay fragments in his lungs and fists, indicating that he was likely buried while still alive.

On the Hamilton County farm near the end of June 1964, forty-four-year-old Clarence Brandenburg gave a speech to an assembled group of a dozen men clad in white robes and hoods. In a later part of the news channel's footage, the Klansmen are seen marching in circles around a burning cross, some of them carrying guns, shouting things including "Freedom for the Whites," and "Bury the n***ers."

"We're not a revengent organization," declared Brandenburg, who was wearing a red hood over his white robe. "But if our president, our Congress, our Supreme Court, continues to suppress the white, Caucasian race, it's possible that there might have to be some revengeance taken." In a second clip, Brandenburg is seen repeating a similar speech, and adding, "Personally, I believe the n***er should be returned to Africa, the Jew returned to Israel."

And then that was that.

The group dispersed, and everyone went home for supper, or a nap, or a beer, or a game of gin rummy, or whatever one does after attending a Ku Klux Klan rally.

This word *revengeance* was later mocked, and Brandenburg's remarks were labeled "self-evidently stupid and silly"—by his own defense lawyer. But that's the thing about white supremacists: their rhetoric is mostly self-evident stupidity and silliness nestled between bursts of horrific vitriol. As cathartic as it can feel to mock, said silliness doesn't make their rhetoric any less deadly serious. Or less deadly.

Right?

Which brings us back to the central question of *Brandenburg v. Ohio*, a question that is as relevant in our current era as it was in the 1960s: How deadly is such rhetoric?

Deadly enough that it should be illegal?

The answer given by the State of Ohio was yes.

Following the broadcast of his speech at the KKK rally, Clarence Brandenburg was arrested on August 6, 1964, two days after the bodies of the murdered activists were found in Mississippi, and charged under Ohio's criminal syndicalism statute, which, like other similar statutes around the country, was originally put on the books primarily as a bludgeon against communist sympathizers and which criminalized advocating "sabotage, violence, or . . . terrorism . . . as a means of accomplishing . . . political reform."

Brandenburg was convicted, fined one thousand dollars, and sentenced to one to ten years in prison. His appeals were rejected by lower courts and by the Ohio Supreme Court. Brandenburg had been laid off from his job at GE in 1958 and had filed for bankruptcy in 1959. So when the ACLU offered to appeal the case, pro bono, to the United States Supreme Court, Brandenburg accepted. His lawyer? A forty-eight-year-old Jewish ACLU volunteer named Allen Brown.

Brown died in 2004, but his friend and colleague Norman Slutsky said of him: "If ever there was a Jewish saint, it was Allen. He was an absolute mensch. One of the most beautiful men I knew." Brown was short, a little on the hefty side, and had a raspy voice, accentuated by his constant smoking. Once a judge reprimanded him for his constant motion during a trial and threatened to hold him in contempt of court if he didn't keep his hand on the podium at all times. During his closing arguments, Brown stuck one finger out, placed it on the podium, and then danced as far as he could, in every direction, with his fingertip still touching the wood. In another case, an obscenity case, Norman Slutsky told of Brown, the Jewish saint, picking up a giant dildo brought as evidence by the prosecution and waggling it in the faces of the jury members, growling: "This may disgust you, and this may disgust you. But it is not obscene." Allen Brown was not a religious man, but he was a true believer in the First Amendment. When he died, his family asked that donations be made to the ACLU.

Also representing Brandenburg on behalf of the ACLU was one of the organization's two national lawyers: a thirty-two-year-old African American attorney named Eleanor Holmes Norton, now the congressional representative for the District of Columbia. Norton had graduated from Antioch College in Yellow Springs, Ohio. A 1960 article in the *Antioch Record* describes how Norton, known then as Ellie Holmes, coordinated efforts between the Antioch chapter of the NAACP, the local ACLU, and other activists to desegregate all of the still-segregated businesses in town. (The only holdout by the time Norton left Yellow Springs was Gegner's barbershop.) In 1964, Norton traveled to Mississippi as legal counsel to the Freedom Summer. She was, in short, no stranger to American racism and no friend to its proponents. In a 1969 interview, reprinted in the *Record*, she said, "If you look closely at the color of my skin and the texture of my hair, you will see that I could only be in this for the principles involved. Self-interest becomes an absurdity."

And so the case in which a Klansman, represented by black and Jewish ACLU lawyers, faced off against the State of Ohio got underway.

In the oral arguments before the US Supreme Court, the lawyer representing Ohio, Leonard Kirschner, made the following argument as to why Brandenburg's speech should be illegal: "If I were to run down Harlem, shall we say, and say 'Bury the Negro,' 'Send them back to the black Africa'—"

Justice Thurgood Marshall, the first African American Supreme Court justice, interrupted: "He wouldn't last that long."

Laughter in the otherwise somber courtroom.

Six minutes later, Allen Brown began his rebuttal by stating that the massive violation of the First Amendment found in the State of Ohio's laws can in fact be illustrated by Justice Marshall's response to Kirschner's hypothetical situation. "Justice Marshall," Brown said, his gravely voice rising, picking up speed, building to something important, "is safe for the moment because the venue is in Washington, D.C., but in Ohio, could be indicted for suggesting a violent reaction by the Negro community."

And then that was that.

The Court's decision was unanimous: Ohio's criminal syndicalism statute, and others like it around the country, was unconstitutional. Advocacy of violence in the abstract is not sufficient grounds for the government to prohibit speech. In order for the First Amendment to be curbed, according to the *Brandenburg* ruling, advocacy of violence must be "directed to inciting or producing imminent lawless action" and be "likely to incite or produce such action."

In other words, the state of Ohio cannot arrest an aspiring white supremacist in a county career center who says, "I believe in killing blacks and Jews." Government officials could intervene only in a case in which he said, "Let's kill this black and this Jew, right now."

A word, here, on white American bigotry and the identities of its obsessions. James Baldwin, in 1967: "One does not wish, in short, to be told by an American Jew that his suffering is as great as the

American Negro's suffering. It isn't." He's right, of course. Michael Schwerner and Andrew Goodman weren't shot because they were Jews—except in the roundabout, romantic, fictional sort of way that links their Jewishness with their conscientious activism. The recent synagogue massacre in Pittsburgh did have a handful of American precedents—the lynching of Leo Frank, the murder of Alan Berg, the Jewish Community Center shootings in LA and Kansas City, and some others—but only a handful, not thousands. Bryan Stevenson's Equal Justice Initiative estimates that 4,075 black Americans were murdered in racial terror lynchings between 1877 and 1950 alone. White supremacists are obsessed with both groups, but their murderous frenzy has been almost entirely directed toward only one. Perhaps this discrepancy is partially due to Jewboy's aforementioned soggy superpower—the ability to blend into American whiteness. At its worst, we have Charles Leb, the owner of a kosher deli in Atlanta who, in 1963, when faced with nonviolent sit-ins calling on him to desegregate his establishment, enlisted the help of none other than the KKK; at its worst, we have Stephen Miller, who has helped give voice to an agenda of white supremacy in the Trump White House. But this discrepancy is also certainly due to the fact that one of the foundational pillars of the United States of America—and one that has never truly been renounced—is the dehumanization, murder, torture, persecution, and wild hatred of black people.

Thanks to Brown, Norton, and the ACLU, Brandenburg walked free. (Though a few years later, this pleasant fellow would be jailed for sixty days for harassing his Jewish neighbor by repeatedly telephoning to berate him with anti-Semitic tirades.) Was the ruling in *Brandenburg* a victory for the forces of revengeance and hatred in this country?

In 1977, the Nazi Party of America sought a permit to hold a parade in Skokie, Illinois, a majority-Jewish village that was home to thousands of Holocaust survivors. Under the standards set by *Brandenburg*, such a parade was obviously permissible: the US Supreme Court unanimously upheld the Illinois Supreme Court's decision to allow the march. The permit-seeking American Nazis were represented in court by the ACLU, as was the case in Charlottesville, forty years later. But we'll get there.

In the meantime, the other side of the coin: after facing pushback from fellow activists for her work in Brandenburg, Eleanor Holmes Norton made a statement, reprinted in the *Antioch Record* in 1969, in which she argued that such cases were more likely to benefit radical activists than Brandenburg's colleagues, and that her defense of racists' right to express their views did not conflict with her "black militant philosophy."

"Actually," she said, "the right wing cases are real plums. When I defend a left winger's right to dissent, I am not saying very much to the increasingly larger body of people in this country committed to repression of extreme ideas. But when I'm defending a racist's rights, the object lesson is dramatically clear."

In the 1973 case of *Hess v. Indiana*, based on the standards established in *Brandenburg*, the Court unanimously ruled to overturn the conviction of antiwar protester Gregory Hess, who was arrested for declaring something along the lines of, "We'll take the fucking street later," within earshot of a cop. And in a 1982 ruling, *NAACP v. Claiborne Hardware Co.*, the court unanimously ruled that the First Amendment, as interpreted in *Brandenburg*, protected a 1964 speech given by Charles Evers, the brother of murdered civil rights leader Medgar Evers, in which he warned black residents of Port Gibson, Mississippi, against violating a local NAACP-led boycott of segregationist merchants. "If we catch any of you going into these racist stores," he said, "we're going to break your damn neck." Even though some residents were indeed later met with violence after violating the boycott, the Court ruled, under the standards set forth by *Brandenburg*, that Evers's speech could not reasonably be construed as intentionally and directly inciting imminent violence.

So where does this all leave us?

Probably in the streets of Charlottesville, Virginia, with hundreds of self-evidently silly and stupid white men and boys bearing Walmart torches and chanting about "Jews not replacing us." The right of the Unite the Right rally to take place had been supported, in line with

Brandenburg and *Skokie* and *Hess* and *NAACP v. Claiborne Hardware*, by the Virginia chapter of the ACLU.

The argument that the horrific violence that took place that day—including a group of white supremacists savagely beating and stomping on a black man named DeAndre Harris as he lay splayed out on the ground of a parking garage, and one white supremacist, from Ohio, ramming his car into a crowd of leftist counterprotesters and murdering Heather Heyer—had far more to do with failures on the part of law enforcement than with any sort of speech that day is, to my mind, a basically sound one. Still, it bears mentioning that after what happened in Charlottesville, the ACLU did draw up a list of guidelines for case selection that, while decidedly not repudiating the Virginia ACLU's decision to defend the white supremacist rally's right to take place, did foreground the tension inherent in defending such speech and clarified that the ACLU will "generally not represent protestors who seek to march while armed."

A few months after the rally in Charlottesville, my wife and I moved back to southwest Ohio. A few months after that, our daughter was born here: tiny, curious, adventurous, brilliant, Jewish.

Our town, Yellow Springs, still feels imbued with Antioch College's progressive spirit and the legacy left by Eleanor Holmes Norton and other activists since. But there are Confederate flags flying in the rural stretches around us, and I've read article after article about white supremacists (around my age) living in the area: the Hitler-admiring white nationalist from Huber Heights; the founder of the Daily Stormer website, whose main pages include "Race War" and "Jewish Problem," based near Columbus. While Jews are not at the very top of American white supremacists' list of bloodlust, these questions, questions of speech and threat and assembly and safety, do not feel purely academic or theoretical to me. There is no flippancy or cavalier intellectualization in my fingertips as I write, here in southwest Ohio, my tiny Jewish daughter napping in the other room, that even after Charlottesville, I think that Eleanor Holmes Norton and Allen Brown and the ACLU were right in their defense of Clarence Brandenburg.

Because in truth, the ideologies of Brandenburg and the tiki torchers are not as divergent from the core ideologies of the American political regime as many think they are. In truth, throughout American history, government suppression of speech and expression has been far more frequently and viciously directed against leftists and radicals, against black militants and Jewish communists, than it has against the various Brandenburgs of this nation. In that light, the Brandenburg case appears as a form of aikido, in which Norton, Brown, and the ACLU harnessed the force of American white supremacism itself as a means of ultimately defending those who would seek to undermine American white supremacism and its American cousins: bigotry, xenophobia, imperialism, and bellicosity. In other words, in challenging the government's right to punish Brandenburg for saying heinous things, a counterintuitive but profound sliver of freedom was wrested from this deeply unfree country.

And for that, here in southwest Ohio, I am grateful.

COHEN V. CALIFORNIA (1971)

The Supreme Court considered this case "at first blush too inconsequential to find its way into [its] books, but . . . of no small constitutional significance": a prosecution under California Penal Code 415 that prohibits "maliciously and willfully disturb[ing] the peace or quiet of any neighborhood or person . . . by . . . offensive conduct." The "offensive conduct" at issue was an antiwar protester's decision to wear a jacket emblazoned with "Fuck the Draft" in a corridor of the Los Angeles courthouse. Writing as amicus, the ACLU urged the Supreme Court to reverse the California courts' affirmation of Cohen's conviction on First Amendment freedom of speech grounds. In a 5–4 decision, the Court agreed, holding that the state may not make the "simple public display" of a "single four-letter expletive" a criminal offense.

Disturbing the War

JONATHAN LETHEM

In May 1968 Robert Cohen walked into a courthouse in Los Angeles wearing a jacket with "Fuck the Draft" stenciled on the back, in order to testify on behalf of a friend. By the time he entered the courtroom, he'd folded the jacket into his lap, but a policeman had noticed him wearing it in the corridor and become incensed. After trying and failing to get the judge to hold Cohen in contempt of court, the irate cop put the nab on him personally. The charge, ironically, was "disturbing the peace." (I suppose we still await a statue called "Disturbing the War.") After an initial conviction, the judgment was overturned in appellate court on the beautiful grounds that Cohen's behavior had been, yes, "offensive" but not "tumultuous"—that is, had incited no other person to a violent response—and that both conditions need to be present to meet the statute's standard for peace disturbance. The state appealed back and won. Cohen's attorneys appealed. Cohen's case reached the Supreme Court three years later.

This case beckoned to me in a few different ways. Truthfully, it seemed like it had my name on it. The spring of 1971 was a fateful one in the relation of my family's life to what was, at the time, an ongoing condition, on my parents' part, of protest of the Vietnam War. My mother was arrested, along with many hundreds of others, during the May Day protest, for occupying the steps of the US Capitol. She was in the early stages of pregnancy with my sister at the time. In the jailhouse to which she and her friends were bused, they were crowded into tiny cells and spent their time incarcerated without food and water (they also protested the conditions of their incarceration by taking what small food they were finally offered, bologna sandwiches, and removing the filler and smacking it up to stick on the wall of the cell: meat graffiti). Eventually an ACLU lawyer attained a settlement from the federal government for wrongful arrest, establishing that the space of the Capitol steps was a public commons from which the protesters had been unjustly removed. Growing up, I was always told that the money from this settlement, though it was just a few thousand dollars, had formed the basis of the fund for sending me off to college. The judgment in favor of my mother and her co-arrestees seems to form a little rhyme with that in favor of Cohen's Fuck the Draft jacket.

I was also, as a kid, a little free speech absolutist and a pottymouth. So was my mother. It would have been right around 1971, when I was seven, that she'd given me a little lecture I distinctly recall (likely it was given several times) about how the sorts of words that our family sometimes used inside the house weren't appropriate for me to repeat at school. This went together with an injunction not to repeat, outside the safe company of a few sympathetic souls, the scalding mockery our parents and their friends applied to the Nixon presidency—he's a schmuck, he's a vampire, he's obviously compensating for a lifetime of sexual frustration, probably just needs a good fuck—word-for-word in front of my teachers or other adults I didn't know.

Now—of course—I wasn't really going to speak these things back to my mother. So I was being instructed to listen to things I couldn't make use of myself for the time being. They were allowed to sink into my expressive lexicon to be retrieved for use at some unknown juncture, according to some as-yet-unspecified future necessity.

And yet, that word, *fuck*—that I also heard with regularity in another place, on the city streets. Kids on the pavement used it as an unfriendly but pungent synonym for the phrases "what are" or "what do" as in the formulations "Fuck you looking at?" and "Fuck you think you're doing walking away when I'm talking to you?"

And I read it in books, like Erica Jong's *Fear of Flying*, which I soon snuck off my mother's shelves. The Zipless Fuck.

And Henry Miller.

And then there was the strange case of Norman Mailer's *The Naked and the Dead*, where everywhere the word *fug* had been substituted—pretty obviously, it seemed. Were soldiers really so discreet?

And the band, the Fugs, who'd taken their name from Mailer's weird euphemism. My mother was pals with one of them, Tuli Kupferberg. And the Fugs had tried to levitate the Pentagon at an antiwar protest in 1967—the same one Mailer wrote about in *The Armies of the Night*.

And the banned books that had been freed, heroically: Nabokov & Co. obscenity trials, *Howl*, the Grove Press, the pulping of J. G. Ballard's *The Atrocity Exhibition*. All of this was part of the cultural world that most thrilled me, and by the time I went to college, I knew, for instance, who Charles Rembar was and had read his book about defending *Lady Chatterley's Lover*, *Tropic of Cancer*, and *Fanny Hill* before the Supreme Court—a book featuring an introduction by Rembar's cousin, Norman Mailer.

Much later, I was allowed to play my tiny part in the public life of "fuck" by a quirk of fate. The *New York Times* chose to excerpt the first sentence from a number of new novels for a promotional feature. I was included, but the first sentence of my book was, "Quit fucking black cops or get booted from the Communist Party." An exception was granted, by unseen powers, to the newspaper's legendarily prudish boycott on that word. There followed a brief stir as I became the occasion of the *Times*'s first publication of the word *fucking* in its pages.

I guess I'd found my juncture.

All this, but I'd never heard of Robert Cohen and his unruly jacket. It had been waiting until now to find me.

The Supreme Court ruled in favor of Cohen's freedom to wear the jacket—narrowly, in a 5–4 split. Cohen was represented by the wonderfully named Melville Nimmer, the State of California by Michael Sauer. Justice John Marshall Harlan II wrote the opinion. He cleared space for defending the utterance by judging *fuck*, in this instance at least, as not an "erotic" word—not therefore a matter of public obscenity yet not an incentive to fighting either: "No individual actually or likely to be present could reasonably have regarded the words on appellant's jacket as a direct personal insult." He then coined the memorable phrase, "One man's vulgarity is another's lyric," which is nearly like a line Bob Dylan would have crossed out of an early draft of "Gates of Eden."

The dissent, written by Harry Blackmun, arched an eyebrow at Harlan's second assertion. "Fuck," in the case of the jacket, was an example of "conduct," not defensible speech. "Fuck the Draft" was "fighting words."

For what it's worth, I like the word, and use it plenty, because I disagree with Harlan here. *Fuck* retains its aura because it is both imperishably erotic and a fighting word. Its magic capacity for oscillation between these signifying powers, as in my mother's language realm and in the books on her shelves, describes its unusual value. Even as capitalism has tried to siphon off fuck's aura through peekaboo appropriations like "Fuddruckers" and "Fcuk Jeans," it holds true. Ask the hip-hop group N.W.A., for instance.

Cohen, who goes under another name now, recently spoke about his case: "I didn't even see the wording on the jacket until the morning before I was headed to court to testify on behalf of an acquaintance. I was and am a patriotic person."

The famous jacket? It had been stenciled and given to him by a female friend, just the night before. "I had a PhD in partying back in those days. I wasn't trying to make a political statement."

Well, fuck, man, you did anyway.

NEW YORK TIMES CO. V. UNITED STATES (1971)

New York Times Co. v. United States is a historic First Amendment safeguard of freedom of the press in the face of government censorship. In 1971, the *New York Times* and the *Washington Post* began publishing confidential documents known as the Pentagon Papers, which revealed that the government had lied to the public about the US role and intentions in the Vietnam War. The United States sought to enjoin the newspapers from publishing these documents, arguing that the president had the power to bar any publication that might injure the public interest. The ACLU submitted an amicus brief to the Supreme Court in which it argued for the critical importance of a free press to an informed public, especially in relation to a war that had so violently divided the country.

The Court ruled in favor of the newspapers, holding that the government had not shown why a restraint on the publications was justified. In his concurrence, Justice Hugo Black wrote that the press must be protected precisely "so that it [can] bare the secrets of government and inform the people." The case established a protection for the press in reporting on government conduct that has been critical in holding government accountable to the people.

Secrets and Lies

SALMAN RUSHDIE

It is shocking, is it not, to those of us living, as we do, in a time of unimpeachable integrity in public life, to discover that there was a time when the government of the United States lied to its citizens, even about matters of life and death, and then went to extraordinary lengths to conceal the fact that it was lying?

During the Vietnam War, the Johnson administration, without telling Congress or the American people, broadened the scope of the war to include the bombings of Laos and Cambodia, increased raids on North Vietnam, and much more. These went unreported in the press. In addition, while President Johnson publicly said that the purpose of US involvement was to protect South Vietnam, he and Secretary of Defense Robert McNamara agreed that the true purpose was to contain China, and they further agreed that this would take a long time, cost a great deal of money, and result in a large number of deaths of American soldiers. None of this was admitted publicly.

The *Report of the Office of the Secretary of Defense Vietnam Task Force*, afterward known as the Pentagon Papers, contained this explosive information in enormous and irrefutable detail. Of the fifteen copies that were made, two were sent to the RAND Corporation, a global policy think tank, where a RAND employee named Daniel Ellsberg read it and knew, as he afterward said, that the report "demonstrated unconstitutional behavior by a succession of presidents, the violation of their oath and the violation of the oath of every one of their subordinates." He photocopied the document and became determined to release it in an attempt to end the war.

On June 13, 1971, the *New York Times* began publication of the documents. The paper was hit with an injunction to cease publication and appealed. The appeal moved quickly to the Supreme Court. On June 18, the *Washington Post*, which also received documents from Ellsberg, had begun to publish too. Judge Murray Gurfein of the US District Court declined the government's request for an injunction, writing that "security . . . lies in the value of our free institutions. A cantankerous press, an obstinate press, a ubiquitous press must be suffered by those in authority to preserve the even greater values of freedom of expression and the right of the people to know."

Now that we have been told that this same press is in fact the "enemy of the people," how innocently those lines read!

This time the government appealed, and the two cases, against the *New York Times* and the *Washington Post*, were heard jointly by the Supreme Court. In an amicus brief, the ACLU stated that if the government's vague test of "information detrimental to the national security" were to be accepted, there would be virtually no limit to censorship of the news then or in the future. And on June 30, 1971, by a 6–3 margin, the Supreme Court found for the newspapers and against the government: "Only a free and unrestrained press can effectively expose deception in government. And paramount among the responsibilities of a free press is the duty to prevent any part of the government from deceiving the people and sending them off to distant lands to die of foreign fevers and foreign shot and shell."

What an absurdly misguided decision!

But to drop the sarcasm, this opinion, by Justice Hugo Black, should be taught in every school and memorized by everyone who attains high public office. It is a part of the bedrock of American democracy.

When I look back at those days, one of my strongest memories is that we were by no means certain that the judgment would go as it did, just as we were not at all sure that, just two days earlier on June 28, 1971, the same court would exonerate the boxer Muhammad Ali.

The great liberal-progressive victories of that time did not seem at all inevitable. It felt as if the future teetered on a knife edge.

These victories were hard won. Both cases could easily have been lost, but because they were strongly, closely, even brilliantly argued, they were won, and we are the beneficiaries of those arguments, among them the arguments made by the ACLU.

"To prevent any part of the government from deceiving the people." I doubt that even during the Nixon presidency (during which the Pentagon Papers case was heard) anyone could have imagined the scale and frequency of the deceptions being wrought on the American people today.

Attacks on the press by the president of the United States—on the "Failing *New York Times*," and the "Amazon *Washington Post*" owned by "Jeff Bozo"—have become an almost daily occurrence, and so it's vital to remember that these newspapers and many others have been, and remain, our best defenses against a capricious, deceitful, and overly mighty executive.

Distrust of the news media had been growing before Trump, and he has done everything he can to feed that distrust. Not long ago, I was lecturing in Vero Beach, Florida, to an almost entirely Republican-voting audience. These folks did not conform at all to the cliché of the Trump voter. They were affluent, white collar, university educated, and read books. Yet they had all drunk the Kool-Aid and bought into the Trump worldview. One questioner demanded, with remarkable heat, "Do you really think the *New York Times* isn't lying to us every day? Do you really believe that?" I tried to defuse the aggression by replying, "Well, yes, I do believe that, sir, except when it's reviewing my books."

But it's not a funny problem. I have some experience of countries in which the powers that be control the information media, and I know that the first step toward authoritarianism is always the destruction of people's belief that journalism is, broadly speaking, pursuing and telling the truth. The second step is for the authoritarian leader to say, "Just believe in me, for I am the truth." Trump's repeated use of "Believe me" is intended to have exactly that effect.

The Pentagon Papers case is a landmark decision in the fight for journalistic freedom and against state censorship. The inheritors of that 1971 decision at the *Times* and the *Post* have thus far acquitted themselves with honor as they seek to do their duty and expose these deceptions. We can only hope that today's Supreme Court will follow in the footsteps of the justices of 1971 and be as resolute in the defense of the freedom of the press as their predecessors were.

ROE V. WADE (1973)

DOE V. BOLTON (1973)

At the time *Roe* was decided, abortion regulation around the country was a patchwork: four states had repealed their antiabortion laws completely, and another thirteen had introduced some reforms, but the remaining thirty-seven maintained near-bans. Under the Texas statute criminalizing abortion, doctors could be jailed for two to five years for performing the procedure. The statute contained only one exception: abortions were allowed to save the mother's life.

But in 1970, two attorneys, Linda Coffee and Sarah Weddington, filed suit on behalf of a pregnant Texas resident challenging the Texas statute and arguing for her right to an abortion. The district court unanimously ruled the statute unconstitutional but would not issue an injunction against it. The case was then appealed to the Supreme Court, where it had to be argued twice: once in front of a seven-justice panel and again after two additional justices were confirmed to complete the Court. By this time, the ACLU's general counsel (and future president), Norman Dorsen, had joined the legal team.

The Court ultimately found the statute violated the constitutional right to privacy, first articulated in *Griswold v. Connecticut* (1965) in a case concerning married couples' right to contraception, and expanded in *Roe* to encompass an individual's right to reproductive choice. The Court ultimately held that (1) states could not regulate abortions during the first trimester; (2) from the first trimester until the fetus was viable, states could regulate abortion to protect the mother's health; and (3) after viability, states could regulate abortion to protect the mother's health and to protect the potential life of the fetus, even if that meant restricting abortion entirely.

Though *Roe* established the right to an abortion, its scope continues to be narrowed in cases such as *Thornburgh v. American College of Obstetricians and Gynecologists* (1986), *Planned Parenthood v. Casey* (1992), and *Gonzales v. Carhart* (2007).

The Ambivalent Activist, Jane Roe

LAUREN GROFF

Jane Roe's nickname was Pixie.

Jane Roe's real name was Norma McCorvey.

By the time Norma McCorvey became Jane Roe, she was only twenty-one, but she'd already had a tough life. Her parents had been alcoholics, and she'd been married at sixteen to an abusive husband. She had a five-year-old daughter who lived with her mother, and she had already given up her second child to adoption. In the summer of 1969, McCorvey was working for a carnival as a ticket seller in Georgia when, on the dark walk home to the women's boarding house, she may have been raped. This was her original claim, but she later retracted it. Still, whatever happened, by the next day when she woke up, she found the carnival had gone on to the next place without her. She stayed in town and got work as a waitress, but soon the morning sickness from her unwanted pregnancy was too rough on her. She somehow made her way back to her mother's in Texas where, when she tried to find an abortion provider, she could not, because abortions were illegal in Texas except to save a woman's life.

Of course, in the 1960s, abortions were illegal nearly everywhere in the United States, and where they were legal, they were so heavily regulated by hospitals that only rich women and the doctors' own mistresses and daughters could get one. A poor, uneducated, unconnected woman like Norma had little chance. For context, in the 1960s, there was no such thing as marital rape; women had no right to refuse sex to their husbands. A woman could be fired from her job for getting pregnant. A woman needed her husband's permission to open a bank account. A woman was not allowed to apply for credit. Due to this prison built out of biology and misogyny and financial constriction, there were an estimated 1 million illegal abortions per year in the United States until 1973.

It should also be mentioned that abortions were illegal despite the fact that abortion has been a common method of birth control in every known human culture and despite the fact that the choice to abort had been a woman's prerogative through centuries of English and American common law. Abortifacient herbs—rue, parsley, blue cohosh, tansy, pennyroyal—grew in most colonial kitchen gardens. Regulations on abortion began to appear only in the early nineteenth century, mostly as a power grab by doctors to eliminate midwives, barbers, and pharmacists from the doctors' own medical turf. Restriction as a way of policing public morals hove into view in the late nineteenth and early twentieth centuries, and by then they had little to do with the stated claim that they were intended to protect the life of the mother: a sterile abortion was, and remains, far safer than childbirth itself.

Because she couldn't get an abortion, Norma McCorvey, in desperation, met with an attorney to begin adoption procedures. When he found out she would have preferred the abortion she couldn't find, he called in two attorneys he knew who were looking for a plaintiff. Their names were Sarah Weddington and Linda Coffee.

What is most startling about *Roe v. Wade* to a twenty-first-century observer is how young and green Weddington and Coffee were at the time. The women were not particularly friends, though they'd met as two out of the five women in their matriculating class at the University of Texas Law School. Weddington had graduated from law school at a mere twenty-one years old and was only twenty-three when she met Jane Roe. Linda Coffee was only twenty-six. Neither had ever argued a trial at court, and neither was able to swing an associate position in a big firm after graduation despite being at the top of their class. Weddington was told during her single interview that it was because the wives of the male lawyers didn't want their husbands working with attractive female associates.

It's true that Sarah Weddington was a former sorority girl with a broad Texas accent who wore her hyperfemininity as armor, with her porcelain face and long reddish-blonde hair and frilly clothes in pastels. But she was an excellent public speaker and nothing seemed to ruffle her. Linda Coffee was a diffident woman, so careless about her appearance that once a male attorney stopped her in the street to run into a drugstore to buy her pantyhose because if he didn't, she was going to sit at court with a giant run in hers. Yet her humble demeanor hid a sharp legal mind and a hard-working soul.

Norma McCorvey was far from an ideal plaintiff due to her difficult past and her shifting story, but she was eager to join the case. The two lawyers gave her a pseudonym to protect her privacy and filed a lawsuit on her behalf against Henry Wade, the district attorney of Dallas County, and soon made it into a class-action lawsuit on behalf of all the women of Texas.

Their argument hinged on the Ninth and Fourteenth Amendments to the Constitution. The Ninth Amendment reads, "The enumeration in the Constitution, of certain rights, shall not be construed to deny or disparage others retained by the people." It is intentionally vague and reserves latent rights that are not listed in the Constitution to the people, including the right to privacy.

The Fourteenth Amendment reads in part, "No State shall make or enforce any law which shall abridge the privileges or immunities of citizens of the United States; nor shall any State deprive any person of life, liberty, or property, without due process of law; nor deny to any person within its jurisdiction the equal protection of the laws."

Norma McCorvey had already had her baby by June 1970, when Sarah Weddington stood to argue the case before a three-judge panel of the US District Court in Texas. It was her first court appearance, but she had prepared deeply, and she and the women of Texas won. The judges decided unanimously that the Texas law was unconstitutional. Yet it was a pyrrhic victory, because the court also decided not to grant an injunction against enforcement of the unconstitutional law, which meant that nothing would materially change in Texas and that abortion providers could still be arrested.

By now, the women had strong supporters from groups like Planned Parenthood, NARAL, and the ACLU, all of whom helped to gather brilliant amicus curiae briefs when the women took the case on appeal to the Supreme Court. Weddington also had to endure the gaslighting and maneuvering of a man tangentially related to the case who tried to take away her right to argue before the Supreme Court. So few women had ever argued before the Court that it was clear a man, he said, should do it. Weddington politely asserted her right.

On the day of the oral arguments before the Supreme Court on December 13, 1971, the tiny hearing room was packed. Sarah Weddington, twenty-five years old, stood to make oral arguments for the second time in her life. She stared out at the six pinkish older white men—and the African American justice, Thurgood Marshall—who would decide whether women had the right to choose how and when they could procreate (the two vacant seats would be filled by Richard Nixon months later). She began to present her case. She was not brilliant, to be perfectly honest.

But the Texas assistant attorney general, Jay Floyd, who argued on behalf of the state, was worse. When he stood to make his oral arguments, he tried to make a joke: "Mr. Chief Justice, and may it please the Court, it's an old joke, but when a man argues against two beautiful ladies like these, they're going to have the last word." The justices winced. Coffee and Weddington looked at him stonily. Floyd was thrown and never really recovered.

The decision took an immensely long time to write. Justice Harry Blackmun, a surprise advocate for liberalizing abortion laws and the most junior justice at the time, wrote the majority decision. He was painstaking and slow. Also, because his background was as the legal counsel at the Mayo Clinic, he wanted to understand the medicine involved in the case. He made the attorneys return and reargue the case once more, which went very poorly for the defense, because the male attorney was so certain the court would tip in his favor that he hadn't bothered to prepare.

Finally, on January 2, 1973, the court issued its decision, 7–2, that abortion was a fundamental right under the Constitution. Norma McCorvey wept when she read about the decision in the newspaper.

That said, *Roe v. Wade* wasn't an unambiguous success for proponents of access to abortion. Just seven years later, the Supreme Court upheld a law that allowed Congress to exclude coverage of abortion from the Medicaid program, thereby effectively preventing many poor women from utilizing this new constitutional right. And then, in 1992, while retaining the understanding that abortion is a constitutionally protected decision, the Court jettisoned Blackmun's framework and replaced it with a standard that allowed states to impose many more barriers to a woman's ability to get an abortion.

Sarah Weddington grew famous from the case: she became a two-time Texas state legislator, worked in the White House, and has a thriving public speaking career.

Linda Coffee went back to her bankruptcy firm and faded into obscurity, which suited her fine: her goal had been to expand abortion rights, not fame.

Norma McCorvey came out as a lesbian, then became a strict Catholic and repudiated her lesbianism, and, in a coup for antiabortion forces, vocally recanted her role in *Roe v. Wade* in the 1980s. She died in 2017. But for years before her change of heart, she'd been proud that she had been the wedge that opened the opportunity for other women—desperate women, poor women, women with health issues, women with too many children, women with no alternatives, women with careers, women whose birth control failed, women who'd been raped, women who were too young, women in school, women who were simply unready for the heavy burden of parenthood, women I know and love, women you know and love—to make the choice that Jane Roe hadn't been allowed to make: to have autonomy over her own body, to take her own reproductive destiny in hand.

O'CONNOR V. DONALDSON (1975)

O'Connor v. Donaldson was the culmination of the efforts of a number of attorneys, most notably Bruce Ennis of the New York Civil Liberties Union, the ACLU's New York branch. The director of the Mental Patients Rights Project, Ennis worked full time on behalf of those who were institutionalized, winning a series of cases that challenged the conditions of confinement of the mentally ill and mentally disabled. Ennis, the author of *Prisoners of Psychiatry* (1972), was a fierce opponent of involuntary civil commitment. Prior to *O'Connor v. Donaldson*, individuals could be held indefinitely in psychiatric facilities, without recourse or review. The Supreme Court dramatically changed this system, ruling that "a State cannot constitutionally confine without more a nondangerous individual who is capable of surviving safely in freedom by himself or with the help of willing and responsible family members or friends."

A Nondangerous Person

AYELET WALDMAN

In 1975, *O'Connor v. Donaldson* finally and firmly established the right of people with mental health disabilities to due process protection under the Fourteenth Amendment. In his ruling, Justice Potter Stewart held that "a State cannot constitutionally confine, without more a nondangerous individual who is capable of surviving safely in freedom by himself or with the help of willing and responsible family members or friends." The decision transformed the status of people with mental health disabilities and of mental hospitals in the United States. According to Bruce Ennis, the singularly idealistic and devoted New York Civil Liberties Union attorney who argued the case before the Supreme Court, in an interview he gave to the *New York Times* on the day the opinion was issued, the result of the ruling was that "mental hospitals as we have known them can no longer exist in this country as dumping grounds for the old, the poor and the friendless."

To those of us who came of age after the civil rights movement, the facts of the case are boggling, compelling, and enraging in equal measure. Thirteen years before the hospitalization at issue in the case, the plaintiff, Kenneth Donaldson, voluntarily checked himself into a psychiatric facility, an experience he describes in his book, *Insanity Inside Out: The Personal Story Behind the Landmark Supreme Court Decision* (1976). During this first hospitalization, Donaldson was by his own account a troublesome patient. He resented being forced to work as a dishwasher and scavenge his dinner from the discards on the staff plates. His grumblings about this and other injustices may well have been part of the motivation for referring him for electroconvulsive therapy (ECT), at the time an agonizing treatment that ward attendants and clinicians sometimes used as a punishment.

Donaldson was strapped down and tormented with ECT twice a week. After twenty-three "treatments," he was finally released.

Following this initial hospitalization, Donaldson was sluggish, hypersensitive, and, for a short period, impotent. He also became understandably suspicious of mental health professionals. As time passed, he began "writing letters to important people. These letters were suggestions, freely given with no expectation of reward other than the feeling of having done one's part." So (possibly) a crank. As a result of these letters, he claims in his book, he was subjected to a campaign of harassment by unknown individuals. "My papers were ransacked in my desk drawer and there was cigarette smoke in the room, though neither the maid nor I smoked." So (possibly) paranoid. He changed his name and then changed it back. He moved over and over again. He had a brush with the law. But all along, he worked, he went to adult education and job training classes, and he raised and supported his family, though he eventually got divorced. Moreover, he was never violent. In fact, those who knew him reported that he was a gentle man.

Finally, in 1956, he moved to Florida to stay temporarily with his parents. Something went wrong during this visit, and Donaldson's father called the police and had his son arrested. It's unclear why Donaldson's father made that initial phone call or why he refused ever to support his son's release. Donaldson writes of having told his parents that he had written an autobiography and sent it off to a publisher. Perhaps that struck his father as delusional behavior. There is evidence that Donaldson expressed to his parents his belief that he had been poisoned by enemies before moving to Florida. What was not alleged was that Donaldson was aggressive or violent to his parents, to himself, or to anyone else. At any rate, his father made the call, Donaldson was arrested, and eventually, after a single, short hearing, he was confined to Florida State Hospital.

Donaldson's greatest misfortune was that once confined to the hospital, he came under the control of a psychiatrist named J. B. O'Connor. At the time of Donaldson's commitment, O'Connor was assistant clinical director of Florida State Hospital. Eventually he was promoted all the way to superintendent. O'Connor seems to have borne Donaldson a grudge, perhaps because the patient had become a Christian Scientist and thus refused treatments like the ECT that had made him so miserable during his prior hospitalization. Donaldson remained confined in Florida State Hospital for the next fifteen years, under the thumb of O'Connor and staff physician John Gumanis. He spent much of that time in an open ward with sixty other men, a third of whom had been charged with crimes. During those long years, he was seen for no more than a total of three hours by a psychiatrist, and even those few hours were devoted to administrative rather than therapeutic topics and tasks.

Again and again Donaldson petitioned for release. A variety of individuals, agencies, and doctors were ready and able to take on his outpatient care and even to have him live with them. These requests were always denied. O'Connor (falsely) insisted that Donaldson's elderly and infirm parents were the only ones to whom he was legally permitted to release him, though by then, Donaldson was in his fifties. O'Connor gave lie to his claim by never approaching the Donaldsons to ask if they would support the release of their son.

Eventually Donaldson's predicament caught the attention of Morton Birnbaum, a physician, attorney, and advocate for people with mental health disabilities who had long argued, including in the opinion pages of the *New York Times*, for the articulation of a constitutional right to adequate treatment. Birnbaum filed suit on his behalf, bringing in Bruce Ennis of the New York Civil Liberties Union. Ennis, like Birnbaum, was a vigorous advocate on behalf of people with mental health disabilities and had won a number of cases, of which he hoped Donaldson's would be the culmination. The suit charged O'Connor, Gumanis, and others of civil rights violations, specifically the intentional and malicious deprivation of Donaldson's right to liberty as guaranteed by the Civil Rights Act of 1871 and the Fourteenth Amendment to the Constitution.

Even as the suit was being filed, O'Connor retired. When word of the suit reached the new acting superintendent of the hospital, he and his staff first threatened to return Donaldson to a locked ward, and then, after pretrial rulings in Donaldson's favor, suddenly released him. The case, however, continued to a jury trial.

At trial, O'Connor's behavior toward Donaldson so shocked the conscience of the jury that they granted punitive damages against him and another psychiatrist. Among other things, the jury found that the doctors had unjustifiably withheld psychiatric care from Donaldson, including grounds privileges designed to teach independent living and occupational therapy.

O'Connor appealed the ruling, and the US Court of Appeals for the Fifth Circuit affirmed the jury's verdict. In response to O'Connor's claim that he had acted in good faith, the court found, among other things, that he and the other defendants "wantonly, maliciously, or oppressively blocked efforts by responsible and interested friends and organizations to have Donaldson released to their custody." The court also granted the right for which Ennis and Birnbaum had long advocated, ruling that if a patient is confined because he needs treatment for mental illness, and not because he is dangerous, due process demands that treatment actually be provided. Involuntary confinement can only be justified by such a quid pro quo.

After this unequivocal victory, O'Connor once again appealed, this time to the Supreme Court. Ennis, who would eventually go on to become the ACLU's national legal director, had never before argued before the Court and later confided to friends that he spent the week before the argument vomiting from nerves. However anxious he may have been, the novice won a profound Supreme Court victory.Though unlike the Fifth Circuit, the Court did not create a constitutionally guaranteed right to treatment, they ruled that Donaldson's prolonged incarceration was a violation of his right to liberty.

As a result of Donaldson's case, state governments were compelled to enact statutes limiting involuntary civil commitment and creating mechanisms for periodic review. No nondangerous person would again be (legally) deprived of his liberty for decades, years, or even weeks and months at a time.

And yet it's hard not to view this victory, though life changing for people with mental health disabilities and system changing for the institutions that had previously incarcerated them without reasonable recourse, as a partial one. What might have happened if Birnbaum and Ennis had been able to convince the Supreme Court to pair its

Fourteenth Amendment ruling with a finding of an affirmative right to treatment? As it stands, the closure of most of the nation's hospitals for people with mental health disabilities did not result in the creation of a well-funded system of community treatment or with increased resources for services like supported housing, job training, drug treatment, or family and parenting counseling. Furthermore, the few budgetary dollars directed toward mental health are most often spent not on the sickest among us but on the "worried well," who are easier, cheaper, and more pleasant to treat, leaving the truly affected to cycle in and out of emergency rooms and short-term civil commitments. Large numbers end up in jails and prisons, which have now become the warehouses of people with serious mental illnesses, where what is most often meted out is punishment and brutality rather than treatment. By conservative estimates, between 6 and 16 percent of the US prison population lives with severe mental illness, and the numbers are far higher when less serious mental illnesses and the illness of drug addiction and dependence are included in those figures.

It is, however, no surprise that we have failed as a society to prioritize the needs of those of us with mental health challenges. Many of us respond to those we view as mentally ill with fear, disgust, and judgment rather than compassion. There are myriad reasons for this intolerance. Deeply embedded prejudices against those we view as less than fully human are as integral to the American character as the fantasy of "rugged individualism," and the most severely mentally ill among us fall neatly into the category of despised other.

There are those of us, however, whose prejudice is a result of the anxiety of overidentification rather than fear of the other. As a high-functioning person with a mood disorder who has written openly about her mental illness, I found myself reading Kenneth Donaldson's case and personal account with an eye toward drawing a distinction between him and me, as if to reassure myself that I wouldn't ever have fallen into such a circumstance. I latched on to his various expressions of seemingly paranoid delusions with a sigh of relief. *I'm not crazy like that*, I thought. *Am I?* It's true I've never been hospitalized, but I came of age in a post–*O'Connor v. Donaldson* world. Were I of my grandparents' generation, it's entirely possible that my occasional bouts of suicidal ideation would have resulted in commitment, and once committed, I, like Donaldson, might have found it all but impossible to convince the arbiters of my incarceration that I should be freed. Moreover, and most important, as a white person of privilege, the system is inclined to trust and believe me, though gender can mitigate that privilege. A woman of color without my resources might even now struggle to convince a court of her "nondangerousness" to herself, if not to others.

In the face of these realities, I find solace in the efforts of the ACLU and its lawyers to demand dignity and the protection of the Constitution on behalf of all of us, including—especially—those least likely to be deemed worthy of it.

WEINBERGER V. WIESENFELD (1975)

In *Weinberger v. Wiesenfeld*, the ACLU argued that the Supreme Court's landmark decision in *Reed v. Reed* (1971), recognizing constitutional protection against sex-based discrimination, prohibited differential treatment among widows and widowers in the administration of the Social Security system. In an 8–0 decision, the Court agreed, thereby vindicating the Wiesenfeld family's right to equality of treatment under the law in the event of spousal death and continuing the development of a robust sex equality jurisprudence.

Father Sues for "Mother's Benefits"

JENNIFER EGAN

A March 11, 1973, *New York Times* article begins: "A woman lawyer from New York and the Women's Rights Project of the American Civil Liberties Union in Newark have joined forces in an attempt to obtain Social Security benefits for a widowed father."

Apparently, a "woman lawyer" was something different from a lawyer in 1973, a distinction unimaginable today. That progress is due in part to Ruth Bader Ginsburg (the "woman lawyer"), who litigated several landmark cases to establish gender equality in American law.

The widowed father described in the *Times* was twenty-nine-year-old Stephen Wiesenfeld of New Jersey. His wife, Paula, had died in childbirth in 1972, leaving him the sole parent of a newborn son, Jason. Paula, a high school math teacher working on her PhD, had earned significantly more money than her husband, who was a freelance computer consultant. For the seven years of her employment, Paula had paid the maximum into Social Security. Had she been male and left a widow behind, that widow would have received Social Security benefits (called "Mother's insurance benefits") to help her raise her child. But because Stephen Wiesenfeld was a father, not a mother, he was denied these benefits despite his wish to be his infant son's primary caregiver.

"I intend to raise my son," Wiesenfeld told the *Times* when Ginsburg, director of the ACLU Women's Rights Project, filed a complaint on his behalf in district court. "I want to be a father to him. I realize I cannot be a mother, but I don't want the tie between us broken."

A three-judge district court ruled unanimously in Wiesenfeld's favor, deeming the Social Security statute discriminatory on the basis of sex and therefore unconstitutional. Caspar Weinberger, secretary of health, education and welfare (later secretary of defense under President Ronald Reagan), appealed the decision to the Supreme Court in 1974. The brief supplied by Ginsburg and the ACLU's legal director, Melvin Wulf, exposed the skein of prejudices that underlay existing practice: "The . . . 'child in care' Social Security benefit . . . reflects the familiar stereotype that, throughout this Nation's history, has operated to devalue women's efforts in the economic sector. . . . Just as the female insured individual's status as a breadwinner is denigrated, so the parental status of her surviving spouse is discounted."

In crackling prose characteristic of Ginsburg legal utterances, the brief argued that the government's calculus would result in a loss for everyone, especially the child, "who supplies the raison d'être for the benefit in question."

"It is invidious discrimination to provide less protection for the families of female wage earners than for the families of male wage earners, to deny to widowed fathers the same opportunity to attend to child rearing that is accorded widowed mothers, and to deny to a child whose mother has died the opportunity to be cared for personally by its sole surviving parent."

To a contemporary eye, these arguments might seem self-evident, but Caspar Weinberger had countered with an array of sallies, including a suggestion that giving benefits only to widows was a way of remedying past discrimination against women. To that, the Ginsburg brief offered this tart riposte: "The case at bar presents a classic example of the double-edged discrimination characteristic of laws that chivalrous gentlemen, sitting in all male chambers, misconceive as a favor to the ladies."

Ginsburg cited recent legal victories (some of which she had helped to bring about) that provided legal precedents for gender equality. One of these, *Reed v. Reed* (1971), involved an estranged married couple in Idaho, Sally Reed and Cecil Reed, both of whom applied to serve as administrators of the estate of their son, Richard, who had died as a teenager. The pathos of these facts—estranged parents confronting the premature death of their child—radiate distractingly through the legal language. Though Richard Reed's cause of death was not specified in the legal documents, it was suicide.

As Richard's parents, Cecil and Sally Reed were related to him equally. But a probate court ruled in favor of Cecil, following an Idaho statute that stipulated, "Of several persons claiming and equally entitled to administer, males must be preferred to females."

Sally Reed sued in district court, which overturned the probate court's decision as a violation of the equal protection clause of the Fourteenth Amendment to the Constitution. But the Idaho Supreme Court, to which Cecil Reed appealed, sided with the original probate court in granting him administration of his son's estate.

"Philosophically it can be argued with some degree of logic that the provisions of [the statute] do discriminate against women on the basis of sex," the decision conceded. "However nature itself has established the distinction and this statute . . . is only designed to alleviate the problem of holding hearings by the court to determine eligibility to administer." In other words, discriminating on the basis of gender (given that "nature itself" created two of them) is a lot easier than having to decide on an individual basis which party is more qualified.

And, the court went on, men generally are more qualified: "The legislature when it enacted this statute evidently concluded that in general men are better qualified to act as an administrator than are women."

According to a description of *Reed v. Reed* on the National Women's Law Center website, Sally Reed reported that her husband had been abusive to her and to their son, whom she'd raised alone until he was a teenager. At that point, Cecil Reed was awarded partial custody of the boy and took out an insurance policy on his life. Richard, known as "Skip," was found dead in his father's basement of a wound from his father's rifle. Hard to imagine a scenario whereby Cecil Reed would have been deemed more qualified than Sally Reed to administer their son's small estate.

The brief that Ginsburg submitted on behalf of the ACLU to the US Supreme Court, to which Sally Reed appealed, pillories the Idaho Supreme Court's decision as "one example of a wider pattern of discrimination against women which infects many areas of American society."

She argued that gender discrimination was not merely unjust but insidious: by assigning second-class status to women, the court was denying them a chance to prove they deserved better: "If a legislature can bar a woman from service as a fiduciary on the basis of once popular, but never proved, assumptions that women are less qualified than men are to perform such services, then the myth becomes insulated from attack, because the law deprives women of the opportunity to prove it false."

The US Supreme Court ruled unanimously in favor of Sally Reed, declaring that differential treatment based solely on gender was a violation of the Fourteenth Amendment's equal protection clause and declaring the Idaho statute arbitrary and unconstitutional. It was the Supreme Court's first ruling against gender-based discrimination under the Constitution. The decision required that hundreds of laws be rewritten and set a crucial precedent.

In her argument to the Supreme Court on behalf of Stephen Wiesenfeld, Ginsburg cited *Reed v. Reed* and a handful of other cases (including another landmark decision, *Frontiero v. Richardson*, which she had worked on in 1973) to claim that the government's move to deny Wiesenfeld Social Security benefits was arbitrary, unjust, and outmoded. "In providing a 'mother's benefit,' but no father's benefit, Congress assumed a division of parental responsibility along gender lines: breadwinner was synonymous with father, child tenderer with mother. Increasing female participation in the paid labor force has placed in clear focus the invidious quality of this rigid sex-role delineation."

In 1975, the Supreme Court ruled unanimously in Stephen Wiesenfeld's favor.

Nearly twenty years later, in 1993, Wiesenfeld was the last witness to speak during four days of confirmation hearings for Ruth Bader Ginsburg's appointment to the Supreme Court. With a lush, graying beard and a congenial air verging on playful, Wiesenfeld, who had never remarried, recounted the facts of his case. "We were among the pioneers in alternate family lifestyles," he said of his wife, Paula, and himself. "It was our plan that I would take on the primary household chores, including those related to the raising of our son, Jason."

Joe Biden, then the chairman of the US Senate Committee on the Judiciary, thanked Wiesenfeld for his testimony and added, "I shared a similar fate that you did in 1972 and raised two children with a professional wife who had passed away, and it is amazing how much has changed."

Stephen Wiesenfeld returned to the Supreme Court in May 2014, nearly forty years after his landmark lawsuit. This time his purpose was to be remarried, at age seventy-one, by Justice Ruth Bader Ginsburg. His son, Jason (at whose Florida wedding Justice Ginsburg had officiated in 1998), and other family members, were also present.

BUCKLEY V. VALEO (1976)

In *Buckley v. Valeo*, the Supreme Court held that limiting expenditures on a political campaign is an unconstitutional violation of the First Amendment's protection of free speech. At issue were amendments to the Federal Election Campaign Finance Act, which sought to regulate spending and fundraising. Under this law, donors were limited to contributing up to $1,000 to a single candidate per each federal political race. The law also limited the amount a candidate could spend on her own campaign, requiring reporting on any contributions above this threshold.

In a per curiam decision, eight justices ruled that restrictions of independent expenditures are unconstitutional, as are limits on a candidate's spending. The Court reasoned that permitting such practices would not necessarily lead to corruption—what Congress intended to prevent in passing the Federal Election Campaign Finance Act—so the government interest was not strong enough to justify curbing free speech.

The Court upheld restrictions on individual contributions to candidates, however, ruling that they don't violate the First Amendment because they are designed to prevent the quid pro quo exchange of political campaign donations for favors, which would be anathema to the integrity of the democratic process.

Spending Money Isn't Speech

How the ACLU Ruined Campaign Finance Laws

SCOTT TUROW

I have been an ACLU supporter throughout my adult life, due in no small measure to my mother's influence. Her dedication to the organization was cemented in the McCarthy era, when the ACLU was an outspoken defender of Americans who were being punished as alleged communist sympathizers. For me, the moment of adherence came in 1977, while I was in law school, when the ACLU successfully represented neo-Nazis who wanted to march under swastika flags through the suburb of Skokie, Illinois, home to many Holocaust survivors. To me, the core promise of the First Amendment is to believe and say what you want about politics. Throughout the years, the ACLU has been perhaps the nation's most reliable defender of the right to express political beliefs of all kinds.

With that said, I am going to challenge the organization's commitment to free thinking and free speech by criticizing the ACLU position on an issue that leaders like Bernie Sanders have called—correctly in my view—the paramount political issue of our time in our country: campaign finance. The ACLU started out wrong on this question and has stayed wrong for thirty-five years, even as events have demonstrated the catastrophic consequence of its views, which are imperiling our democracy and grotesquely depreciating the commitment to equality that was declared unequivocally at the time of our nation's founding.

Although most Americans would find it hard to believe today, in 1974, in the wake of Watergate, the Congress passed, and President

Ford signed, wide-ranging restrictions on political contributions and campaign spending. Led by Senator James Buckley of New York, who had been elected as a member of the Conservative Party, an odd coalition of political bedfellows that included, quite prominently, the New York office of the ACLU challenged these restrictions in court. Buckley and the ACLU viewed spending money on politics as indistinguishable from political speech and thus entitled to the near-absolute protections of the First Amendment.

The case, *Buckley v. Valeo* (Valeo was the secretary of the US Senate and a party only for formal, legal purposes), reached the US Supreme Court in 1976. The resulting opinion is, by some counts, the longest ever handed down by the Court and can be summarized only with a sense of peril. Nonetheless, the key holdings, shorn of nuance, are relatively straightforward. Because of the appearance (or reality) of corruption when elected officials accept money from those who also seek to influence them, campaign contributions to candidates for public office are properly subject to governmental restriction. By contrast, a candidate or independent party's spending on politics is tantamount to speech and is strictly protected by the First Amendment. *Buckley*, in effect, set off the money wars in American elections, because it said that political spending can't be limited. Even worse, perhaps, it struck down any limits on spending by an individual, meaning that billionaires could run for office and self-finance. To quote Sarah Palin, albeit in a different context, "How's that workin' out for ya?"

There is so much wrong with *Buckley* and the ACLU's position that I have a hard time containing my rage, which starts from the fact that an organization that is supposed to be dedicated to free speech has taken a position that effectively limits the speech of others.

Writing in the *New York Times* about twenty years ago, I called *Buckley* "the *Dred Scott* decision of the twentieth century," referring to the nineteenth-century case that affirmed treating slaves as property that could be returned to their owners across state lines. I have had a blessed career as an author, but if I had to bet on any words I have written being quoted one hundred years from now, it would be those.

Buckley's distinctions were largely unworkable. A contribution, after all, is spending by an individual. As the years have worn on, the

ACLU has supported decisions eroding most limitations, including the duly reviled *Citizens United* decision, which granted even fictional entities like corporations the right to spend without limit on politics, as long as that money was "independent" of a particular candidate's campaign.

No notion is more central to the American political vision than the one expressed in the opening lines of the Declaration of Independence, paraphrased from the seventeenth-century British political philosopher John Locke, that "all [persons] are created equal, and are endowed by their Creator with certain unalienable rights." That vision, by its nature, gives every American citizen equal influence over our political process. That fundamental political equality is enshrined in the constitutional principle of one person, one vote.

Strikingly, that idea of political equality among all citizens was supported not just by the natural law philosophy that prevailed centuries ago, but also by contemporary political theory. John Rawls's *A Theory of Justice* (1971) has been without question the most widely respected work of political philosophy written in my lifetime. In his book, Rawls proposes that a just society would be constructed behind a veil of ignorance in which the governing principles would be composed by their authors with no idea of where we stood in the social hierarchy, no notion of our wealth, our gender, our race, our intelligence, our geographical location. Not knowing how any of us would come out in the pecking order, we would all quickly agree from the start that the only arrangement that is just and fair is to give each citizen an equal voice in governance.

Thus, a system that gives a greater political voice to the rich, because they are able to "say" more is, quite literally, un-American. The greatest analytical flaw of the ACLU position is its refusal to consider that point and what flows from it: the capacity of the rich to drown out the voices of those who are less affluent due to the ability of the rich to say so much more. If I held a political meeting and the speakers there were inaudible because one person had shown up with an electric megaphone through which he or she was relentlessly shouting, there is no doubt Megaphone Person could be shut down by the police for disturbing the peace. *Buckley* and the cases that follow it give Megaphone Person an absolute right to shout over the other speakers.

By contrast, *Buckley* said, "The concept that government may restrict the speech of some elements of our society in order to enhance the relative voice of others is wholly foreign to the First Amendment." Justice Brett Kavanaugh, for example, has hailed that declaration as "one of the most important sentences in First Amendment history."

But permitting the exercise of any right without regard to its impact on other citizens is fundamentally out of keeping with the political understanding of the Constitution's framers. In his *Second Treatise on Government*, John Locke, the guiding philosophical spirit of our nation's founding, wrote, "Men being . . . all free, equal and independent, no one can be . . . subjected to the political power of another, without his own consent." Creating a system, in the guise of the First Amendment, that elevates the political power of one group over that of other citizens violates our nation's first principles.

This "natural law" understanding is pivotal to our democracy. All persons are born with an equal right to hold and express political opinions. "Free speech" in this light is inherently equal and unlimited. Those who want to talk politics sixteen hours a day can do so. But money, as we all know, is distributed unequally in our society. And tying political rights to wealth is so wrong-headed, so deeply unfair and unjust, that it is hard to believe that an organization dedicated to "civil liberties" could ever have adhered to those views.

Constitutionalizing unlimited political spending was a disaster in principle and has been almost apocalyptic in its effect. Special interest groups, because of their ability to coordinate contributions and spend without limit on behalf of the politicians who do their bidding, wield immense influence over our body politic. Worthy candidates without independent means decline to run for political office because they must spend at least half their time chained to their phones and rattling a tin cup while they beg for money. Billionaires, by contrast, whether Ross Perot or Michael Bloomberg or Howard Schultz or Donald Trump, can run for the highest office in the country without any base of support to start except their own open checkbook. The resulting system always carried the risk that some unlettered billionaire idiot could use his resources to overwhelm his primary opponents and end up in the White House.

What exacerbates my criticism of the ACLU is its stubborn unwillingness to survey the smoking political wreckage and acknowledge its mistake. Instead, the organization has lifted its banner and proudly led us all over the cliff. The ACLU has slavishly followed the logic of *Buckley* and even submitted a brief in support of *Citizens United.* That's right, the ACLU, our ACLU, advocated for one of the most wrong-headed and widely reviled decisions of the US Supreme Court in recent times, even though if you go to the ACLU website you find no forthright admission of that fact. (As someone who likes the ACLU, I still find it deeply offensive that an organization dedicated to freedom of belief and expression hides from its own actions out of apparent fear of diminishing its contributor base.) The idea that corporations (or unions or other associations) ought to be able to spend freely on political expression is preposterous. It has nothing to do with the reasons corporations exist, and the idea of granting political rights to fictional persons, who do not hold the right to vote, makes no more sense than creating free speech rights for dogs. The shareholders of corporations, the members of unions, and the supporters of associations like the National Rifle Association or Planned Parenthood all have every right to their beliefs and to speak and advocate for them. But recent events have demonstrated dramatically what the problem is in endorsing unlimited corporate political spending. Foreign citizens can own and control American corporations. How then can we prevent foreign governments from spending wildly on our elections through the guise of the corporations they control?

The closest the ACLU has come to acknowledging the mistake they made in *Buckley* is to say, "The ACLU believes that the system of electing candidates to federal office is badly in need of repair. We will continue to advocate for reform of the current system, including in support of our longstanding commitment to public financing of campaigns."

This is little more than a fig leaf, a makeweight that frankly appears to be aimed at appeasing angry contributors like me. First, unlimited spending has already led to the collapse of public financing systems.

Public financing of presidential campaigns was part of the 1974 legislation that the Supreme Court approved in *Buckley*, but because candidates could raise far more privately than the Congress—subject to special interest influence—was willing to appropriate, they eventually walked away from the public financing system for presidential races. Even supposed reformers like Barack Obama did that.

Second, the *Buckley* approach to the First Amendment inevitably becomes the hatchet used to bust up any rational public financing scheme. In order to make sense, a public financing system must either require candidates to take part, with no right to spend on their own—that's a violation of the First Amendment under *Buckley*—or must give the candidates who participate in the public system resources equal to those of their privately financed opponents. But the US Supreme Court, following the *Buckley* principles, has decided that giving publicly financed candidates funds to match the expenditures of the privately financed punished the constitutionally protected expression of the privately supported.

I know that people on the ACLU board and many constitutional scholars will read my remarks and say that I am making this sound easier than it is. The law is at its most artificial in drawing distinctions. Words and ideas are not little boxes with sharp edges. But as decisions pyramid on top of each other, legal concepts end up unmoored from common sense. The *Buckley* court wrestled with issues that have been lost in the years since. The Constitution guarantees "freedom of speech," and "speech" in common understanding in 1789 and today is the verbal utterance of an individual. The more we expand the absolute protections of the First Amendment beyond the right of an individual to say, write, and think as she or he chooses, the more vexing distinctions become.

Spending money is conduct, just like shooting skeet or playing music. And so is spending money on politics. Political spending clearly has expressive elements, but the government has always had the right to regulate outward behavior because of its potential impact on the rights of others. The American courts accept the right of the government to enact narrowly tailored, content-neutral regulation of expressive conduct in other contexts. I have followed with considerable amusement the long-running battle in the US Court of Appeals for the Seventh Circuit over Scabby the Rat, a twelve-foot balloon union protesters have erected at a construction site where they are striking, who has been consistently deemed to violate the local sign ordinance in Grand Chute, Wisconsin. No one can explain to me why the right of union members to send a message vital to their livelihoods, which also expresses political beliefs in a community not deep in pro-Union sentiments, is due less constitutional protection than *Citizen United*'s right to blast Hillary Clinton. There is nothing about campaign finance regulation, both contribution and expenditure limits, that is incompatible with our core understanding of the First Amendment.

Reversing *Buckley* and *Citizens United* is going to take time. But the intellectual underpinnings are there. In fact, *Citizens United* overruled prior precedents that supported campaign spending limitations and that by itself gives a subsequent Court ample ground to reject *Citizens United* as an abandonment of the principle of stare decisis. But no organization can play a more critical role in leading us back toward reason than the ACLU, because its support for these decisions is so often cited by the kinds of conservatives who love *Buckley* because they don't believe the government should hinder property owners' rights to do whatever they like with what they have. It should be evident by now that if the ACLU really believes that public financing of campaigns is the best answer to the current stinking mess, repudiation of *Buckley* is the first step.

It is high time for the ACLU to make the declaration that comes hardest to human beings: "We were wrong. We apologize to all Americans for a bad decision made with good intentions. We will work tirelessly to correct our mistake."

BOB JONES UNIVERSITY V. UNITED STATES (1983)

Prior to 1970, the Internal Revenue Service (IRS) granted tax-exempt status to private schools, colleges, and universities without consideration of the discriminatory nature of their admissions policies. Following an injunction from the District Court for the District of Columbia in *Green v. Kennedy* (1970), the IRS no longer provided this exemption to schools that had racially discriminatory policies in place. One of the schools affected by this new change was Bob Jones University, a religiously affiliated nonprofit that interpreted the Bible as prohibiting miscegenation. The university banned interracial relationships on campus and refused to admit students in interracial relationships. In the mid-1970s, Bob Jones and Goldsboro Christian Schools sued the IRS, seeking restitution of their tax-exempt status. The Fourth Circuit Court of Appeals ruled that racially discriminatory policies, even those stemming from religious beliefs, violated clear federal policy against discrimination in education and thus could not be considered for tax exemption. The plaintiffs appealed to the Supreme Court. The ACLU joined with other civil and human rights groups to provide amici curiae briefs urging that the appellate decision be affirmed. The Supreme Court held that the government has a fundamental and overriding interest in eradicating racial discrimination in education, which "prevailed, with official approval, for the first 165 years of this Nation's constitutional history." Since 1983, *Bob Jones University v. United States* has served as a reminder that the religion clauses of the First Amendment do not trump compelling government policies against discrimination.

Bob Jones Builds a Wall

MORGAN PARKER

When I first learned about myself, the African American, I was made to believe that the origin of my species began here on American soil, tilled by my enslaved ancestors, blah blah blah. I was invented here on this land, already owned, already assigned a specific function; a contained and delineated place. I was a fairly recent phenomenon, an advancement of science and global commerce. There were Africans, there were Americans (Caucasians?), and there was me. Hanging on the arm of a mystifying subgroup, unwelcome and unchosen.

White people taught me all this stuff, by the way, at my white Christian school, where everyone had so much respect for African Americans and everything we've been through as a people. Delivered to these great United States from the darkness of Africa, where we lived in huts and bathed in buckets of river water and did not know about the Gospel. We are the story of a very brave people, just like people in the Bible. I'm not "really" like people in the Bible, this is very clear, because the people in the Bible are white, and my illustrated Bibles and textbooks are filled with pictures to prove this. But these long-suffering people—slaves—that's where it all started for me. I'm not African; that's a whole different people we don't know about. I am an American—but not exactly. African American. I hate the way they say it. I hate the way I come with an asterisk.

Decades later, I am still trying to unlearn and reeducate myself. I am still trying to untangle a heavy and long-held belief that I do not deserve love. That I do not belong anywhere; that my presence is always an interruption; that I am a stain, an unwelcome splotch of ink or blood on crisp white bedsheets.

Until 1971, Bob Jones University, a private Christian school in Greenville, South Carolina, refused to admit African American students. The university's God-fearing leader, Bob Jones Jr., zealously honored his father's vision for a campus free of any secular, atheist, earthly, or liberal influence—from the New International Bible, to the teaching of evolution, to racial integration.

There is so much for me to say about how the prevalence of religious beliefs supporting institutional practices like these have wriggled their way into my consciousness; how over the years, my interactions with white Christians have twisted and injured the way I see myself and my place in this country. There is even more to say about how people like Bob Jones Jr. think, and how institutions like his operate so resolutely; how devout religious leaders derive from the teachings of the Bible such ugly and cruel conclusions. They all have so much to say—to preach—about me and my place in this country. On Easter Sunday 1960, Bob Jones Jr. delivered a very-special-episode sermon over the Bob Jones University radio airwaves, and subsequently published it for sale at the Bob Jones University bookstore under the title *Is Segregation Scriptural?*

The title of the sermon is not really a question, yet a question mark dangles, taking the joke too far. At a bar in Washington, DC, a white couple next to me touches each other's thighs, gregariously filling space with their conversation and echoing laughter. I tell myself that their display, like a stock photo in a picture frame, is not meant to taunt me or remind me of my otherness. My otherness is of course in the joke of my aloneness. (Why can't I get that hymn out of my head, out of my body?) I hear the man remark to his companion, "It all makes sense now."

That's how I feel reading *Is Segregation Scriptural?* That's how I feel sitting alone, hunched over several plates of appetizers, flirtatious couples orbiting my lonely dark planet. It is very clear to me what I am allowed to expect and want from my American life, and too easily, I follow the rules. I do not trespass. Maybe because I hate myself, but maybe because I know I am hated. In Washington, DC, right now, in February 2019, a national emergency has been declared, and the emergency concerns borders. It all makes sense now.

As a product of white evangelical education—albeit among the so-called progressiveness of Southern California, as opposed to the deeply embedded racism of South Carolina, and a solid thirty years after Bob Jones's Easter sermon—I know what is and isn't scriptural, and I know how to argue in Bob Jones's dialect. It's the same rhetoric I encountered in chapels and classrooms where I sat, befuddled, terrified, and ashamed, as youth group leaders or pale Bible teachers presented rigorously fabricated interpretations of scripture. There are some slick acrobatics involved in using biblical text to prove your doctrine, bending the world to your vision of it until other points of view vanish. A kind of speaking that creates truth from scratch, without question. This is what it says, and who can argue with God's words? This impassioned genre of speech, this art of war, is well suited for fundamentalist evangelical white Christians and people like me, who are bullheaded. Therefore, I'm calling bullshit on Bob Jones's whole platform.

Anyone can use the Bible to prove anything. Much like a poem, its interpretation may be subjective. Its authors are consistently debated, and either way, long gone, so the text is fair game. Words don't mean the same thing for one person as they do another. Rather than seeking the text's intention, analyzing it in its historical context, as one would a poem, many preachers—whom, it should be noted, are not always theological scholars but self-appointed messengers—approach the text with their personal convictions, politics, and feelings about what constitutes faithfulness, what constitutes right. Words do not always awaken the same fears or the same people.

In the introduction to his book *God's Trombones: Seven Negro Sermons in Verse*, James Weldon Johnson writes of the great impact of "old-time preachers" on the "sense of unity and solidarity" among slaves and their descendants. "It was the old-time preacher who for generations was the mainspring of hope and inspiration for the Negro in America," he says, noting that their "power for good or ill was very great." Because "they were the first of the slaves to learn to read, and their reading was confined to the Bible," the Negro preacher's brilliance was in the ability to translate and freestyle, such that "a text served mainly as a starting point and often had no relation to the development of the sermon."

Words are always blooming with possibility. The languages of words and bodies and actions and looking can be the dearest gift—a pathway to empathy and love. At its most beautiful, language is the secret weapon for understanding how we relate, how we make sense of the terms of our weird world. Or it can be another kind of weapon, sharpened in the hands of the stubborn or the extremist or the fear mongering. Words are ductile, delicate, and loaded like that.

We entrust our spiritual leaders as interpreters of a higher and more enlightened power—we are swayed by their reasonings, like a poet's or a president's. It is dangerous to insist that the Bible's words are absolute, literal, unflinching, and to manipulate the Bible as a secondary source to back up the claims of the primary source, which, really, can be whatever. What can we learn from the text? is a markedly different question from, Where in the text is my point proven? How might this text transform my understanding of the world? It's a departure from, Where does the text align with what I personally believe about the world?

The standpoint of Bob Jones's Easter message is particularly American, rooted in his perspective of American life in 1960 South Carolina—and his alone. His mission isn't to interpret God's Word but to convince his constituents, neighbors, and anyone else listening to the radio, that his way of seeing is the right way of seeing. How Jesus might have seen American life in 1960 South Carolina. (Because Bob Jones and God, it seems, share the same mind? I wonder what it feels like to think this about yourself.)

First, Bob is mad. Anger is no vibe to bring to an argument, and certainly not, as he puts it, "one of the most important and timely messages I have ever brought." I am a woman, so people are always reminding me to leave my emotions out of it, but no one has reminded Bob that emotions compromise your chances of ever being taken seriously; therefore my opponent has entrapped himself in this vulnerable position. Still, before he even begins, he's already patronizing his listeners and already: "Do not let anything disturb you. I want you to hear this message through."

Do not let anything disturb you. A theme is established. It hangs in the air throughout the sermon, in the bedrooms of each supposition. It always comes back to this language. Disturbance, protection. Vigilance. Unrest, peace, purity.

Second, Bob is fucking terrified. He knows something terrible looms and threatens—something satanic, a word he capitalizes. This has gone too far, Bob thinks. This is an emergency. He hones in on a single word in a single verse in a single chapter in the Book of Acts, Acts 17:26: "And [God] hath made of one blood all nations of men for to dwell on all faces of the earth, and hath determined the times before appointed, and the bounds of their habitation." "That says that God Almighty fixed the bounds of their habitation," Bob Jones reiterates, blasphemously disregarding the rest of the verse and neglecting to analyze the passages surrounding it. "That is as clear as anything that was ever said."

Citing anything out of context is completely irresponsible debate etiquette, but Bob Jones introduces the verse apropos of pretty much nothing, only attributing the passage to Paul, whom he considers to be "the greatest man who ever lived . . . greater than Moses." I buy this, because in the white evangelical interpretation, Moses is hailed as a sort of Abraham Lincoln, nobly leading slaves to freedom. I don't really understand the Paul thing, though, because what I remember about Paul is that he was once named Saul. In my interpretation, Paul is arguably the Bible's greatest example of transformation and progressiveness. Paul signifies and sanctions the godliness of reinvention—his greatness is in his growth. I would say that Paul is a symbol of the righteousness gained from expansion, from change and course correction. I would say that self-improvement, and a spirited drive to better one's community, is one of the most exemplary acts of faith, a heartening display of service. Bob Jones fearfully condemns progression and adaptation as against God's intention. Unless it concerns the rehabilitation of the formerly African.

* * *

One of the first doctrines I learned from my zealous teachers-slash-missionaries was that the world split between those inside and those on the outside—a truth made unwaveringly clear as landscapes and demographics transformed on the drive from school to our house. My side of town felt darker, less pure; my family's values not stringent or steadfast enough. I feared for us and pitied us. Was it even possible for us to see the world washed in so much warm light? Why couldn't joy and devoutness come more naturally? Was it because we were African American?

What I learned was fear. Every interpretation of scripture was a warning. In every Bible class lesson, every youth pastor's message, and every memorized Bible verse, I heard or else. The line between good and bad, clear as anything. You are in, or you are out. There was Christian and there was secular—no murky waters, no room for uncertainty, no excuses.

That word: *secular*. The way my elementary school teachers' faces contorted angrily as they spat it—railing against Harry Potter, or skirts above the calf, or *South Park*, or *NSync. The way my friends offered to pray for me and my ongoing struggle to resist temptation, to resist the dangerous allure of the secular world. Do not go outside the lines. That villainized outside world. Everything of it will only doom you to hell.

African American culture, of course, is itself inherently secular. Probably because of the rap music. Probably because of residual influence of our godless African ancestors. If I was going to wrangle myself a spot in heaven—the black part of town in heaven—I would have to become an entirely different person. I would have to clamp down my impulses to argue and shout and be unique. I would need to stay still, remain quiet and earnest—I would need to prove myself to earn an asterisk on my African American status. This is how I became "not really black, though." How could I be, if I was among them?

Much of the groundwork on which Bob Jones builds his message is a bizarre variation on the classic "I have black friends" defense, which, it should be noted, is never convincing, and definitely never asked for. He talks at length about a Chinese couple he once met, concluding, "All right, he is a Chinese. He married a Chinese woman. That is the way God meant it to be." He says, "Chinese people are wonderful people. The Japanese people are ingenious—they are wonderful people. The Koreans are wonderful people. The Africans are wonderful people. In many ways, there are no people in the world finer than the colored people who were brought over here in slavery in days gone by." Of course, Bob preaches again and again, the Bible makes crystal clear the importance of lines between peoples. It's what pretty much the whole book is about if you're looking at it that way. Being led astray. Purity. Disgracing your line. That's what feels as violent to me as a deep slash across my back—the straight and solid line.

"When nations break out of their boundaries, and begin to do things contrary to the purpose of God and the directive will of God," the preacher gravely reminds, "they have trouble." Boundaries and borders and walls and limitations are essential to godliness—any other ideology is of the secular world.

The boundaries of our habitation include countries of origin (which Bob Jones liberally conflates with race), restaurants, public pools, train cars and buses, and of course, wedding chapels and sexual relations. Build a wall around all these things, all these different kinds of bodies, and "we will have no trouble." No threats to God's plan. No national or spiritual emergencies.

There is another way to read the Bible, to interpret God's will: that what God demands of us is not borders or walls or separatism, but love.

Caught up in the fervor of his South Carolinian perspective, Bob Jones seems to have forgotten that these United States were founded by rebels who broke out of the bounds of their habitation and created a new established order. Borders and oceans were crossed. America, the land of imported races, and still yet one nation under God. Freedom is a dangerously ambitious slogan to apply to a nation, and a hypocritical ideal to apply to a religion.

Which brings us to another horrifying and reckless assertion Bob Jones makes, which I can only interpret as a justification of slavery. This claim happens subtly but confidently. He first pronounces, of course, that slavery was wrong. "But God overruled," he reasons. "When they came over here"—and I could spend paragraphs on the use of this word *came*, not to mention the fixation on victims, *they*, rather than *perpetrators*—"many of them did not know about the Bible and did not know about Jesus Christ; but they got converted. Some of the greatest preachers the world has ever known were colored preachers who were converted in slavery days. . . . God Almighty allowed these colored people to be turned here into the South and overruled what happened and then he turned the colored people into wonderful Christian people."

There you have it: a neat little scriptural justification of American slavery; lemonade out of the single most disgraceful human rights violation America has ever committed, a legacy that will continue to plague our country until its end. That little slip-up.

"Did you colored people ever stop to think where you might have been if that had not happened?" The smugness. The moral superiority. "Now, you colored people listen to me. . . . You might be over there in jungles of Africa today, unsaved." The motherfucking nerve. That goddamned question mark.

Bob has worked himself into incoherent fury and fight. In all the backflips to loosely connect Jim Crow segregation to one little Bible verse, his sermon has completely lost its way. He darts from warped discussions of war with Japan; to rambling about how the good white people of the South have helped build churches for the good colored people in the South; to a claim that the places in America with the most trouble are the most integrated (New York, California . . .); to shouting out his favorite Chinese people; to, yes—the reminder that we colored people should be altogether grateful we were brought here, that God allowed us to be. When he's gotten too far off message, he returns to the word *boundaries*, to the necessity of restriction and purity and how things were "meant" to be. We are allowed to be here—with an asterisk.

As do most self-righteous white men who have only ever been granted authority, Bob Jones has absolutely no handle on the concept of subjectivity.

According to Bob, after God adjusted his unflinching and crystal-clear will and "permitted the slaves to come over to America," it was us African Americans who didn't follow God's will—a baseless accusation that our purpose in being (no, coming) here was "so that the colored people could be the great missionaries to the Africans." Instead, we settled in. We crossed the borders of our assigned plantations and started having sex with the good white people, trampling the divine order. "The white people in America would have helped pay their way over there. By the hundreds and hundreds they could have gone back to Africa and got the Africans converted after the slavery days were over." This is news to me! In all my years of hearing, "Go back to Africa," I never knew there were checks being waved around.

Could and would are theoretical assumptions, reserved clearly for white slave owners whose sins were forgiven, for whom God graciously amended his will. "We are having turmoil all over America"—and you might think Bob Jones refers to the racist crimes of the Jim Crow era, generally considered to be disturbing and satanic—among them, lynchings, church bombings, and constant violence against wonderful Christian people—but instead, he damns "propagandists" who "slander God Almighty" by "preaching pious sermons . . . about rubbing out the line between races—it makes me sick." It's obvious he refers not only to the aspirations of the entire civil rights movement, all those who "put their own opinion above the word of God," but specifically Martin Luther King Jr., whose peaceful, gentle, and obedient style evangelicals across the board love—like are obsessed with. I remember asking about Malcolm X in an elementary school classroom and quickly being met with horror stories about dangerous, gun-wielding thugs who served only to distract from the Christian—American—progress achieved by Dr. King. I mean, come on. I have never met a white Christian who didn't like that guy.

In 1960, six-year-old Ruby Bridges needed to be escorted to her integrated public school by US marshals after receiving death threats. In 1960, months before Bob Jones insisted on the radio that "no two races ever lived as close together as the white people and colored people in the South and got along so well," four negro college students refused to leave the counter of a Woolworths and were met by spit in their faces, cigarettes burned into their skin. This was in Greensboro, North Carolina, 189 miles from Bob Jones's Greenville, South Carolina.

Six years earlier, *Brown v. Board of Education* had ruled the segregation of public schools unconstitutional. This was a decision of the secular world, upholding their own political agendas above God's will, straying from his indisputable Word as did Eve in the garden, damning our nation to oppressive, satanic influences. In 1967, *Loving v. Virginia* legalized interracial marriage in the United States. Bob Jones University began to admit negro students only four years later, in 1971—provided they were married, and to another negro.

Meanwhile, in 1970, the Internal Revenue Service had amended previous regulations to specify that only private schools without discriminatory admissions policies be allowed to claim a tax exemption status. Bob Jones, steadfast in his commitment to keep black pussies like mine from curdling the purity of the white race, the crucial bounds of our habitation, ignored this, opting instead to file suit petitioning the school's revoked exemption status on the basis of the First Amendment. In 1975, still involved in a drawn-out legal battle with the courts and determined to make the case for their entitlement to tax cuts, the university conceded to allow admission to single negroes—provided they were not engaged in, or known to advocate for, interracial unions. The university was still illegally receiving tax cuts, filing suit to petition their revoked exemption status on the basis of the First Amendment. And anyway, interracial marriages, dating, and intimate relationships were prohibited under the school code of conduct, and continued to be until 2000.

No wonder that in 1990, my place in my white evangelical school felt like a favor. Why I didn't bother thinking of myself as ever getting the guy, modeling the Christian values of white families contentedly smiling at the grace they feel from the inside out. Why I felt that because of my color, I could never be fully saved, always given a pass for my blackness, which, in scriptural language, carried with it corruption, imperfection. On chapel days, we gathered for prayer and worship before a sermon from our school pastor. In one song, we begged, "Wash me white as snow." Those were literally the lyrics. I know because they were taught to me by good white Christians. No wonder. It all makes sense.

Obviously Bob Jones Jr. has taken a few detours in his sermon to explain that God may selectively allow the egregious sins of a purportedly Christian nation; that slavery wasn't that bad; that Negro life in the South is actually great; that Martin Luther King Jr. is a propagandist with satanic motives; that he knows some lovely Chinese people; and that travel funding reparations have been readily available to former slaves all along. Still, the agenda behind this particular segregationist sermon is to defend his university's racist admission practices. The title of the sermon is not really a question. The message—buried as it is in absurd flights of revisionist accounts of past and present race relations in the South—is specific and pointed. It is the mixing. Ever the thoughtful ally, the pastor makes sure to explain his intention to build a coloreds-only Bob Jones University. Separate, but, you know—separate.

"God never meant to have one race," he proclaims assuredly. Interracial mixing must be prohibited at all costs, even the cost of equal education. Don't even think about going to bed with a black woman, not on Bob Jones's watch. "God never meant for America to be a melting pot to rub out the line between the nations. That was not God's purpose." (Bob Jones is permitted to say this, as it has been established that he and God are of one mind.) "I say it makes me sick!" he bellows, as if our very presence, our sheer proximity, scourges him with the physical force of a tumor or contagion. How dramatic—as if getting too close to us is a hazard to a white Christian body.

I have loved white men or boys in my life, and some may have loved me back, but to my core, I cannot and never did believe they could, fully. They wouldn't end up with me, certainly. Neither of us could imagine me in the frames on the walls of their WASPy, or suburban, or midwestern homes. My high school boyfriend, who lasted such a short time and ended with such disdain that I do not even count him in my list of boyfriends (thereby clearing the list), was sat down by his father quickly after I entered the picture and warned about the troubling challenges we might face as an interracial couple—especially, he stressed, if we had children. Were we really prepared for this burden and difficulty? Was he sure this was worth it? It was 2004, and I was sixteen.

I always felt insufficient. I still do. I wasn't aware of the psychological damage brought on by these early beliefs about my unlovability and inherent shortcomings until I realized how it haunted me with black men too. And women, and success, every glimpse of satisfaction and hope for desirability. Any relationship prospect, the prayer to be welcomed inside—I am not right, I will never be enough, I will never be the one. How could I not believe it, the hymn buzzing in my head? This shit adds up.

Another word for insufficiency is *niggardly*. Words are ductile and illuminating like that. It does not matter whether Bob Jones was aware of the damage he was doing as he railed against integration—and specifically, interracial dating and marriage, the evil blurring of racial boundaries. It doesn't matter if he knew viewpoints like his would run me off, distrusting even God's sense of benevolence. What is said is the message, and what is done is the message.

Employing another classic defense beloved by white people whom no one has asked to prove they aren't racist, Bob Jones makes sure to underline the fact that "only a small percentage of southern people held slaves," that "a great many people in the South in the old days did not believe in slavery." I am always being reminded of good white people, being asked to state for the record that I don't hate all white people. Here, I find the schism of thought between us and them. They are personalized where we are theoretical. They, as individuals, can be singled out as exceptions; they can be one of the good ones. They can be excused from any guilt or responsibility for African American plight if they themselves did not own slaves—and we are haunted by the facts, by the deeply fucked-up reality that our American consciousness stems from inequality, insufficiency. There are those who have—who have always been able to have—and those who barely have identities.

Bob Jones believes in justification over philosophy. I believe in questions—and, like Paul, growth. The possibility of restructuring one's frame of mind, a sunny sliver of hope in a misguided world. Imagine being a spiritual leader who instructs only defense, and never creation. Who piously insists that our foremost responsibility to the world is not to flood it with more goodness, but resist and prohibit everything of it. Imagine being the sort of person who believes, unwaveringly, that the only good and pure world is an unchanged one.

It is somehow always about money, of course. It always comes back to this language. "The commercial aspect was dominant," Bob Jones admits of the good Southern whites who did not believe (conceptually?) in slavery yet still participated. "People bought slaves and sold them." There is no way to justify slavery, insists the preacher who has endeavored, sneakily, to do just that. It was wrong, but it happened; it was a slip-up, for which God found a way to "overrule" and make right. It wasn't really their faults. "Some good people fell for it and went ahead with it," he says, while calling proponents of integration satanic. Is not integration—including cohabitation, interracial sex, equal voting rights and blended education—a consequence, a natural and inevitable outcome of the finances of slavery? In every account I've heard, it was the slave owner who got in bed with the slave.

If we separate ourselves, draw up borders and differentiations, we can more easily profit off one another without guilt. If we never budge, if budging is an affront to our God, it's easy to condemn immigration and integration; the disappearing lines of habitation; the sense of being invaded—interrupted. Do not let anything disturb you. In theory, it's easy to fear the infiltrating swarms of people demanding to be counted as such. In practice, do we not rely on the unwelcome, the Other, for their crucial role in our comfortable, money-thirsty lifestyles?

Ever since my transformation on the slave ship—my unbecoming, my skin made retail—my worth has been measured in my contribution to the bottom line. My penance for invading the bounds of habitation is unending. In all mixed communities, I am asked to explain myself, to come to my defense. I am worth the trouble, I plead with every word, I make up for myself in value. It is always about spinning peoples into monies. Now, folded in to American society, technically free and reluctantly allowed a place, I am an unrented apartment, sitting there with no return. Bleeding money.

In Bob Jones's America, I keep myself in check. I do not ask for more, I do not push my luck, I do not tempt men into corruption, I do not try to be someone I never can be. I never, ever, touch your sons—my acceptance depends on my aloneness, at the very least my innocuousness. Maybe in Bob Jones's America, the only Africans left are only the model Christians, the preachers and missionaries and select service workers. Maybe in Bob Jones's America, walls are everywhere—around the South, around California, around every city's Chinatown, around every oversexualized African (American). In Bob Jones's America, we know our place. We stay there.

In 2019, in every heart and every state, we are still trying to figure it out, or trying not to. Debating for years and centuries whether a kind of life even matters; if someone named alien or illegal can also be named a person; if there was justification; if there are enough borders; if God meant for any of this, these folks, to befall our nation of good people. I know there is no use in refuting—even with their own language and reasoning—what people like Bob Jones are committed to regarding as gospel, just as I know it is no use to ignore them. But I know this is what made me, and what haunts me, a black woman who cannot allow herself to be loved or wholly welcome. I want to dismiss this absurd, blasphemous sermon and everything it stands for, everything it defends. But now that I've read it, it all makes sense. I will always hear it and know that it is somewhere inside America, and that as an American, its words are inside me too, convincing my perspective to run, hide, or bow invisibly. Holiness means I need to disappear. This is what hums like an itch as I eat alone, in a sea of color-matched pairs swimming around me. There is no place for me here, on the other side of a border I never knew was there.

Damn you, preacher. The only way to know and honor any kind of God is to see and praise every universe, to understand how they give each other breath. We, the immigrants and African Americans, we hybrids and interlopers, who have crossed the borders of habitation into the unknown, and willingly taken up the dark, brutal story of these United States: we have done nothing but love this nation, nothing but try desperately to make this nation love us. We have forgiven your trespasses, offered you grace and unconditional mercy. We have taken up your crosses. We have died for your sins.

CHURCH OF THE LUKUMI BABALU AYE V. CITY OF HIALEAH (1993)

In an era where Supreme Court decisions are highly polarized, in both 5–4 votes cast and in the eyes of the American electorate writ large, one may forget that the members of our nation's highest court do at times find unanimous consensus. One such decision was *Church of the Lukumi Babalu Aye v. City of Hialeah*. The Supreme Court, led, ironically, by the Court's perennial swing vote, Justice Anthony Kennedy, held that a law targeting a particular religion must satisfy "strict scrutiny" to pass constitutional muster. In other words, any law of this nature must be narrowly tailored and serve a compelling government interest to be constitutionally valid. The Court found that an ordinance by the city of Hialeah banning religious animal sacrifice did not meet those requirements, violating the First Amendment's free exercise clause.

The juxtaposition of the Court's holdings in *Church of the Lukumi Babalu Aye* and the recent *Masterpiece Cakeshop, Ltd. v. Colorado Civil Rights Commission* (2018) highlights the complexity of the ACLU's fight for civil rights and religious freedom. In *Masterpiece Cakeshop*, the Supreme Court cited *Church of the Lukumi Babalu Aye* in its decision, holding that the Colorado Civil Rights Commission, like the City of Hialeah, was unconstitutionally hostile toward a baker who refused to furnish a same-sex couple with a wedding cake based on his religious beliefs. Nevertheless, the Court implied that the decision was narrow, focusing on what they deemed to be the antireligious bias of some of the commissioners. The Court affirmed the "dignity" of gay people and couples and acknowledged their entitlement to protection against discrimination.

Some Gods Are Better Than Others

VICTOR LAVALLE

By now it's a cliché to hear about the conversation between a black parent and child where the parent tells the child she'll have to be ten times better—or a hundred times better—than her white peers if she wants to succeed in the United States. This has become a commonplace, damn near boilerplate, which is actually heartbreaking if you slow down and think about it. So let's do that, shall we?

The underlying point of this parental wisdom, of course, is that the cards are stacked against the black or brown person in the workplace, in school, even in line at the supermarket. Your standard is different from someone else's and, to make it worse, those other people won't even acknowledge it. My wife and I see this in school interactions where our son and the other brown-skinned boys are singled out as problem kids. Meanwhile, their white male friends are described as "energetic" or "enthusiastic." To use a sports analogy (please forgive me if you hate sports), the goalposts aren't set at the same distance.

Again, this sounds like a cliché, a point so obvious that one risks making other people's eyes roll. But something magical happens when you don't simply take such a thing for granted, when you hammer home the thuddingly clear truth every time: people can't ignore it if you keep reminding them. I suspect that's what clichés are actually meant to do: to hide something in plain sight. It's the kind of clever plan that would make a James Bond villain gasp with envy. This country doesn't treat everyone equally? That's, like, so obvious. Why do we even have to talk about it?

The *Church of the Lukumi Babalu Aye* and *Ernesto Pichardo v. the City of Hialeah* came before the Supreme Court on November 4, 1992, and was decided on June 11, 1993. The facts of the case go like this: In

April 1987, the Church of the Lukumi Babalu Aye leased a plot of land in Hialeah, Florida. There they planned to build a church. In theory this shouldn't be a problem—America, land of religious liberty and all that—but the Church of the Lukumi Babalu Aye is part of the Santeria religion. You may begin to see the problem now.

Or maybe you don't. I shouldn't presume. To this day, many people's idea of the Santeria faith comes from some throwback horror movie like *The Believers* or the 1988 horror movie *The Serpent and the Rainbow* or the 1987 horror movie *Angel Heart*. Sensing a pattern? (Not to mention that the last two are actually about Voodoo, or Hollywood voodoo, but people tend to mix up both Santeria and Voodoo into a general "bad" religion category.)

The point of most of those movies seems to be that the practitioners make soul-selling deals with evil forces, they often indulge in highly sexualized rituals, and they make bloody sacrifices of animals.

The first one of these is untrue, the second really a matter of perspective, and the last, unfortunately for the Church of the Lukumi Babalu Aye, turns out to be true. Animal sacrifice is an aspect of the Santeria faith.

Which brings us to the town of Hialeah, Florida, and how the townsfolk reacted when the church leased a plot of land with the intention of building a church in the Santeria faith.

Hialeah went batshit.

This particular form of batshit came in the form of the Hialeah city council passing four ordinances aimed at the church and its practices. Two of them "forbade the offering of sacrifices, a sacrifice being defined as killing an animal unnecessarily in a public or private ritual or ceremony, and not for the sole purpose of sustenance." The third ordinance forbade the keeping of animals intended for sacrifice. And the last "confined the slaughtering of animals to a slaughterhouse."

Soon the American Civil Liberties Union represented the petitioners.

Now I have no doubt there are plenty of people who don't see an issue here. The practice of animal sacrifice may seem cruel, downright evil, and any laws that banned the practice fall on the side of righteousness for those who sympathize. But you have to remember what I wrote about the goalposts, the changing of standards based on whom, exactly, one is evaluating. The ACLU joined the fight on behalf of the church because it simply wasn't up to the Hialeah city council to decide which religion's practices were deemed lawful and acceptable and which ones were, as they say, beyond the pale.

Pete Rivera, a Santeria high priest, was quoted in a *USA Today* article that focused on this case. Rivera "says the animals he sacrifices die more humanely than animals killed in slaughterhouses." Anyone who has even casually learned about the conditions in American slaughterhouses would be hard-pressed to argue. And yet the Hialeah ordinances made sure to preserve the rights of slaughterhouse owners. There wasn't even a clause about making sure those slaughterhouse deaths were handled with any care.

Another point made in an article in the spring 1993 issue of *Reform Judaism* underscored the hypocrisy: "There is no question that these ordinances do single out those who kill animals out of obedience to religious command, while not touching those who kill animals for any other reason—for food, scientific research, pest control, euthanasia for sick pets, animal population control, or hunting for sport. Can the government ever forbid for religious purposes an activity it freely permits for all kind of non-religious purposes?"

The answer to this question should be obvious, but those Hialeah ordinances were upheld in 1989 by a US district judge and, two years later, "a three-judge panel of the Eleventh Circuit Court of appeals unanimously affirmed this ruling."

Talk about having to be one hundred times better than your peers! When I read about this case, I found myself reeling at the idea of how hard these judges must have contorted themselves to miss the intentional targeting of a specific religion.

The case went all the way to the Supreme Court, where, I'm happy to say, the nine justices unanimously called bullshit on those lower court judges and the wack-ass city council of Hialeah. They struck down the ordinances as clear violations of the free exercise clause of the First Amendment.

I'd like to point out that these nine judges were almost all appointed by Republican presidents: Reagan, Nixon, and Bush appointed seven of the nine justices. You had guys like Antonin Scalia and Clarence Thomas, no friends of Santeria I am sure, who still had to concede—or outright defend—the right of the Church of the Lukumi Babalu Aye to practice its faith as its adherents saw fit. Imagine that.

If I despair at anything in this case, it's simply the layers of powerful people—a city council, a crew of judges—who were willing to overlook the obvious violation. Laws must be applied equally to all American citizens. Imagine having to go all the way to the Supreme Court to have such a basic right affirmed. So I feel sincere gratitude that a body like the ACLU stood to meet that challenge to individual freedom and fairness under the law. Without such support, the powerful always run rough over the powerless. Long may the friends of the powerless reign.

Ashe!

HURLEY V. IRISH-AMERICAN GAY, LESBIAN, AND BISEXUAL GROUP OF BOSTON (1995)

The celebrations that occur in Boston on March 17 carry with them a storied history dating back to the earliest days of the United States. The date represents not just the traditional feast of Saint Patrick, held close by Irish immigrants, but also the evacuation of royal troops from the city in 1776. Boston commemorates the day with a city holiday, the highlight of which is the Saint Patrick's Day–Evacuation Day parade organized by the South Boston Allied War Veterans Council, known to draw as many as one million onlookers.

In 1993, members of the Irish-American Gay, Lesbian, and Bisexual Group of Boston (GLIB) sought to celebrate both their Irish heritage and queer identities by marching in the parade under an organizational banner. Their application to participate was denied despite no written criteria or procedures for admission established by the council. The Supreme Judicial Court of Massachusetts held that the exclusion of GLIB violated the commonwealth's public accommodations law, which protects people from discrimination in public places, including discrimination on the basis of sexual orientation.

In a 9–0 decision, the US Supreme Court reversed the decision of the Supreme Judicial Court, holding that compelling the inclusion of GLIB in the parade violated the organizers' First Amendment rights. In its amicus brief, the ACLU—while supporting the organizers' First Amendment rights—urged the Supreme Court to remand the case to further develop the facts regarding state involvement, which it believed would alter the First Amendment calculus. The City of Boston had allowed the council to use the city's official seal, provided printing services to the organization, and helped fund the parade. The Court, however, ducked the issue, finding that the issue of state action was not properly preserved. LGBT groups continued to be excluded from the parade until 2015.

Queer, Irish, Marching

MICHAEL CUNNINGHAM

In 1995 I was arrested, along with about ninety others, for marching with an LBGTQ contingent in the Saint Patrick's Day parade in Manhattan.

The parade, which was first held in New York City 250 years ago, had, for some time, barred LBGTQ people from marching as a group with any kind of banner declaring our sexual orientation as well as our Irishness.

For years prior to 1995, LGBTQ groups marched anyway, replete with a banner. Former mayor David Dinkins marched with the LGBTQ faction in 1991, and he, along with the other marchers, was jeered at, spat upon, and doused with beer.

In 1995, however, in *Hurley v. Irish-American Gay, Lesbian, and Bisexual Group of Boston (GLIB)*, the US Supreme Court unanimously declared it legal for the Irish Council to prohibit LGBTQ people from marching in the parade. The opinion, delivered by Justice David Souter, asserted that private citizens organizing a public demonstration can't be compelled by the state to include groups that convey a message the organizers don't wish to convey. Souter wrote, "One important manifestation of the principle of free speech is that one who chooses to speak may also decide what not to say." Private organizers of a public event were, then, exercising their right to free speech by silencing whomever they chose to silence.

So, as of 1995, it became not merely a difference of opinion but actually illegal for LGBTQ people to march in a Saint Patrick's Day parade if we weren't wanted by the parade's organizers.

What, then, could we do but join the 1995 parade anyway, with multiple banners?

Now that we were breaking the law, we were subject to arrest if we refused to disperse. About ninety of us refused to disperse. About ninety of us were arrested.

Full disclosure: My Irish surname notwithstanding, I'm queer but I'm not Irish. My paternal grandfather, third generation, took the name Cunningham because it seemed like a better bet for getting on in America than his actual name, Grig, which is Croatian and was once, surely, Grigoslav, or something like that.

I'm Croatian, not Irish, though I didn't learn about that until my early twenties, when my father found some old letters among my grandfather's personal effects.

America is, of course, full of people bearing invented names and, by implication, invented histories. I, with my own invented name and history, had never marched in the Saint Patrick's Day parade before. But I believe that any living person is Irish enough to publicly face down discrimination no matter where, or who, it comes from.

Full disclosure number two: I'm a white gay man, I pass for straight on the streets, and I haven't suffered anything remotely like what much of the world has in store for its queer citizens.

Which made it all the more surprising for me when, on that Saint Patrick's Day in 1995, before the police took us away, I saw the sidewalks of Fifth Avenue crowded with people jeering at us, spitting on us, throwing eggs, and dowsing us with beer.

Some of them were children. Some were elderly.

I particularly remember a woman around eighty, eminently respectable looking, shouting, "Get out, fags."

She was probably someone's grandmother. She might, in theory if not in fact, have been the grandmother of one of the queer marchers. She could more easily have been the unknowing grandmother of a queer grandchild or two or three, who happened not to be marching in the parade.

I suspect it's white and male of me to have been so shocked by the vehemence of the hatred. I hope you'll forgive me for my naiveté, and for stating what will be, for many, the obvious: We were only marching, respectfully, as a group, with banners declaring ourselves to be among the LGBTQ Irish. We were not chanting or causing a disruption of any kind. Still, the jeers, and the eggs, and the beer kept flying.

Soon after we'd passed the woman who wanted fags to go away, we were arrested.

I should tell you a little about getting arrested for an act of civil disobedience, if it's never happened to you.

If, for instance, you're merely marching in a parade from which you've been legally banned, the police order you to disperse. Should you obey, that's that. Should you refuse, however, you're resisting arrest and are summarily arrested. You're handcuffed, put into a police van, and taken to whatever jail is closest.

Like some other marchers that day, I'd already been arrested, with ACT UP, any number of times, for civil disobedience and resisting arrest. We of ACT UP, however, were usually causing considerable disruption.

We were invading, and closing down, the New York Stock Exchange. Or we had handcuffed ourselves together in a human chain around a New Jersey pharmaceutical company that was refusing to share the results of its research into a promising AIDS vaccine. Or we were walking, en masse, covered in fake blood, into a speech being given by George H. W. Bush at the Waldorf Astoria.

We caused disruptions like that because first Ronald Reagan and then George H. W. Bush essentially never mentioned the AIDS epidemic during their presidencies. We caused disruptions like that because the Centers for Disease Control refused either to fast-track approval of promising new AIDS drugs—the established protocol took at least two years—or to release incompletely tested AIDS drugs to people who were dying, people who understandably felt that any yet-to-be-revealed side effects would still be preferable to death.

We caused disruptions like that because hardly anyone not directly affected by the epidemic was doing anything at all. We caused disruptions like that because we couldn't think of any other way to draw attention to the fact that hundreds of thousands of people were dying and no one in power seemed to notice, or care.

We didn't want to get arrested. Hardly anyone wants to get arrested. It was simply the inevitable result of causing the kinds of disruptions that might attract at least a little bit of attention.

Getting arrested for civil disobedience, and for resisting arrest, is a process similar to what I imagine it must have been like to go to some government agency or other in the days of the Soviet Union, when people stood in line for six or seven hours just to get a document stamped.

Going to jail is, more than anything else, crushingly dull. It takes about six to seven hours, moving from holding cell to holding cell, getting fingerprinted, etc. Weeks later you appear in court, where the judge almost inevitably dismisses your case, with the understanding that you'll be better behaved for the next six months.

The police at the parade were brusque but not brutal. We were, after all, queer activists whose primary quarrel was not with the police. We were, for the most part, cooperative, and they, for the most part, were distant and weary, people with a job to do. That said, it surely made a difference that the majority of us were white.

But no police officer has ever, in my various experiences of getting arrested, been as hateful as that old woman standing on Fifth Avenue. I can still see perfectly her livid face and spittle-spewing mouth. She wore a prim, green felt hat.

The hatred today is not like what it was that day in 1995, but the battle does continue, to no one's surprise. In 1999, at the Bronx parade, where six marchers were arrested, Karin O'Connor, an organizer of the parade, said, "We're celebrating a Catholic holy day. We're marching for Saint Patrick, and people who march should be in line with what we're celebrating, Irish pride and Irish Catholic pride." A gay group, she added, does not fit in at a Catholic celebration.

One wonders where that leaves the people who are queer, Irish, and Catholic.

In 2017, in Boston, OutVets, a group of LGBTQ veterans, was barred from participating in the parade, although they had marched in previous years. That said, after some politicians announced that they wouldn't join the parade if OutVets was banned, the organizers reversed their decision, and OutVets became the parade's lead group.

In 2016, the New York City Saint Patrick's Day Parade, Inc. officially allowed Lavender and Green, the Irish LGBTQ organization, to march in the New York City parade. In 2017, notoriously homophobic

Vice President Mike Pence (of Irish descent) marched for several blocks with the Irish contingent in the Washington, DC, parade.

And Ireland, after all, was the second country to legalize gay marriage, in 2015. Leo Varadkar is now, in 2019, Ireland's first gay prime minister.

I wonder how that old woman, if she's still alive, would feel about all that.

Progress has been made. But only up to a point.

There are, at this writing, thirty-six cities and towns in the United States where Saint Patrick's Day parades are held. It remains legal for any of them to bar LGBTQ people from marching. In 2018, in the New York borough of Staten Island, the local parade committee voted to ban LGBTQ groups. Staten Island Parade president Larry Cummings said, "Our parade is for Irish heritage and culture. It is not a political or sexual identification parade."

I suspect a number of Irish people would be surprised to hear that their heritage and culture has nothing to do with politics or sexual identification. I mean, have you ever been to Ireland?

The beat goes on, as Sonny and Cher put it. History tells us that any people who are determined simply to exist will outlast those who'd rather they not exist.

Here's to the next Saint Patrick's Day parade, then. And the next, and the next.

RENO V. ACLU (1997)
ASHCROFT V. ACLU (2004)

Reno v. ACLU and *Ashcroft v. ACLU* are quintessential First Amendment cases. The federal government deemed a given form of speech socially harmful and took steps to silo it away. In *Reno*, the Court ruled the Communications Decency Act's definition of *obscenity* was too broad and imprecise, censoring an enormous swath of otherwise legal speech, and therefore fell afoul of the First Amendment. In *Ashcroft*, the Court struck down the Child Online Protection Act as overbroad and ill tailored to its purpose, and therefore also unconstitutional.

In both cases, the ACLU shouldered the burden of making uncomfortable arguments in order to protect free speech, adhered to its higher principles in fighting to protect a core American freedom from overzealous legislators.

"Because Girls Can Read as Well as Boys"

On Protecting the Children

NEIL GAIMAN

Two weeks before I was born, in October 1960, D. H. Lawrence's novel *Lady Chatterley's Lover* was put on trial for obscenity. It was a jury trial, and at the end of it, the book was found not to be obscene. I was born on the day the book, in its cheap paperback edition, went on sale (and sold out, all across the United Kingdom). Mervyn Griffith-Jones, the prosecutor, had asked the jury in his opening statement, "When you have read it through, would you approve of your young sons, young daughters—because girls can read as well as boys—reading this book? Is it a book that you would have lying around in your own house? Is it a book that you would even wish your wife or your servants to read?" Normally, only the last sentence of this is quoted, making fun of the antiquated attitudes of lawyers who had failed to realize that the sixties were just about to happen, and sexual intercourse was, as Philip Larkin put it, about to begin: after all, wives in 1960 were allowed to choose their own reading material, and the servant classes were being replaced by labor-saving devices.

The question that hangs in the air, though, always, and that colors conversation of censorship is the first half of Griffith-Jones's question: Would you approve of your young sons, or your young daughters, reading this book, seeing this image, being exposed to this idea?

As adults, one of our responsibilities is to protect children. Some of this protection takes the form of keeping children away from images, from ideas, from stories, from films that we do not feel they are ready for.

Not all adults agree on the boundaries of this protective sphere, and not all children are the same. And "children" is a slippery concept, defined differently in different places. Where does childhood end? Would you protect a six-year-old from the same ideas or images you would protect a seventeen-and-a-half-year-old from? And how do "community standards," the nebulous but still legally real idea that different people in different places have different views on what is or isn't acceptable, fit into all this?

We want to protect our children. But legal arguments, like the one made in the *Lady Chatterley's Lover* case, presume something about children that is not actually true: they assume that children read and parse fiction that contains sex in the same way that adults do.

Children want to know things. They are curious. But they tend to explore within their comfort zone.

Children are good at exploring and pretty good at figuring out their comfort zones. On the whole, they would tend not to pick up horror fiction, or even go to Judy Blume to learn about sex, before they are ready. But when they are ready and curious, they explore. It's how they make sense of the adult world waiting for them. And children will make mistakes in their exploration. They will go too far. I remember, bored, waiting for my mother, as a boy, and picking up the only reading material around, which turned out to be a well-documented, respectable, illustrated publication about murder methods in World War II concentration camps and on Nazi experiments on human subjects who were mostly, like me, Jewish. I had known we had lost many relatives: discovering how, and discovering how human beings could kill other human beings, became the stuff of my nightmares.

(Quick! Define *children*. At what age does childhood end? In 2007, a Florida appeals court upheld the successful prosecution of a sixteen-year-old girl and a seventeen-year-old boy as sex offenders, in this case as "child pornographers," for taking a photograph of themselves naked and one of them "engaged in sexual activity" [something they were legally of age to do] because the girl had emailed the photos to the boy as keepsakes. Should they have been prosecuted? Should the prosecution have been upheld? And if they had wanted to search the Internet for information on how to have sex safely, or for birth control, or even for legal advice on whether it was safe to take naked photos of themselves with their phones, should this be forbidden or encouraged?)

I write for children. I write for small children. They like destruction and creepy things, they like small journeys into the dark that end safely. I write for older children, who like stories about families and about death and danger. I write for adults. In writing for adults, I always find myself writing, in whatever disguise, about sex and about death. Writing for children, I try and write about hope and the complexity of the world, about bravery and doing the right thing. But there is always death present in the stories. I leave out the sex, because younger children tend to respond to sex in their fiction in the way that children respond to a drunk adult throwing up in the street: there's curiosity there, but also aversion, the knowledge that this is part of an adult world that is inevitably waiting for them but is filled with weird-ass things that adults inexplicably do. But several of my adult novels have been honored as adult books that older children would or should read, and they have sex in them, and darkness.

There will always be curiosity about the adult world. There will always be ways to explore that. (I was twelve or thirteen when William Peter Blatty's *The Exorcist* went around the school, passed from hand to hand, from boy to boy. The page with the crucifix masturbation, just like the pages in the unabridged class dictionary that contained the swear words, was the page the book fell open to.)

The Internet began as a place where government employees and academics could exchange information with each other. And then it grew, unplanned and, for the most part, unregulated. The Internet is a delivery system. It can deliver a Batman cartoon or a porn video. It can deliver tweets or blogs or adverts, money or movies or gardening tips. It can offer you all the world's information, or most of it, entertainment and violence, delights and dangers of all kinds. Anything you can encounter in the world outside you can find a version of on the Internet. So the question becomes, How do you regulate something so huge, so slippery, so potentially filled with pitfalls? And how do we protect our children from everything in the world? Our six-year-olds as well as our seventeen-year-olds?

As a parent, I want to keep my children safe from all dangers and threats. (I put my hands over my twelve-year-old daughter's eyes during *Pan's Labyrinth*, during the bloody bits, and told her what the subtitles were saying. She didn't want to stop watching, but she didn't want or need the images of blood in her head. But it would have been a lesser film if Guillermo del Toro had been forced to take those moments out of his movie, eliding the adult content to protect the children.)

And governments, responding to that impulse, took the simplest option. They tried, when the Internet became a thing, to make the Internet a place that would be safe for children.

The way we most often try to codify an official response to large and unruly questions is to fence them in with laws. The first significant attempt by the US government was through Title V of the Telecommunications Act of 1996, better known as the Communications Decency Act (CDA). It was signed into law by President Clinton in 1996 and attempted to target indecency and obscenity on the Internet by making it a crime punishable by two years in jail, a $250,000 fine, or both, to engage in speech that was "indecent" or "patently offensive," if that speech could be viewed by a minor.

Within five months, a panel of three judges in Philadelphia had blocked part of the CDA. In July 1997, a federal court in New York struck down a further section, arguing that its reach was too broad. This culminated in *Reno v. ACLU* (1997), where twenty plaintiffs, including groups representing cyberspace rights and gay and lesbian rights, and the ACLU, challenged the act on the grounds that its provisions would criminalize expression protected by the First Amendment—and specifically that the terms *indecent* and *patently offensive* were both vague and constitutionally overbroad. The Supreme Court agreed, and a landmark 7–2 opinion delivered by Justice John Paul Stevens firmly ruled that the CDA placed an "unacceptably heavy burden on protected speech" that "threatens to torch a large segment of the Internet community."

"The interest in encouraging freedom of expression in a democratic society outweighs any theoretical but unproven benefit of censorship," wrote the Court. "We presume government regulation of the content of speech is more likely to interfere with the free exchange of ideas than to encourage it."

The government tried again. In 1998, Congress introduced the Child Online Protection Act (COPA). It criminalized the posting on the Internet, for "commercial purposes," of material that was "harmful to minors," to the tune of a $50,000 fine and six months in prison. It defined material that was harmful to minors as:

> any **communication, picture, image, graphic image file, article, recording, writing, or other matter of any kind that is obscene** or that–
>
> (A) **the average person, applying contemporary community standards**, would find, taking the material as a whole and with respect to minors, is designed to appeal to, or is designed to pander to, the prurient interest;
>
> (B) **depicts, describes, or represents**, in a manner patently offensive with respect to minors, **an actual or simulated sexual act or sexual contact, an actual or simulated normal or perverted sexual act, or a lewd exhibition of the genitals or post-pubescent female breast**; and
>
> (C) taken as a whole, lacks serious literary, artistic, political, or scientific value for minors.

Immediate and obvious problems with this (apart from the oddness of the word *simulated*, which puts a photograph of an oil painting of a naked woman into the same category as a photograph of a naked woman) would be that applying "community standards" to the entire Internet, the most conservative and restrictive communities in the United States would be able to set the standard for everywhere else, in the United States or in the rest of the world. "Community standards" change from place to place, but any of the communities in any of those places could object to what they saw, and the Internet would bow to the most restrictive and the most easily upset. And there is always someone, somewhere, who will object to something.

COPA left "for commercial purposes" vague; even if a website is not obviously selling you something, it can still exist for commercial purposes. And what if it is trying to inform you? COPA could have criminalized gynecological websites, websites with information about sexually transmitted diseases, sexual advice columns, and art history sites. It would have meant that adults would have needed to input credit card information before accessing any "commercial" website with adult content, including LGBT information, causing privacy issues (and ignoring the possibility that people under age eighteen can have, or obtain, credit card numbers). And above all, it tried to apply local law to the Internet, which is not local: adult content is not only found on US websites.

The case went back and forth between the Third Circuit and the Supreme Court from 2002 until 2009, when the Supreme Court declined to hear the third appeal, effectively striking COPA from the books.

Ashcroft v. ACLU (2004), which ended COPA, was a landmark case. It upheld the injunction, predominantly on the grounds that there were less restrictive ways of tackling the issues than the ones that COPA was attempting to put in place. Justice Anthony Kennedy delivered the majority opinion, explaining that "content-based prohibitions, enforced by severe criminal penalties, have the constant potential to be a repressive force in the lives and thoughts of a free people."

(Though *Ashcroft v. ACLU* is the more recent and more often cited, it is intimately entwined with *Reno v. ACLU*, and observations from the latter cut to the bottom line over the debate on online restrictions. Justice Stevens's majority opinion in 1997 argued that "the interest in encouraging freedom of expression in a democratic society outweighs any theoretical but unproven benefit of censorship.")

Justice Kennedy also pointed out that "the factual record does not reflect current technological reality—a serious flaw in any case involving the Internet. The technology of the Internet evolves at a rapid pace."

This, as we've seen from attempts by legislators in both the United States and other countries to understand the influence of social media on the 2016 election, remains a critical issue, and one that's not going to be solved any day soon. COPA's attempt to criminalize pornography and sexual content on commercial sites hosted in the United States would have been powerless in a world where users (including children) could simply jump the fence into the big wide world. Nobody is an island in cyberspace, and no country is either. Even islands aren't really islands any longer. The people who make our laws are always one step behind this new realm they're trying to control, with its strange and flexible geographies.

Overreaching attempts to protect the rights of some are bound to have an adverse impact on the freedoms of others. A recent example has been Tumblr's 2018 decision to ban pornography from its platform, incensing a number of users (including young people, sex workers, and members of the LGBT community) who had relied on it as a relatively safe space for interaction.

Which brings us back to where we came in: the attempt to ban books like *Lady Chatterley's Lover* in order to protect the children.

The decisions in both *Reno* and *Ashcroft* make explicit reference to the rights of adults, the former in part decided on the grounds that the CDA was an abridgment of the First Amendment because it didn't allow parents to decide what material was acceptable for their children. In 2007, Senior Judge Lowell A. Reed Jr. of Federal District Court, in the decision that the Supreme Court declined to hear or to overturn, stated that "despite my personal regret at having to set aside yet another attempt to protect our children from harmful material," he was blocking COPA because "perhaps we do the minors of this country harm if First Amendment protections, which they will with age inherit fully, are chipped away in the name of their protection."

Children live in a world of adults, and they, in their turn, will become adults one day. We do not and we cannot protect children from the adult world by making the adult world a place safe or fit only for children, and the Internet is, for good and for evil, a part of the world, the world as represented by information. As adults, we owe it to our children to protect them, yes. As a positive thing: through communication, by choosing and permitting, as best we can, strictly or permissively, what they encounter, in the world, on screens and on pages. We have to talk to them, inform them, have the awkward and embarrassing conversations we might rather avoid but are necessary if they are going to navigate the adult waters ahead of them. It's our responsibility to do that.

We do it by helping our children to grow and to learn. We do it by letting them explore and by setting the bounds of their exploration ourselves. We do it by helping them. We don't do it—we can't do it—by removing the adult books from the shelves of a library and by trying to make the whole world into a nursery. If we do, we will find ourselves scraping away the freedoms of the adults who will come after us in our attempts to protect the children they are now.

CITY OF CHICAGO V. MORALES (1999)

Under Chicago's 1992 Gang Congregation Ordinance (GCO), it was a crime for criminal gang members to loiter in a public place. In practice, this meant police officers could order to disperse any group of two or more people they believed to contain gang members. Anyone who didn't obey violated the ordinance and was subject to some combination of a $100 to $500 fine, six months in prison, and 120 hours of community service.

During the three years of its enforcement, the GCO resulted in roughly eighty-nine thousand dispersal orders, leading to approximately forty-five thousand violations. The majority of people targeted were black or Latinx, many of whom had no gang affiliation whatsoever. In *City of Chicago v. Morales*, the ACLU represented plaintiff Jesus Morales, arguing that the ordinance was too vague to satisfy the Fourteenth Amendment's due process, and therefore unconstitutional.

Generally a criminal law will be found unconstitutional for vagueness if an ordinary person cannot understand what conduct it prohibits and it authorizes or encourages arbitrary and discriminatory enforcement. Writing for the Court, Justice John Paul Stevens found that the GCO violated both prongs of the vagueness test. Under the common law, *loiter* means "to linger in a place with no apparent purpose," but is that the definition an ordinary person will know? Similarly, how long must the "loiterers" remain dispersed? How far must they go? The ordinance provided no answers to these questions.

On the second prong, the law granted police officers absolute discretion in enforcement. With no formal guidelines for identifying who was loitering versus who lingered with a purpose, officers were free to enforce the ordinance according to their own personal whims and biases. Officers could order everyone to disperse, or no one at all. The law was accordingly struck down as an unconstitutional infringement on personal liberties.

We Gather

JESMYN WARD

The Supreme Court struck down Chicago's antigang loitering law, which disproportionately targeted African American and Latino youth who were not engaged in criminal activity. The law had resulted in the arrest of 45,000 innocent people.

When I was a child, Easter was a major holiday in my community. Most of us were black, semidevout Catholics, so we rose early on the holiday, attended Mass in pastel and cream outfits specifically sewn or purchased for the day, wore full-skirted dresses and crisp ties. After Mass, we changed into less formal outfits, again specifically sewn or purchased for the day. My grandmother was a seamstress in her youth, so sometimes she made my brother's and sisters' outfits, tailored them to our short torsos, long legs, slim arms.

After the midday Easter meal, we all went down to the local baseball park where our team was part of the regional Negro league; our team was the DeLisle Yellow Jackets, named after an especially pernicious wasp-like insect plentiful near woods where there are deer trails. They are at their worst during the late spring, when they swarmed us whenever we walked outside and bit us so badly we were left with raised red welts. The swelling and pain took days to subside. Our baseball players wore black and yellow and white uniforms, and they were good enough that every year, they were given pride of being the home team on Easter Sunday. One man was DJ and sportscaster all at once, narrating the game and then playing blues records during breaks between innings.

At the edge of the field was a tiny, low-ceilinged building that contained pool tables, a small dance floor, and a bar. This was our local hole-in-the-wall blues club.

Most years, it was already warm by Easter, so while we children played games behind the bleachers and took our tooth money to the concession stand for pickles and candy and, when we were hungrier and had a generous adult's cash in hand, fried fish, the adults took breaks from the humid spectacle of the outside and sought the dim, cool interior of the club. Challenged neighbors to rounds of pool. Sipped a cold beer or wine cooler. Stomped the dance floor.

When I was a child, my small town felt isolated. There was a hub of four long roads where all the people I knew, more than half of whom I was related to, lived. The one convenience store was owned by a local family. There was one Head Start, and one elementary school, one Catholic church, one fire station, one ballpark/hole-in-the-wall blues club, and wilderness around, stretching farther than my small legs could walk. Our year spun a procession of community gatherings, where we came together to celebrate our living, our survival. Mardi Gras. Easter Sunday. Mother's Day BBQ at the park. June church bazaars. Halloween/fall festivals at the elementary school.

An older gentleman I met from Texas once told me this: everything changes. He had watched the desert pare away the houses and storefronts of his hometown, the old die, the young flee, until his town disappeared. I was nineteen when I met him, attending college in California, and when he said this to me, I felt the pain of recognition. My town too was changing. The old DeLisle disappearing, plot by plot, as new people moved in and settled the wilderness, razed the pines, cleared acres to cultivate scraggly, threadbare grass lawns. The old DeLisle reduced gathering by gathering as our institutions faltered, our community-affirming holidays out of favor due to organizers getting old, fatigue, poverty. When I moved home briefly in my late twenties, the only community gathering still in existence was the Easter ball game.

That year was an anomaly. It was cold, and perhaps this is why the young adults who attended the game did not want to actually sit in the park and watch. We milled and gossiped and laughed and ate and drank on the sidelines, but before the afternoon waned, many of us left. We migrated to the local park, around a mile away, where we could at least sit in our cars in the small lot rimming the playground, crank our heaters, and play music that wasn't blues. Sometime during the afternoon, one fresh-dressed, hoodied young man let loose his 6 by 9 speakers to sing, and he pulled out into the road, which sported no traffic at all, and rode down the block very slowly, windows rolled down, perhaps swerving a bit, to regale us with music. To show off his car, freshly washed and waxed, tires burnished with Black Magic tire gel.

Soon he was joined by another young man, another car. And another, and another, all serenading us, all smiling, usually with a compatriot in the passenger seat, whose hair was braided tightly to his scalp, whose line was less than twelve hours sharp, mugging for the growing crowd on the sidelines in the parking lot, making us grin with the pleasure of being alive under the weak spring sun, blood rushing to the music, the growl of the tires, breathing and singing and beating in the dying day. Soon there was a procession of cars driving up and down the block, an impromptu musical parade.

The police hired for security at the ballpark down the street noticed. The next year, on our way to the ball game, we rode past the park and saw the parking lot blocked off. Four county sheriff cars posted around the park to prevent anyone from parking, and another two at a fire station nearby. More parked on the shoulder of the road around the ballpark to prevent would-be attendees from parking and socializing anywhere that wasn't the ballpark. I glared at all of them, anger and sourness roiling in my gut, unable to articulate what it felt like to be policed.

Before that moment, I'd had some experience with what it meant to live in a police state. I'd grown up in Mississippi, after all, a place where Parchman Prison Farm, a plantation prison that stole many from black communities all over the state, reenslaved them over decades, could and did exist. In DeLisle, county cops had stopped me more than once, asked me to exit my car, interrogated me over who I was and where I was going and who was with me, and then never gave me a ticket or reason for pulling me over. I'd heard of others in my community who suffered the same—black women who were more vocal about their resentment at being racially profiled, who were then handcuffed by police for pushing back. What I could not articulate at the time was this: What happens when a community is policed to the point that public gatherings are criminalized, when community members are prevented from coming together to affirm we are alive we are alive we are alive? What then happens to that community?

In 1992, the city of Chicago passed the Gang Congregation Ordinance that prohibited individuals from loitering in public places. A city commission argued that violent crime was escalating due to street gangs and that loitering gang members intimidated "ordinary" residents. The ordinance meant that police officers had the power to ascertain that one or more people in a certain place were gang members, loitering with no purpose, and could then order them to disperse, and then arrest them if they disobeyed that order. Morales, among forty-five thousand innocent others, was charged with violating said ordinance. In the end, the Supreme Court ruled in favor of Morales, holding that under the Constitution, police officers do not have unlimited discretion to define the nature of the loitering, and such laws must be subject to sufficiently specific limits.

This desire to police the other, to rob the alien other of the very human pleasure of gathering in public and sharing community, is not new. Black boys as young as twelve were charged with loitering in Mississippi in the 1930s and 1940s and 1950s and sent to Parchman Prison to be reenslaved. The Gang Congregation Ordinance resulted in forty-five thousand innocent people, mostly black and brown, being arrested. New York City's infamous stop-question-and-frisk program, which is still currently active, has been the conduit for rampant racial profiling and illegal stops. According to the NYPD's own reports, nearly nine out of ten stopped-and-frisked New Yorkers have been innocent.

Sometimes I marvel at what it might feel like to be a white American. Especially a white American male. To walk out of my front door and enter public space and to be free of preconceived notions of who you are, of your morality or lack thereof, your work ethic or lack thereof, your intelligence or lack thereof, your ethical standards or lack thereof. To walk through the world unjudged. And then I often wonder what it is like for white men to not have to worry about the types of judgments that are particular to my sex: What must it be like to not have to worry that your work is worth the same as everyone else's, to not have to worry that if you are sexually assaulted or harassed, you will be blamed for it because of how you dressed or spoke or drank or stood or sat? What must it feel like to exist in the outside world unencumbered by the threat of not only racial but also sexual violence?

Sometimes I think I have experienced something of what it must be like to move through the world a bit more freely. When I left Mississippi for college in California when I was eighteen, the farther I got from the South, the lighter I felt. I looked up more often instead of watching my feet as I walked. My shoulders, perpetually curved as a cowed animal's, began to straighten. I had conversations with classmates wherein I would relate stories of racism from my past, and in the telling, I would realize how I'd accepted the bullying, internalized it, accepted it as my due because I was black, and this was Mississippi. In leaving Mississippi, this place where every other street is named for a Confederate, where politicians pose with Confederate flags, where they make flippant remarks about public lynchings at campaign events, I felt a little safer, a little lighter in public. This is the kind of place where Cruisin' the Coast, a gathering of mostly white, older people who tool around the different small towns of the Gulf Coast in restored antique cars, produces just as much, if not more, traffic and congestion business as Black Spring Break in Biloxi, and while Cruisin' the Coast is celebrated, BSB is heavily policed, restricted, and the outcry to cease the event increases every year. This denial of community gathering does this too, teaches us that we are less than human, that we don't deserve to feel that sense of joy of being serenaded, or the sense of kinship when an arm is flung over your shoulder, or that sense of ease when someone you have known for years tells a good joke, and you turn your face to the sky and laugh.

I am ever grateful for the work the ACLU does to root out this racist behavior legitimized in law, wherever it occurs, in Mississippi, where they've brought suit against the Madison County Sheriff's Department to challenge racially motivated policing or Chicago or elsewhere, but it is disheartening to know that this happens all over the country, even when not codified in law. This belief that black people, brown people, queer people, trans people, disabled people, women are perpetually less is the great American Gorgon, and these endless terrible laws and behaviors are its myriad heads, regenerating one after another. Rooting us in place with one glance, miring us in inequality. This is how we are frozen in stone. Sometimes I believe this is an endless battle. And in a rare moment, I believe maybe we are our greatest heroes, ACLU and all. On these moments, I think: onward, to freedom.

ZADVYDAS V. DAVIS (2001) (*amicus*)

At its core, *Zadvydas v. Davis* is a case about due process rights and who possesses them. The second Bush administration argued that undocumented immigrants could be detained indefinitely, even if there was no realistic hope of deportation. This amounts, essentially, to life imprisonment without any hope of parole. When Mr. Zadvydas filed his habeas petition, the ACLU and other rights groups immediately filed spirited amicus briefs on his behalf.

Writing for the majority, Justice Breyer declared that all persons in the United States possess due process rights and that the indefinite detention of undocumented immigrants is unconstitutional because it constitutes arbitrary imprisonment. The Court reasoned that undocumented immigrants are not convicted criminals, so imprisoning them for long periods of time is both a rights violation and an affront to individual liberty. What's more, the Court held that the lack of procedural safeguards in the immigration legal system (such as judicial review) increased the likelihood of inappropriate detention. Accordingly, indefinite detention of undocumented immigrants was struck down; the government is required to release nondeportable persons after six months. In *Clark v. Martinez*, the Court would extend this principle to inadmissible immigrants, i.e., those who are detained because they are barred from entering the United States. Undocumented persons are therefore protected from indefinite detention when both leaving and entering are impossible.

This issue is by no means settled. Immigration authorities have pivoted to other justifications for violating undocumented persons' due process rights. The ACLU continues to fight such abuses, whether by direct representation, amicus briefs, or simply raising awareness of these injustices.

Stateside Statelessness

MOSES SUMNEY

The first time my African father was deported in 1980something, he had snuck onto a plane out of France with a fake passport in his satchel. Upon landing in Boston, he was immediately seized by authorities. Caught. In holding, a sympathetic border security agent gave him clear instructions before carting him back to a return flight: "This is the best country. This is where you want to be. Don't stop trying to get in. Have your children here. Try and try again to come back." Soon after, America expelled my father back to his port of last departure, Paris, instead of back to Accra, Ghana's capital, where he originated from. It was sheer luck and logistics that saved him from being sent back to his country of origin, because it would have been virtually impossible to leave Ghana for the Promised Land that is North America.

The path back to country of origin was not so simple for Kestutis Zadvydas of the *Zadvydas v. Davis* ruling. Although a legal resident of the United States, he was born to Lithuanian parents in a displaced-persons camp in Germany. He was not recognized as a citizen by Lithuania, Germany, or the United States (although he likely held a green card after his family migrated to the US). After serving two years in prison for a blue collar crime, he was further detained and ordered deported. Federal immigration law stated that once a person had been ordered removed, the US attorney general must complete the extraction process within ninety days. Failing that, the immigrant could either be released back to the public or be detained indefinitely until removal became possible. Since both Lithuania and Germany refused to take him, Zadvydas remained in prison for two additional years (after completing his initial two-year sentence). After a long battle, the Supreme Court ruled that it was indeed unconstitutional for expats to be detained for longer than ninety days without confirmation of verifiable, imminent acceptance from their country of origin.

The case posed foundational legislative questions about immigrants in America: Do non-citizens have constitutional rights? Are the rights of "aliens" inalienable? Can deportees be detained indefinitely if their country of origin will not acknowledge them? But it also asked philosophical questions, existential questions of humanity: Where do you go when no one will claim you? Who are you if you can't clearly be identified?

As my excursion into researching *Zadvydas v. Davis* begins in a tea café in London, I am struck by the immense privilege my US passport has granted me in my lifetime, especially as I've achieved a basic level of financial self-determination. The United Kingdom has recently instituted a Registered Traveler Program for citizens of certain nations (it isn't difficult to imagine which ones), so that an approved foreigner can enter the UK expeditiously and stay for up to six months at a time without rhyme, reason, or visa. This means that I can come to Great Britain literally whenever I want, sail right through customs without waiting to see a border agent, and stay for as long as six months. To reset that entry period, all I must do is briefly step out of the country, perhaps take a two and a half hour train ride to Paris and come back. After being here for a month, I realize my experience contrasts greatly with the way my parents entered Europe in the 1980s, before they finally settled in America and started a family. I breeze through the gates, but they snuck in.

After falling in love in a Ghanaian village in the 1980s, my parents knew it would be best to migrate to a Western country before having children. This is a common mentality among Africans who covet upward mobility; the only way to climb the echelons of Ghanaian society was to go abroad and return with foreign currency. Having Western citizenship would ensure that their kids had everything they didn't—a chance at a better life, but most important, global autonomy. Because, as they soon found out, traveling country to country is no small feat when you hold an African passport; it's often impossible. And getting a visa to go to America was harder than smuggling a camel through the eye of a needle. So even though America was always their end goal, they moved first to Nigeria, then Germany, then France, then Great Britain, then Canada, before settling in California in the early 90s. It was an immigration process that took ten years, a long game of international hopscotch that had to be played because almost no country would grant them legal entry—especially the United States.

My family is well acquainted with the North American purgatory of casually wondering when it's your turn to be deported. Just a few years ago, well into my twenties, my parents sat me down (over the phone) for the first time and unveiled some family secrets about their road to living in America. After residing in Quebec for two years, following a two-year stint in France, my father moved to California to plant the seeds for my mom and older sister joining him. He saved up while working as a janitor, and once he had enough to provide for them, sent for my mom and sister. But, of course, my mother couldn't get a visa. She embarked on a migration that by now was familiar to my parents: she snuck across the Canadian border in the middle of the night. Or at least tried to. She was stopped by Canadian border security while trying to enter Michigan, and was rejected. Caught. Instead of driving six hours back home as instructed, she holed up in a motel near the border for a week. Now that she had been discovered, she was at great risk of being deported, and it was only a matter of time before they came back for her. Lying on her back on that stiff motel bed, my mom could fearfully foresee a carceral future in which she was trapped in a transitory state similar to that of Zadvydas, and many other immigrants who were awaiting their fate in jail before inevitable deportation. Except this was Canada, not the US, and my mom was female, not male, and, to complicate matters further, she was several months pregnant with me.

Maybe this pregnancy provided the determination and grace that kept her from being freighted home immediately. Legend has it that a cavalcade of immigrant mothers rode up in the middle of the night, slipped her into their chariot of fire (the back of a cargo truck), and successfully stowed her away to California.

I have to interrupt this fugitive drama to interject that I myself wonder how much of this story is accurate. Like most oral histories, the facts get distorted and diminished in the retelling, and the details of this pilgrimage have changed every time I've spoken to my mom. I chalk that up to her propensity for dramatic flair (yes, it's hereditary), mixed with a lifelong habit of concealing the truth for the sake of safety. There is something about concealment that transforms the truth. As for my father, he won't even let me share the specific details of how he crossed over from Canada for fear that it will expose him and disrupt future migrants from taking the same path.

Reading *Zadvydas* while I await a refill on my Earl Grey tea (the French waitress in this east London café insists that I must try it the "right" way, black with a slice of orange, instead of ruining it with soy or almond or oat milk), I wonder where, exactly, would they have sent my mother if she was caught again on either side of the border? Where would my family have been shipped off to if we had been discovered, paperless, in the 1990s? Back to Canada where my sister was born? Back to Europe, where my parents had spent all of their twenties building their lives? Or back to Ghana, from whence they originally came, but hadn't been in over ten years? Faces and places in Ghana would now have been foreign to them; they would not likely be smoothly accepted by their peers. Where do you go when no one will claim you?

Questions like these inspired my parents to keep our origin story a secret from us children, for fear that we would slip up on the playground, or at the post office, or at the doctor's office, and reveal our illegitimate status. Maybe we would accidentally tell our friends at church that our mother didn't have documents, and those snot-nosed kids would tell their conservative Christian parents. We remained in the dark, even as we moved back to Ghana in the early 2000s, and back again to California six years later.

As of early 2019, Ghanaian-American expats are having their identities questioned more than ever before. In early 2019, it was announced that the Department of Homeland Security had imposed sanctions against incoming visa requests from Ghanaian nationals as a blanket penalty for the Ghanaian government refusing to accept seven thousand fresh deportees from the US. In response, the Ghanaian government has insisted that it must verify each individual deportee of Ghanaian citizenship before accepting them back onto Ghanaian soil, holding up deportations. And then there is the infrastructural issue of finding accommodations for each person once their citizenship is confirmed; Ghana's population is smaller than that of California's, and one can imagine that social resources must already be at capacity if people are so eager to emigrate in the first place.

Pressuring the Ghanaian government to accept potential deportees is the current administration's way of circumventing the immigration law established by *Zadvydas v. Davis* and its associated cases (such as *Clark v. Martinez*). Since detaining deportees indefinitely beyond ninety days is unconstitutional, penalizing innocent Ghanaians seeking visas is a clear attempt to strong-arm Ghana into accepting the deportees before the purgatorial period runs out, and the US is legally required to release the would-be expellees.

I wonder what will happen to each of these citizens, stuck in limbo between two nations that don't want them. I think of the dread I feel when I drive into an intersection during congested LA rush hour traffic, and get stuck in the static crossroads, neither here nor there, at risk of collision from either side. I think of how I feel when I get lost driving through Accra's Tetteh-Quarshie interchange at night, having just barely missed an exit because the freeway signage is elusive and the lighting is not illuminating. How I feel when lost on a train platform in central London, unsure if I'm going north or south or east or west, only sure that time is a finite resource I can't control. In these moments coming and going become interchangeable: "Nowhere" becomes an inhabitable place, a zip code ending in an infinity loop of zeros that I seem to occupy indefinitely. We get our sense of self from a sense of home. We are taught to root our identities in feelings of belonging and community. We are programmed, across customs, to define ourselves by our origins first and our preferences second. But who are you if you can't clearly be identified?

It has already been so difficult throughout my lifetime for Ghanaians to emigrate—even the well-connected ones. We hear so much about the parasites trying to illegally get into America, but not enough about how difficult *legal* entry is, especially from countries oppressively deemed the "Third World" (propagating the idea that they are so underdeveloped that they might as well be the bottom-most tier of the planet). The fact that most illegal immigration occurs through overstayed visas, not fence-hopping, is ignored. I've learned this firsthand through my half brother, ten years older than me, whom I did not meet until we moved back to Ghana when I was ten. My father had him shortly before he met my mother and left Ghana, but was unable to bring him along. Once my parents reached America, my brother tried to join us, but the US Embassy denied him a visa, year after year, decade after decade, until he was thirty years old. Even after my parents were legally granted naturalization, and even after my father's near-twenty years of accumulated US residency, the government denied my half brother a visa because there was no guarantee that he would return to Ghana if he visited us. Nor did they allow him to immigrate, because they refused to accept that our tax-paying family could sustain him.

Learning I had an older brother when I was ten may have been confusing, but learning for the first time in my twenties that my parents had been illegal immigrants felt like discovering I was adopted, or that I had been a phantom of my assumed self all along. Suddenly, so many things about my childhood made sense. My parents were almost always self-employed or working odd jobs; my mom was a seamstress for much of my childhood, sewing African clothes for San Bernardino women who wanted to connect with the motherland, and my dad was a taxi driver who often picked us up from school in his cab and broke taxi codes by planting us in the front seat while he picked up passengers throughout the Inland Empire. At some point they ran a thrift shop in downtown San Bernardino. We went to private school, but didn't realize that my parents worked there as custodians and assistants in order to pay the discounted tuition. My sister and I were the only black students in our Colton school—truly a feat considering San Bernardino had such a large black population. Being the alien was not alien to me.

By the time my older brother was finally granted a visa in the 2010s, any fantasy semblance of constructing a quintessential American family had dissipated. I had gone off to university, and my family had decided that after twenty or so years courting America, they just didn't want to date it anymore. Besides, they had what they needed—passports for their kids, citizenship for themselves: clinging to a dying economy would be overkill. Over the course of three years, ravaged by the recession, we had downsized from a five-bedroom, two-story stand-alone house to a two-bedroom apartment for five people. My mom took a government job with the county, but it still wasn't enough. The American dream had long given way to night terrors by the time my brother finally arrived. And though he made it over the pond, he found it hard to make it in America without a support system.

Although one of the more obscure court cases to the common public, *Zadvydas v. Davis* has recently been made relevant by the Trump administration's horrific immigration policies. Families are detained and split apart, children separated from parents and caged in pop-up detention centers. I am acutely aware that if I had been born ten years later than I was, to, say, a Latin American family, or if I had crossed from the Southern border instead of the Northern border, I could have had a much different story. Instead, my citizenship has never been called into question.

My identity, however, has always been in flux. The funny thing about emigrating is that many migrants are trading an emotional sense of security for a residential one. As my parents climbed the rungs of that American dream™, I found that my sense of place was constantly under siege. "Where do you go when no one will claim you?" is not just a jurisdictional question. It is a psychic one, an emotional one, a spiritual one. Oscillating between nations as a child—living both on the western coast of Africa and the western coast of America back-to-back and back again—taught me that citizenship does not guarantee safety. Where you're born does not indicate where you belong. I've never lived anywhere and not been the odd one out. I'm the African in America, the American in Africa, the African American among white Americans, the American African among black Americans. Similarly, our family never seemed to have the kinds of communal bonds that I learned to expect from years finding solace in literature instead of going out to play with kids who thought I was weird.

Taking up residence in a country that is not originally "yours" is like signing a deal with the devil—you accept that you may never have a cultural sense of community in this new land, you might not find a restaurant that cooks the food of your homeland, you may never see your family again. But! Your children will have passports and be able to travel. If they can afford it. And maybe if they aren't left with an inherent sense of alienation and divorce from their roots, they might even return "home." That's, of course, if you don't get kicked out of the country first.

Although *Zadvydas v. Davis* established that non-citizen residents of the United States do have constitutional rights, as a first-generation American, I constantly feel taxed to acknowledge questions like "What right do immigrants have to the *bountiful* resources of their adopted country? Why are immigrants deserving of our sympathy, when they've already exploited our resources?" At the risk of generalizing or oversimplifying a non-monolithic issue, I like to focus less on what immigrants are running to and more on what they are running from. For West African immigrants (not unlike Latin and Central American immigrants) are trying to correct, on an individual basis, the sociopolitical trappings of neo-imperialism. That is to say, these nations are territories that have been politically destabilized, resourcefully depleted, culturally corrupted, and exploited by the United States and its allies. If developing countries had been allowed to self-actualize without foreign interference, fleeing them would be far less necessary. Immigration (legal or otherwise) is a Band-Aid that attempts to heal the deep injury of colonization. And so we move, to where the grass is greener and the water comes out of the faucet hot. It's a kind of fucked-up reparations, except instead of being handed a salve for decades of oppression, non-citizens are doing it for themselves.

When I call my dad to seek approval to reveal our story to the public for the first time, he jovially insists I share: "I didn't come here 'illegally.' What they call illegal, I call *alternative entry*. They stole Africans and illegally moved us to this country. So you could say me coming was me avenging my lineage. I didn't come here 'illegally'—I came by all means necessary, to pay my taxes, get my masters and PhD, and go back home. I tried for ten years to enter the country legally and they denied me based on technicalities. What they couldn't deny was my heart and my ambition."

Back in London, I'm not convinced by the slice of orange with which the French waitress has colonized my Earl Grey tea. I like my tea the way they do it in Ghana, which is the way the British taught them to do it during imperialism, after they stole tea from the Indians. The way I insisted on having it when I went to visit family in Accra two months ago. Black, with milk, and slightly sweetened. Except I want almond milk instead of cow's milk, because my American nutritionist has made it clear that dairy is not good for my system. And I'll have it with honey instead of sugar because sugar is evil and, yes, honey converts to sugar in your digestive system, but it's at least good for your throat. See, I've been having allergic reactions lately for the first time in my life. It's been pointed out to me that when in a new climate, a new city or county or state or sovereignty that doesn't sit well with your body, having raw, locally sourced honey helps your body adjust and rid your system of symptoms that scream "I'm foreign!" I take a sip of tea and sniffle. There isn't enough honey in the world.

IMMIGRATION AND NATURALIZATION SERVICE V. ST. CYR (2001)

Enrico St. Cyr's victory in *Immigration and Naturalization Service v. St. Cyr* represented the first time in over a decade that an immigrant prevailed over the Immigration and Naturalization Service (INS) before the Supreme Court. The case, argued by the director of the ACLU Immigrants' Rights Project, Lucas Guttentag, stood as a powerful preservation of noncitizens' habeas rights.

The INS soon ceased to exist. The post-9/11 creation of the Department of Homeland Security divided its powers between US Citizenship and Immigration Services (USCIS), US Immigration and Customs Enforcement (ICE), and US Customs and Border Protection (CBP). St. Cyr, however, provided critical precedent for later cases, especially *Rasul v. Bush* (2004) and *Boumediene v. Bush* (2008), that addressed and protected habeas rights for Guantánamo Bay detainees.

The Way the Law Leads Us

GEORGE SAUNDERS

Let's say that in 1977, you were me and were caught going 80 mph in a 35 mph zone, in your dad's Chicken Unlimited company van, while cranking the Foghat. Let's just say that. You plead guilty, pay the fine. Twenty years later, in 1997, when you are older and wiser and teaching at Syracuse University and have a beautiful wife and two darling daughters, Congress changes the law: going 45 mph over the speed limit is now a felony. A cop shows up at your door and arrests you and puts you in jail—because, by the way, the new law is going to be applied retroactively.

Should you get to plead your case before a judge?

This (roughly speaking, and with a few adjustments) is what faced thousands of people in 1996.

The adjustments: (1) I was a US citizen; the people in question were lawful permanent residents (LPRs), aka legal immigrants, aka green card holders; (2) for "speeding," substitute: "crimes of various types, sometimes minor, but deemed to be deportable"; and (3) for "puts you in jail," substitute: "deports you immediately without possibility of further appeal."

Before 1996, if you were a legal immigrant to the United States and committed a crime that made you deportable, you were entitled to a hearing before an immigration judge, where you could present an argument for relief from deportation under section 212(c) of the Immigration and Nationality Act. This didn't guarantee you wouldn't get deported; it just guaranteed that you'd have a day in court—a chance to put forth what, in the legal world, are called "individual equities," essentially, the mitigating factors that might argue that the country was better off with you in it than with you kicked out of it.

Then, in 1996, with the passage of the (terrifyingly titled, at least to my ear) Antiterrorism and Effective Death Penalty Act of 1996 (AEDPA), the situation changed: if you were a legal resident and committed any of a broad category of crimes, including very minor ones, you could now be deported immediately (no appeal possible) to your country of origin, regardless of the fact that you might have a house, a family, and/or a business in the United States, and none of those in your country of origin, where you may have lived only as a baby, and whose language you might not even speak.

To further complicate matters, some courts held that the AEDPA could be applied retroactively: that is, it was applicable to people whose crimes predated the passage of the AEDPA and to those who had made plea deals pre-AEDPA on the understanding that they would not be deported, and even to those who had already completed their sentences.

Some of these cases seemed to have come out of bad absurdist novels. Take, for example, Gabriella Dee, a Canadian with a doctorate in biology, teaching college in Pennsylvania under a temporary visa who, while applying for a green card, being a college professor and all, answered forthrightly that, yes, she had, in fact, been arrested before, once, ten years earlier. While she was a student in Canada, her visiting Israeli boyfriend had expressed a desire to see the United States but couldn't get a visa. So, as Anthony Lewis reported in the *New York Times*, "A fellow student . . . drove her across the border; the Israeli walked across without going through immigration, and they picked him up. I.N.S. agents immediately stopped them. A magistrate found Ms. Dee guilty of a misdemeanor and fined her $25."

In 1996, ten years after the event, her green card review triggered . . . a deportation order. Imagine the feeling that evening in the apartment, presumably strewn with half-graded student papers, that Dee shared with her American husband—the shock, the sadness, the isolation, the frightening transition that now suddenly loomed ahead of this person who, outside of what was basically a juvenile prank (and was treated as such by law enforcement), had done everything correctly.

Or consider Jesus Collado. As described by NYU law professor Nancy Morawetz, in the book *Immigration Stories*, Collado came to the United States from the Dominican Republic in 1972, when he was seventeen. He had a girlfriend younger than he (she was sixteen, he was eighteen—something like Rolf and Liesl in *The Sound of Music*, if Rolf and Liesl had lived in New York City) with whom he had a consensual sexual relationship (okay, here we depart somewhat from *The Sound of Music*). Her parents disapproved and brought statutory rape charges against him (departing entirely from *S.O.M.*). His lawyer advised him to plead guilty, in exchange for no jail time, and he did; he was convicted of a misdemeanor, received probation, and went on with his life. He got married (to a different woman, thus avoiding many future tense Thanksgivings with the in-laws), had kids, ran a successful restaurant in New York City. Then in 1997, returning from a trip overseas, he was handcuffed and detained at the airport by immigration inspectors. In this case, the sterile phrase "denial of 212(c) rights" meant this: Collado, who had, since that early (arguably contrived/punitively motivated) run-in with the law, been living an utterly normal, positive, productive life, found himself in detention, awaiting deportation to a country with which he had no real connection and in which he had not lived for twenty-five years. And he had no legal recourse: neither he nor his wife and daughters would be allowed to speak to a judge about what kind of husband, father, or person he was, or what kind of life he had been living over the course of those twenty-five years.

Tens of thousands of people were in similar, potentially life-wrecking, situations.

Danny Kozuba had come to Dallas from Montreal as a small child. He enlisted in the US Army, served in Vietnam, and went on to run a kitchen-installation business. In 1990, he began serving a three-year term in prison for drug possession. He was released in 1993, but after passage of the AEDPA, he suddenly found himself facing deportation, despite his forty-three years of living in the United States. Was that forty-three-year period punctuated by a rough patch? Well, apparently.

Or at least a period during which he had possessed drugs and been caught doing so. Had he served his time? He had. But post-AEDPA, his punishment was to be renewed, and ongoing, and we only need compare his situation with that of a hypothetical native-born American in the same situation to detect the extent of the unfairness. Imagine the many other people of Kozuba's age and generation who had possessed drugs, been caught, done their time, and were now back in the world. What was the difference between Kozuba and this imaginary peer group? He had been born in Canada, about an hour from the border, and brought here as a child. Was this really a meaningful difference, one that justified the catastrophic disruption of his now law-abiding American life?

Junior Earl Pottinger was another child immigrant. He came to the United States from England at the age of three. He had served a brief prison sentence for attempted sale of a controlled substance and then, on his release, as Morawetz describes it, "Pottinger thought he was going home to his mother and brother in New York. Instead, he was whisked away to an INS detention center in New York and then transported to a remote detention facility in Oakdale, Louisiana. When he sought 212(c) relief before an immigration judge his request was denied . . . and he was summarily ordered deported." By the time his ordeal ended, Morawetz writes, Pottinger "had spent far more time in detention fighting for a 212(c) hearing than he had spent in prison serving the sentence for his crime."

Morawetz described one type of legal resident imperiled by the AEDPA: "LPRs who either had long forgotten their brush with the criminal law or assumed that any deportation consequences would be measured against their individual equities."

But the AEDPA also now applied, moving ahead, to all legal immigrants convicted of crimes that made them deportable. So, if you were a lawful permanent resident and committed a crime deemed to be deportable, that was it: you could be taken into custody and deported as soon as possible, and that was that.

To make all of this worse and even more Orwellian, also in 1996, Congress enacted, and President Clinton signed, another draconian immigration law, the Illegal Immigration Reform and Immigrant

Responsibility Act (IIRIRA), which included a provision that, the INS argued, made it impossible for immigrants like Collado and Pottinger to go to federal court to challenge their deportation orders.

So according to the US government, these tens of thousands of people would be exiled from their home and families without even having a day in court.

Tracking the historical progress of this issue toward the Supreme Court (or trying to, if one is as big a legal dunce as I am), one gets a notion of the intense and highly technical type of lawyering done by the ACLU. Following passage of the AEDPA, there were upward of ten thousand deportation orders, and many of those affected had no lawyers, or had lawyers without experience in the federal courts, who were not aware of the larger work being done around this issue, or that the ACLU was involved. Relevant cases, happening all over the United States, had to be identified and tracked without the benefit of databases, websites, social media, this all having occurred in, roughly speaking, a pre-Internet world. "Merely keeping track of cases was a Herculean task," Morawetz wrote.

The particular case that finally brought this discussion to the Supreme Court was *INS v. St. Cyr*. Enrico St. Cyr, an émigré from Haiti, was serving a prison term for a drug charge; he had sold around a hundred dollars' worth of cocaine and been sentenced to three years. He had pled guilty, and the resulting conviction made him deportable. But in the meantime, passage of the AEDPA had made it impossible for him to request that an immigration judge permit him to remain in the United States based on his ties in the US—a common form of relief before the 1996 law. After his release from prison, he was taken into custody by the INS. St. Cyr had no family in Haiti and, to make matters worse, would be jailed upon arrival in Haiti and kept, as Morawetz somewhat understatedly puts it, "in harsh conditions," even though, in the view of the US government, he had served his time.

The effort to push back against the AEDPA and IIRIRA was led by Morawetz and Lucas Guttentag of the Immigrants' Rights Project (IRP) of the ACLU, who ultimately argued the case before the

Supreme Court. The ACLU "placed 212(c) relief in the context of an immigration process which requires two steps before anyone is deported. First, there must be a determination whether a person is deportable. Next there must be a determination whether the person is eligible for and deserving of any relief. Only after these two steps can a person be deported."

On June 25, 2001, the Court ruled in favor of St. Cyr, establishing that immigrants have a right to challenge the legality of their deportation through habeas corpus proceedings (or an adequate substitute procedure). The case "changed the fate of thousands of legal immigrants facing deportation proceedings," according to the *New York Times*. St. Cyr was released in July 2001, having spent six years in custody—three for his crime and another three in INS custody—as he awaited deportation. The government offered no recourse or relief to those who had already been deported under AEDPA, arguing that the St. Cyr ruling did not grant these individuals any right of return. Many of these people remain deported to this day, their lives having been altered forever.

In essence, *INS v. St. Cyr* asked, Does a legal immigrant who has committed a crime for which he or she is deportable have the right to a review by a federal court? The Court answered: Yes. Can that immigrant be deported without the opportunity for a *habeus* review? The Court answered: No. The case, wrote Morawetz, serves as "a sober reminder of how difficult it is to protect immigrants from harsh and illegal deportation laws and litigation that curbs access to the courts." It speaks also to the question of the separation of powers enshrined by the Constitution. That is, can the executive branch (the attorney general, in these cases) simply throw someone out of the country? The law, in other words, serves as an acknowledgment of the possibility that sometimes one part of government gets things wrong, and in such a case, the courts have a legitimate role in setting things right. It asked, implicitly, a critical question about due process (a right that many of us take for granted) that resonates powerfully today: Who exactly is entitled to due process, and why?

* * *

Wait a minute, our alert, perhaps somewhat right-leaning, reader—let's call him "Len"—may ask at this point. This ruling gives a person convicted of a deportable crime the right to appeal before he or she is deported. But do we mean *all* deportable crimes?

Even unto, let's say, murder?

There is a temptation, when describing a law one deems bad, to bring forward only the most egregious examples of its application, that is, to highlight the most sympathetic cases, a temptation to which, I admit, I have succumbed above. But a law must also be evaluated as it applies to everyone to whom it might be applied—even, and especially, to the worst-case scenarios. Here we might ask, experimentally, on Len's behalf: Okay, let's say there's a legal immigrant who has been convicted of a brutal murder. Does even that person have the right to be heard by a judge before being deported?

INS v. St. Cyr concluded: Yes, even this hypothetical immigrant/convicted murderer, having served his time, is entitled to his day in court.

To which Len might ask bluntly: "Why should such a person, who is not even from here, but only here by our generous consent, be allowed to continue to stay here after being convicted of such a terrible crime? Why bother? Why should we have to endure the extra trouble and expense of ensuring that such a person gets a court hearing? Why not just throw him out and be done with it?"

Is this an entirely irrational position? After all, what do we lose by deporting this hypothetical murdering fellow without giving him a chance to appeal? Are we a better country if we get rid of him, no questions asked, or if we give him a chance to appear before a judge?

The law, we feel intuitively, *reflects* our public morality. We are against stealing, and so we make laws that reflect this belief. We observe that smoking is bad for our health, and ban it in public places. But at certain higher altitudes, the law also helps us *construct* that morality, helps us *discover* it. Reading about *INS v. St. Cyr*, I was struck by the way that the law, led by the ACLU's efforts, kept feeling around for—moving in the direction of—what was right, for what most closely tracked the

Constitution's intent. This process seemed to function something like a rigorous mathematical proof, or, God help us, the writing of a novel: hundreds of small decisions and logical/legal crossroads, traversed via rigorous application of objective criteria, gradually leading to a conclusion that might surprise us, or feel counterintuitive, or which we might even find repellent. In this way, the legal process can be seen as a sort of machine that operates via precedent, the function of which is to ask: What do we really believe? Or: What *should* we really believe?—a complex logical operation that is smarter and more compassionate than we naturally/habitually are capable of being; a machine whose innards apply legal and logical rigor in order to produce a result we must honor, because that machine (unlike us) runs entirely on our highest principles. The result, having been so produced, is available for us to ponder. If we study that result carefully, we may gain a better understanding of our democracy and its highest intentions.

So, complex machine, we ask you: What is the benefit of extending the right to appeal to our hypothetical murderer, as you have done via *INS v. St. Cyr*? If you claim that this is a good thing, *why* is it a good thing?

Who has not, in these Trump years, noticed a change in the way we think and talk about immigrants? Seeping out from the far right into the larger culture is the notion that immigrants, even legal immigrants, are somehow irredeemably *less*: deficient, tainted by their origins; surreptitious usurpers, trying to take things away from us "real" Americans; undesirable; suspect; irredeemably and regrettably Other. It's not a new American idea, but it is making an unwelcome comeback. The tacit intent of this type of thinking is to discourage immigrants from coming and, if they have already come, encourage them to leave. And "immigrant," on the street and on the Internet, is often code for "nonwhite person," and "nonwhite person" often incorrectly signifies, to certain people, "immigrant."

The immigrant falls even lower on the scale if he or she is, in fact, here "illegally," that is, here after staying past the expiration of a visa, or without having gone through the legal process of being admitted. But for many, there was (and still is) no viable legal process, no line to join. Legal exclusions have been present for some groups throughout our history. The first immigration law passed by Congress, the Naturalization Act of 1790, provided that only "free white person[s]" could become naturalized citizens. There followed a steady process of racial and ideological exclusions: in 1882, the Chinese, the uneducated, the mentally unwell, those with infectious diseases were excluded; the Japanese were excluded in 1902, anarchists in 1901, the illiterate in 1917. Inspection stations appeared at the southern border in 1891. National quotas were first established in 1921; the Border Patrol came into being in 1924. Even today, a Mexican national who is a close relative of a US citizen can face a wait of more than twenty years for a visa. Filipinos, Chinese, and Indians also face years-long delays, while people of other nationalities face no significant wait time at all. That is to say: the notion of who can come here and how and if they may stay is an evolving notion, one about which, at various times in our history, we have felt in different ways.

We find, in the contemporaneous discussion around the AEDPA and IIRIRA, a pre-echo of our present discourse, in which it seems that many of the parties inveighing against immigrants may possibly never have met one or, to put it more generously, have only a vague, negative, projective notion of who comprises the immigrant population in our country. (Senator Phil Gramm of Texas, in 2000, arguing against a reform bill that would have modified the AEDPA to address some of the excesses discussed in this essay, suggested, in a hyperbolic and, of late, familiar tone, that the reform "welcomed money launderers, tax evaders, perjurers, fugitives from justice, alien smugglers and an assortment of other scoundrels to live among us." He did not include "rapists and murderers," but this was, you know, the year 2000, a simpler, gentler time, God help us.)

At the other end of the spectrum of ways in which one may feel about immigration is a view that sees no distinction, really, between citizen and occupant: if a person is here, she is here, and deserving of all the rights of the citizen. Her presence is what predicates our protection of her rights, rights that are presumed to have existed always and everywhere, in perpetuity. Her presence here, we might even say, gives us an opportunity to avail her of these rights in which we so fervently believe, regardless of how she got here. This view values a person's dignity and physical well-being over her legal status; presumes good intentions on her part; would prefer to err on the side of too much mercy over too little, especially given the inherent vulnerability of the type of person in question.

Why must we resist this view of immigrant-as-less? Because: it contradicts our founding principles. We believe, or claim to believe, that all men are created equal. We do not say "all Americans" or "all native-born Americans" or "all citizens," or "everyone who has filled out the proper paperwork," but "all men," by which we now understand ourselves to mean "all human beings." The due process clause of the Fifth Amendment does not refer to the rights of citizens only, but to the rights of "all persons."

A human being far from home, in a country into which he or she was not born, is still, according to the best version of our founding principles, a human being, and entitled to all of the rights therein. And a human being anywhere who has committed a crime, we believe, should be entitled to her day in court, by which we really, ultimately, mean: we should not cut her off from the human by denying her a chance to explain who she is and how her situation came to pass. It is a beautifully human thing, I think, to build in this fail-safe—an admission of our own limitations, the ritual enactment of a sort of auto-humility that stops us from potentially doing a needlessly harsh thing in error. We have, this way of thinking says, sufficient largesse to show abundant compassion; it does not sully us to do so but ennobles us.

So, when we find a person like our hypothetical immigrant murderer, who has done his time within our country, we have a choice: Do we make an exception to our usual view of personhood, saying, "Sorry, these rights, in which we supposedly so passionately believe, are only for citizens," or do we err on the side of the larger interpretation: these rights are for all human beings, and we will do our best to grant them to as many people as we naturally can, including you, hypothetical murderer, by virtue of the fact that we find you here among us. So much do we believe that all human beings are created equal, with certain inalienable rights, that we delight to offer these rights to any and all we can. Rather than hovering protectively over these rights, doling them out like a miser, we celebrate them and offer them with joy and confidence, as we might a precious gift to a dear friend.

The law, here, seems to say: It is correct and enlightened that our government should make the space for such an appeal to occur—for anyone and everyone. It endorses a view of life that understands the value of particularity and specificity and the wisdom of human interlocution—the notion that the complexities of a truth are best communicated by one human to another theoretically sympathetic human, in person.

Could there be—could there ever be—a case where our convicted murderer, through the courts, overturns his deportation order and is allowed to stay, and we are happy about that? A case where this person's individual equities, weighed against the crime for which he has paid the penalty, argue for relief from deportation? In a sense, having concluded that this person's presence within our border and our understanding of justice confer on him his right to a day in court, we actually don't need to worry about this. That's for the judge to decide. But let's go ahead and worry about it. We might view this consequence of the ruling as an endorsement of a fundamental belief in human malleability—in a human being's potential to change. Might a convicted murderer's individual equities conceivably be such that a judge could be persuaded that the country would in fact be better with him in it than out of it? Well, the ruling seems to imply, it's a big world and anything can happen. Or maybe the ruling is saying: Look, the cost of assuming that such a transformation is possible is less to us than the cost of assuming it is impossible; that is, it is more in keeping with our vision of ourselves to believe in the possibility of such a transformation and to allow a mechanism by which such a transformation might be recognized than to categorically deny it.

* * *

One last thought: To extend this way of thinking beyond the realm of *INS v. St. Cyr*, and for the sake of argument, we might also conclude this: a human being far from home, in a country not his or her own, even he or she who has not followed the local convention on the paperwork, is still a human being and still entitled to the rights therein. That is: anyone within our borders is going to get—we are going to fight to see that he or she gets—treated according to our founding principles: as if he or she, in his or her rights to full personhood, is every bit our equal, regardless of the method by which he or she came to be here.

It seems to me that part of what the ACLU does for us is force us, through rigorous application of the law and a dedicated seeking after its meaning, to understand our principles at their highest level. Having attempted to see what our beliefs really mean, at high altitudes, in rarefied atmospheres, we are more capable of living into them down here on the ground and more likely to protect them with the appropriate energy.

LAWRENCE V. TEXAS (2003)

Lawrence v. Texas struck down a Texas law defining same-sex sexual activity as a crime under state law, simultaneously striking down sodomy laws in twelve other states. The Supreme Court's ruling made same-sex sexual activity legal in every state and territory of the United States.

On September 27, 1998, John Lawrence and Tyron Garner were arrested by Texas police after police entered Lawrence's home, having been called to investigate reports of a "black man going crazy with a gun." (These reports had come from Garner's jealous partner.) The police allegedly found Lawrence and Garner engaged in sexual activity in Lawrence's bedroom and arrested both men.

In *Lawrence*, the Court found that the Texas Penal Code, which criminalized sodomy, violated the due process clause of the Fourteenth Amendment. Justice Anthony Kennedy, writing for the 5–4 majority, overturned the Court's prior ruling in *Bowers v. Hardwick* (1986), which had previously upheld the constitutionality of sodomy laws and had found no basis for the constitutional protection of sexual privacy.

Live from the Bedroom

The Culture War

MARLON JAMES

This is not an essay about lynching. But the curious landmark case of *Lawrence v. Texas* made me think about it all the same. And not just because it was inflamed by two different kinds of panic over a specific fear in the unpoliced white imagination, what writer Greg Tate once called "the black sex machine gone berserk." Quick recap: When Robert Eubanks, a white man of Harris, Texas, called the police on his friend John Geddes Lawrence Jr., a white, gay fifty-five-year-old medical technologist, and mutual friend Tyron Garner (black), it was because he noticed that Lawrence and his on-and-off-again lover had hit it off way too well, and while he went out to get soda, he jealously surmised that they were getting it on. Many white people profess ignorance at how racism actually affects black people yet demonstrate full awareness of how to use it for the most damage. Eubanks called the police, counting on their hair-trigger reaction, yet more likely discounting how bloody these encounters usually play out.

But Eubanks, in an action that would go viral with white women twenty years later, called the police on a black person having too much fun. And like quite a few white men from the good old South, Eubanks knew exactly what to say to get his revenge. He called the police to report not a sex but a gun crime, specifically "a black male going crazy with a gun" at Lawrence's apartment. The recklessness of Eubanks's imagination remains stunning, but the black gun in the white mind has often been inseparable from the black cock. As for hard black cocks, the police claimed to have seen that and more when they stumbled on Lawrence and Garner in flagrante delicto. If nothing else, Eubanks was as excellent a reader of racial assumptions as he was of sexual chemistry. Garner was two things in the Middle American fancy wrapped into one: big black gun as phallic symbol and a big black penis as gun substitute. It's remarkable how a case that would go on to make great strides for sexual orientation started out with white America's warped perceptions about race. This was a case that could have gone to the Supreme Court for very different reasons had the police chosen to act differently—meaning had they assumed that Garner was the kind of threat Eubanks claimed he was. But whatever it was the police saw those two men doing, both were arrested and charged with a misdemeanor under Texas's antisodomy law.

But back to lynching. And with it a side on bestiality. Supreme Court Justice Antonin Scalia, in his dissenting opinion, argued that in the wake of the *Lawrence v. Texas* decision—which invalidated sodomy laws in twelve other states, making same-sex sexual activity legal in every US state and territory state—laws against bigamy, same-sex marriage, adult incest, prostitution, masturbation, adultery, fornication, bestiality, and obscenity would not prove sustainable.

Slippery-slope theory is a common trope of conservative thinkers, as is conflation, but the opinion was nonetheless curious given that in states like Texas, acts of bestiality were actually legal. Texas made it illegal only in 2017 on condition that lines such as "act involving contact between the person's mouth or genitals and the anus or genitals of an animal or fowl" were struck from the law. As for lynching, that became illegal only in 2019. I make this wide digression to point out that whether it was overturning an unjust illegality (consensual sex between men), or outlawing a long-accepted legality (lynching black men and women, sex with a donkey), there's a sense in America that justice too often comes too late.

You don't have to be gay to see the ripple effect of *Lawrence*. For one it overturned *Bowers v. Hardwick* (1986), a Supreme Court decision that even a few members of the Court knew should never have happened: it upheld a Georgia statute that sexual privacy did not deserve constitutional protection. Intimate sexual activity was one of our freedoms after all; at least it was to benefit from due process.

Lawrence v. Texas paved the way for gay marriage and, with it, curiously enough, a wave of gay men who would have disapproved of both Lawrence and Garner.

But the details of the actual case remain fascinating because it shows two clashing visions of America finally going to war, both clutching the Fourteenth Amendment like a Bible: those demanding that freedom for all should mean all, and those demanding that traditional values must mean that what many consider freedom isn't freedom at all but leeway to deviate from morality. There are more things you should know. Antonin Scalia's dissent is fascinating in its frightfulness, especially when you consider that *Lawrence* was not that long ago. He found this judgment in line with the infamous homosexual agenda, an abstract concept that seemed sprung from a fake document, like a Protocols of the Elders of faggotry.

Except in this case Scalia brandished a working definition. He laid it out as "the agenda promoted by some homosexual activists directed at eliminating the moral opprobrium that has traditionally attached to homosexual conduct. The Court has taken sides in the culture war, departing from its role of assuring, as neutral observer, that the democratic rules of engagement are observed." He did not stop there but went on to conclude in a way similar to long-standing opponents of civil rights legislation that this was a turn against the way the American people chose to evolve and that the Court showed it was "impatient of democratic change." This is important because even in the wake of gay marriage, and homosexuals voting for Trump, even world-famous gay stars are still being bashed and beaten, and many other world-famous people have been inching back to that time when they could still get away with being publicly homophobic.

The Court's decision was more in line with a liberal version of where America could possibly go, but I wonder if Scalia's remarks aren't a more accurate capture of where America might still be now. We (meaning us liberals) like to think that progressive legislation eventually produces progressive change of thought, but the Trump years have loudly and violently proven this not to be the case. We also like to ignore that progressive triumphs nearly always come with violent right-wing backlash, scrambling to conclude that the Manson murders, for example, were senseless when they were simply racist. Manson wasn't trying to end the sixties' dream; he was trying to get black people framed for the murder so that it would start "Helter-Skelter," a race war.

Racism and anti-Semitism came unhooded in 2017 despite decades of civil rights. Speaking of civil rights, the Supreme Court rolled back on protections the very same week it approved gay marriage. *Roe v. Wade* is constantly under siege, this time to wither it from the branches, not the root. Bakers are taking to the courts for the right to not bake cakes for same-sex weddings, funeral directors are refusing gay corpses, and for an administration that came in with the help of so many homo-millions, the rollback against protections of LGBQ and, in particular, trans people has been alarming.

I migrated to the United States in fall 2007. Some people flee to, some run from, some do both. I left Jamaica to save my life, but contrary to the connotation immediately raised by coupling "Jamaica" and "gay" in the same sentence, I was only fleeing myself—or, rather, a version of myself intent on killing me. This version of myself couldn't imagine a place where I could hold another man's hand for more than four seconds, could never even imagine admitting to being gay in the first place.

The previous sentence is not true. I imagined it all the time. I lived in the fantasy of it, delaying as long as I could the reality of it never happening. Other times I disconnected from it completely and imagined two other men living out wildly romantic lives, usually two handsome white men, as if my imagination had turned into a drama on the WB network. No gay person running to America fools himself into expecting a country decked out in rainbow colors or that you can't be gay-bashed in New York City. But we run in the hope that we will not be excluded from life, liberty, and the pursuit of happiness because we flex queer. Note that those three words are all abstractions, and gay Jamaicans younger than me are far more interested in pursuing them in their own country. And lawmakers are constantly chafing against *Lawrence v. Texas*, playing with it, trying to corrupt it, and using it as a basis to claim that it restricts the very Fourteenth Amendment that made it possible. Scalia himself asserted that the same rationale that overturned *Bowers v. Hardwick* could be used to send women back in the closet with the coat hanger.

But what drew me to these United States was the idea that simply being myself was protected by law, even if at the time I didn't know what that self was. This is a crucial thing for those of us who never had a chance to grow into ourselves in our home countries. We migrate to America to simply become. And while *Lawrence v. Texas* arrived far too late for far too many, for people like me, it came just in time.

RASUL V. BUSH (2004)

On January 14, 2004, the ACLU joined a coalition of sixteen legal, human rights, and religious organizations to submit an amici curiae brief in support of the petitioners in *Rasul v. Bush*. Shafiq Rasul, along with Asif Iqbal, David Hicks, and several other co-petitioners, was part of the first group of prisoners to be held and interrogated at the Guantánamo Bay detention camp. The question before the Supreme Court was whether Guantánamo detainees had the right to challenge their detention in federal court, or if the US government had the legal ability to hold them indefinitely, without explanation or oversight.

Habeas, Guantánamo, and the Forever War

WILLIAM FINNEGAN

Are we at war? The United States has committed troops to military conflicts in dozens of countries since World War II without a single declaration of war. Not in Korea, not in Vietnam, not in Iraq. The legal basis of these commitments has varied, but the scope of judicial authority has been consistently unclear and never more so than in the "forever war" that we've been fighting, erratically, semi-secretly, since 2001.

After the September 11 terror attacks, the US government at the highest levels was determined to strike back and prevent further attacks. A joint resolution of Congress, passed within days, gave President George W. Bush the authority to use military force against those responsible for the attacks on New York and Washington, DC. This authorization was soon followed by the invasion of Afghanistan as the United States and its allies sought to destroy the al-Qaeda leadership, which included the planners of the 9/11 attacks, and their bellicose hosts, the Taliban regime. This authorization was also used to establish a military prison at Guantánamo Bay Naval Base, an American installation in Cuba, where the first group of prisoners arrived in January 2002.

Guantánamo was chosen carefully, according to John Yoo, then a lawyer in the White House Office of Legal Counsel and a key Bush official in the planning of the war on terror. It was isolated but accessible, and it was not technically on US territory. It might serve as an island outside the law. The administration quietly developed interrogation and detention policies and practices with little apparent regard for US law, human rights law, or the laws of war, including the Geneva

Conventions. The United States wanted actionable intelligence, and by almost any means necessary. Prisoners were subjected to waterboarding and other abuses generally considered to be torture. Some disappeared into CIA-run "black sites"—secret prisons—scattered across the globe. Others were sent to jails in countries such as Egypt and Syria where they could expect to be tortured, and were. Because some detainees have never been officially acknowledged, it is impossible to know precisely how many have been held. Nearly eight hundred have passed through Guantánamo. The 2001 military authorization, which has been cited as the legal basis for operations across the globe, is still in force today, just as Guantánamo continues to house, if that is the right word, prisoners who have never been charged.

American attorneys, concerned about the status of Guantánamo detainees and convened primarily by the Center for Constitutional Rights, were initially unable to contact detainees. Instead, they had to find "next friends"—usually relatives, often parents—of the detainees to bring actions on the detainees' behalf in US courts. One of the first actions to assert the rights of detainees, filed in district court in Washington, DC, in early 2002, was for two British nationals, Shafiq Rasul and Asif Iqbal, and an Australian, David Hicks. All three had been captured in Afghanistan. Indeed, all three had been sold to American special forces, who were paying a bounty, by a coalition of local militias known as the Northern Alliance.

Their complaint, filed by a consortium of American lawyers, challenged their detention, asserted a right to counsel, and sought to end their ongoing interrogation. None of them had been a member of a fighting force, they claimed, and they were thus incorrectly classified as "unlawful enemy combatants"—a poorly defined category, in any case, adopted by the Bush administration. They argued that their detention violated, among other things, Fifth Amendment due process rights. The court had jurisdiction, they said, under the federal habeas corpus statute, which guarantees the right of a prisoner to challenge his or her detention. The government filed a motion to dismiss on the basis that the court lacked jurisdiction.

The district court agreed and dismissed the complaint, giving two main reasons. *Johnson v. Eisentrager*, a 1950 Supreme Court decision, had considered a petition from a group of German intelligence officers who were being held by the US military after having been captured in 1945 in China, where they were still assisting the Japanese puppet government in Nanking although Germany had surrendered. They had been convicted by a US military commission of violating the laws of war, then transferred to an American-run stockade in occupied Germany. The DC Circuit Court of Appeals had ruled in their favor, under the Fifth Amendment's due process clause and the habeas statute. But the Supreme Court had reversed. Justice Robert Jackson, writing for the majority, found that because the petitioners were enemy aliens held outside the United States and already convicted of crimes committed abroad, they did not have the right to a habeas appeal. "Eisentrager controls the outcome in this case," the government argued in *Rasul v. Bush,* and the district court agreed.

But to reach that conclusion, to answer the jurisdictional question, the district court found it had to determine the status of the naval base at Guantánamo. This was not war-torn Europe. Did the United States exercise territorial sovereignty? If so, that would indicate jurisdiction. In the lease agreement with Cuba, the United States can operate the base for as long as it chooses, but Cuba retains "ultimate sovereignty" over the territory. The detainees, like the *Eisentrager* petitioners, were therefore outside US territory, the court reasoned, and had no right to US judicial review. The DC Circuit Court of Appeals agreed. *Eisentrager* had barred the extraterritorial application of the Fifth Amendment's protections to aliens, and that meant Guantánamo. Whether the aliens were enemies or not, the court lacked jurisdiction.

According to their attorneys' brief to the Supreme Court (the Court had granted certiorari), submitted in early 2004, three of the petitioners, Shafiq Rasul, Asif Iqbal, and David Hicks, did "not even know they are the subjects of this litigation." At that point, the three had been in Guantánamo for two years. Rasul and Iqbal later spoke at length about their experience in US custody. Their account is harrowing. First, they barely survived their time after being captured by the Northern Alliance militia. After the US military bought them, American soldiers kicked them, beat them, starved them, shackled them, hooded them, stripped them naked, threatened them with dogs, forced them to stay awake for days, forbade them to speak, forbade them to pray, held guns to their heads, forced them into stress positions past the point of permanent injury, locked them in cages in isolation, and interrogated them for months, until each of them confessed to practically anything they were accused of just to get the torment to stop. Is this you in a photograph at a meeting with Mohammed Atta? Whatever you say. Is this you at a rally with Osama bin Laden? Yes.

In oral argument before the Supreme Court, the solicitor general, Theodore Olson, began his remarks on behalf of the government by declaring, simply, "The United States is at war." This seemed to be the central, definitional issue around which the arguments, the precedents, the soaring points about the rule of law, and the fine points of jurisdiction turned: If the United States was in fact at war, what sort of war was it? Where were its boundaries? Under what rules should it be conducted?

John J. Gibbons, a former federal judge from New Jersey, in oral argument for the petitioners, readily acknowledged that the United States was at war and that a habeas petition filed by a lawful combatant from "the battlefield" or any location near it should be dismissed out of hand. He praised the *Eisentrager* decision, even though *Eisentrager* provided the basis for much of the government's argument in *Rasul*. Gibbons seemed to accept that war by its nature creates a zone in which the country's political and military leadership must operate according to military necessity, untrammeled by the oversight of domestic courts. The Court's concern, expressed in *Eisentrager*, about the war effort being drowned in "enemy litigiousness" if enemy aliens were granted access to federal courts was justified.

But this was Guantánamo. It was eight thousand miles from the Central Asian battlefield, barely a hundred miles from the US mainland. As a practical matter, the war effort would not be impeded by considering the claims of Guantánamo detainees. The United States had been exclusively in control of the enclave for a century. "Cuban law has never had any application inside that base. A stamp with Fidel Castro's picture on it wouldn't get a letter off the base." Gibbons, a soft-spoken jurist who had served in the Navy during World War II, could offer these details with some confidence, having been assigned for a year to an ordnance facility at Guantánamo.

Several points distinguished the *Rasul* petitioners from the German nationals in *Eisentrager*, according to Gibbons and his colleagues. They were not citizens of an enemy nation, but rather of close allies. More important, the *Eisentrager* petitioners had been tried before a properly constituted US military commission in China, where some defendants had been acquitted and others convicted. They had therefore been accorded due process, their status as enemy war criminals established. They were filing habeas petitions, moreover, from a recently conquered corner of Germany, not from a quiet US base in the Caribbean where American law had long applied. The Court's denial of their claim had been on constitutional, jurisdictional, and practical grounds; it did not want to compromise "wartime security" by interfering with the president's authority as commander in chief.

These elements all differed fundamentally from the creation of an offshore prison where detainees could be held indefinitely with no due process—never charged, never tried. Thus, *Eisentrager* was not a guiding precedent. The habeas statute and the Fifth Amendment's due process clause both assured the petitioners access to American courts. The Geneva Conventions, a binding treaty, also argued strongly for them. It was, again, a legal fiction to say that Guantánamo was not under US jurisdiction. Indeed, Justice Ruth Bader Ginsburg expressed impatience with what she called "the metaphysics of ultimate sovereignty."

The Court took all these points and, in June 2004, it reversed the lower courts by a 6–3 majority. Justice John Paul Stevens, writing for the majority, reached back into British common law prior to American independence for examples of the historical reach of habeas corpus beyond national borders. Congress had made explicit in 1842 that federal habeas rights extended to foreign nationals, and the government had conceded in *Rasul* that an American citizen held at Guantánamo would have access to American courts. Justice Anthony Kennedy, writing in concurrence, distinguished the practical considerations in *Eisentrager* from those in *Rasul*—differentiating, in effect, between wars. Whereas in *Eisentrager*, "the existence of jurisdiction would have had a clear harmful effect on the Nation's military affairs," the same could not be said of *Rasul*. Under the habeas statute, which requires only that a court have jurisdiction over a detainee's custodians, the district court clearly had jurisdiction. The Court ordered the district court to consider the merits of the petitioners' claims.

Justice Antonin Scalia, writing in dissent—he was joined by Chief Justice William Rehnquist and Justice Clarence Thomas—offered a sharply different view of the war on terror. The *Rasul* decision was "an irresponsible overturning of settled law in a matter of extreme importance to our forces currently in the field." The "present war" appeared, in Scalia's argument, as existentially dangerous as World War II. This decision would, as the "more circumspect" 1950 Court had foreseen in *Eisentrager*, open our courts to millions of enemy prisoners "abroad." Indeed, the *Rasul* majority had avoided even explaining "*why Eisentrager was wrong*" (emphasis in original). That was presumably because the Court did not consider *Eisenstrager* wrong. Scalia foresaw a future in which Guantánamo prisoners would be able to "forum shop" through all ninety-four federal judicial districts. "For this Court to create such a monstrous scheme in time of war, and in frustration of our military commanders' reliance upon clearly stated prior law, is judicial adventurism of the worst sort."

Rasul v. Bush was a major victory for habeas corpus, which, while being constantly renegotiated, remains a cornerstone of the rule of law. The *Rasul* ruling was statutory, however, not based on the Constitution, and relatively narrow. It ordered judicial review of detentions at Guantánamo regardless of a prisoner's citizenship, but nothing specific beyond that. Congress, the Bush administration, and the lower courts all set to work to weaken, further narrow, or simply, in the case of Congress, cancel the outcome of *Rasul* with new legislation. The most notable short-term effect of *Rasul* was to open Guantánamo to lawyers to meet with their clients.

But the Supreme Court continued to rule in favor of habeas rights. In 2008, it rejected a military commission system established by the Defense Department as illegal under the Uniform Code of Military Justice and the 1949 Geneva Conventions. Then it found the congressional action to suspend habeas rights for Guantánamo detainees unconstitutional under the suspension clause, which states, "The privilege of the writ of habeas corpus shall not be suspended, unless when in cases of rebellion or invasion the public safety may require it." This was the first time the Court had struck down a federal statute using the Suspension Clause, and it went some distance toward defining what kind of war the war on terror is—not, for a start, one that merited the suspension of habeas.

Habeas corpus has been suspended before, of course: by President Abraham Lincoln during the Civil War, without consulting Congress, citing dire military necessity in and around Baltimore (Congress authorized a national suspension two years later); by President Franklin D. Roosevelt, informally but effectively, and selectively, during World War II, citing a wholly imaginary threat to justify the internment of more than 100,000 ethnic Japanese, most of them US citizens. The lasting shame of that internment was invoked in *Rasul* by the filing of an amicus curiae brief under the name of Fred Korematsu, a Japanese American welder who fought his internment up to the Supreme Court, where he lost. (In 1998, Korematsu, vindicated by history, received the Presidential Medal of Freedom, the nation's highest civilian award.)

The Court's 2008 ruling on the suspension clause blocked further congressional interference with the habeas rights of Guantánamo detainees. Still, many basic questions were left unanswered, including the admissibility of evidence in these detention reviews (hearsay was being allowed by the district court) and the reach of the Court's habeas rulings into other notorious corners, beyond Guantánamo, of the military's new prison system—places such as Bagram Air Base in Afghanistan and Abu Ghraib in Iraq. Prisoner arrivals at Guantánamo slowed to a trickle after *Rasul* and then stopped altogether, and releases steadily reduced the facility's population, and yet virtually none of these releases was court ordered and none was to the United States. (Congress forbade release to the United States specifically and repeatedly, even for the most harmless detainees, the most blatant cases of mistaken arrest, and even when the detainees had nowhere else to go.) The political pressure brought by court cases has been a factor in some releases, certainly, but the habeas process has rarely, if ever, been allowed to run its legal course.

Two of the original *Rasul* petitioners—Rasul and Iqbal, the British citizens—were actually released during the Supreme Court's consideration of their case. (The lawyers had added more petitioners, including twelve Kuwaitis and a second Australian.) It seemed that the main crimes the prisoners had been forced to confess to—the meetings in Afghanistan with bin Laden and Mohammed Atta—could not possibly have occurred. MI5, the British intelligence service, which had been collaborating in the interrogations, simply looked at employment, police, and passport records that showed the detainees, just as they had claimed, working and going to college in the British West Midlands during the period in question. David Hicks, the original Australian petitioner, was later convicted by a military commission of having fought with the Taliban, served a short sentence, and returned to Australia in 2007.

But the military commissions have barely functioned, and forty prisoners remain in Guantánamo today, the majority still uncharged. Five have been cleared for release but remain locked up. President Barack Obama, who vowed to close the prison, failed. His administration did try to move the case of Khalid Sheikh Mohammed, the alleged mastermind of the 9/11 attacks, who was reportedly waterboarded 183 times, from Guantánamo into the civilian court system, scheduling him and four alleged co-conspirators for trial in the Southern District of New York in 2011. The objections of Congress and local authorities in New York to a criminal trial were so fierce and frightened, however, that the administration was forced to fall back. The status of most of the remaining Guantánamo prisoners is a hapless, law-free muddle—too difficult to try, too dangerous to release. Their plight shows, among other things, the moral jeopardy, the legal rot, that grows when we remain too long on an ill-defined war footing.

KITZMILLER V. DOVER AREA SCHOOL DISTRICT (2005)

In *Edwards v. Aguillard* (1987), the Supreme Court ruled that a Louisiana law requiring that creationism be taught whenever evolutionary science was taught violated the establishment clause of the First Amendment since it advanced a particular religious belief. *Kitzmiller v. Dover Area School District* extended that reasoning to school district policies requiring the teaching of "intelligent design" as part of the biology course curriculum. District judge John E. Jones III found that intelligent design is not science and "cannot uncouple itself from its creationist, and thus religious, antecedents." Therefore, he reasoned, a policy requiring the teaching of intelligent design would, like a policy mandating the teaching of creationism, advance a particular religious belief in direct violation of the Constitution.

Who's Your Villain?

ANTHONY DOERR

Someone Burns the Monkey Mural

In 1998, in a leafy corner of eastern Pennsylvania, a graduating senior at Dover Senior High School paints a sixteen-by-four-foot mural of hominids jogging left to right across a treeless landscape. The primate farthest to the left scampers like an ape, the ones to his right become successively less apelike, and the one farthest to the right runs like a human.

Monkey becomes man. You get it.

For four years the painting sits in room 217, propped in a chalkboard tray, apparently gnawing away at the sensibilities of certain folks, until one weekend in 2002, just before the school year begins, when the grounds supervisor orders his crew to burn it.

Soon afterward, science teachers at Dover High start hearing whispers that the school board is filling with people with an aversion to Darwin's theory of evolution. One board member, a former corrections officer named Bill Buckingham, even carries a photo of the now-incinerated mural in his wallet, telling people that he "gleefully watched it burn."

In 2003, Buckingham becomes chair of the school board's curriculum committee, which means he's in charge of evaluating new textbooks. When he receives a routine request from Dover's ninth-grade teachers for a new edition of *Biology*, perhaps the most widely used biology textbook in the United States at that time, Buckingham leafs through a copy and finds it "laced with Darwinism," as though the book were a pile of marijuana sprinkled with PCP.

"It wasn't on every page of the book," he says, "but, like, every couple of chapters, there was Darwin in your face again."

In search of an alternative, Buckingham contacts the Thomas More Law Center, a Christian nonprofit in Michigan, whose motto is "The Sword and Shield for People of Faith" and whose website header features a cross, a sword, an angry bald eagle, and a misty painting of George Washington praying in the snow. One of its cofounders is the founder of Domino's Pizza. The Thomas More Center tells Buckingham about a 1993 textbook, *Of Pandas and People*. The book displays a bamboo-holding panda on the cover, starts with a quote from Carl Sagan, includes some cool-looking diagrams, and seems legit—until you actually read some of it.

Pandas, for example, ignores the fact that species go extinct (they do), implies our planet could be thousands of years old (it's 4.543 billion years old), claims that the fossil record doesn't include transitional fossils such as limbed fish (wrong), says big dogs can't breed with little dogs (they can and do), argues that giraffe necks are long because their legs are long (huh?), and declares that the different forms of life on Earth spontaneously blooped into existence "with their distinctive features already intact—fish with fins and scales, birds with feathers, beaks, and wings, etc."

How did so many different-looking creatures show up here fully formed? Easy: they were designed by "an intelligent agent."

Oh. This Is About God?

Yep. And nope. Look, the diversity of life on Earth is mind shattering, and I can absolutely understand how someone might disbelieve the fact that, over incomprehensible eons, platypuses, woodpeckers, microscopic tardigrades, pterodactyls, and Kerry Washington all evolved from primordial microbes you can't see with the naked eye. That sounds crazy. Humans share 60 percent of our genetic material with bananas? Crazy 2.0.

I also get how the discoveries of science—especially the ones that seem to continually prove our insignificance—can scare people. It was scary when we figured out that the Earth wasn't the center of the solar system, and it was even scarier when we figured out that there were 2 trillion galaxies in the universe. What about the soul? What about transcendence? As Pascal put it three and a half centuries ago, "When I consider the short duration of my life, swallowed up in an eternity before and after, the little space I fill engulfed in the infinite immensity of spaces whereof I know nothing, and which know nothing of me, I am terrified."

And I also understand that the inner workings of life are so cool and so complicated that some folks feel they must conclude we were designed by an almighty Designer. Think, for example, of the astonishing number of things that have to go right so you can read this sentence: your irises have to correctly dilate your pupils, your retina has to convert the light bouncing into your eye into electrical impulses, your optical nerves have to relay them to your brain at the speed of light, and your brain, floating in total darkness, has to create meaning from black hieroglyphs on a white background. It's astonishing!

But the existence of complex life-forms does not prove that God schemed up every creature on the planet and set them here fully formed like a child placing LEGO figures on a table. If an intelligent agent designed all the creatures on Earth, why have 99.9 percent of the species that have ever lived gone extinct? That doesn't sound very intelligent. If we humans were designed, why would we get hiccups and hernias? Why do we grow wisdom teeth and appendixes and male nipples? Why do we have big chunks of fish DNA in our genome?

Gods might be everywhere, gods might have ignited the first spark of life on our planet, gods might be floating above our heads judging us this very second, but the only scientifically viable explanation for the origin of species is evolution.

The Parents Lawyer Up

Of Pandas and People doesn't specify whether its "intelligent agent" is the Abrahamic God, E. T., or the rainbow serpent of the Australian aborigines, but Bill Buckingham, curriculum chair on the Dover school board, is pretty sure he knows who it is. As he puts it, "Two thousand years ago someone died on a cross. Can't someone take a stand for him?"

In fall 2004, when Buckingham fails to convince the school superintendent to purchase 220 copies of *Of Pandas and People*, he gets in front of his church and raises enough money to buy sixty, which are then donated anonymously to Dover High. And on October 18, the school board votes 6–3 to approve Buckingham's motion that before any science teacher in the district teaches evolution, she'll have to read a four-paragraph statement explaining that the concept of intelligent design is a viable alternative to Darwin's theory of natural selection. She'll also have to announce that copies of *Pandas* are freely available to any kids who want to check them out.

Dover High's science teachers refuse to read the statement, so the superintendent and his assistant read it instead. Freaked-out parents, including a mother of two named Tammy Kitzmiller, get in touch with the ACLU, and in December Kitzmiller and ten other Dover High parents (many of them devout Christians) file suit in the Middle District of Pennsylvania, alleging that the school board is violating their constitutional rights by thrusting religion into their kids' science class.

Judge Jones Goes to School

Ten months later, *Kitzmiller v. Dover Area School District* goes to trial in Harrisburg. The parents are represented by attorneys from the ACLU, Americans United for Separation of Church and State, and Pepper Hamilton, a Philadelphia law firm. The school board is represented by the Thomas More Law Center. The presiding judge is a salt-and-pepper-haired fifty-year-old named John E. Jones III, a Republican recommended by Senator Rick Santorum and appointed in 2002 by President George W. Bush.

Because it is a civil suit, no jury is present; instead the jury box bustles with reporters. For most of the next forty days, something extraordinary happens: a white-and-blue-paneled courtroom in rural Pennsylvania becomes a classroom in which, interspersed with local witnesses, a series of paleontologists, molecular biologists, geneticists, and theologians educate Judge Jones and the reporters in attendance about the ever-growing avalanche of evidence supporting Darwin's theory of evolution.

Robert Pennock, a biologist and philosopher at Michigan State University, explains how experiments with fast-replicating organisms like *E. coli* allow biologists to see natural selection happen in real time. Berkeley paleontologist Kevin Padian, looking as if he has just brushed dinosaur dust off his khakis, shows the court slides of feathered dinosaurs and hippo-like whales, transitional fossils that *Of Pandas and People* claims do not exist. Brian Alters, a science education professor from McGill University, calmly explains that "claims of supernatural intervention in the origin of life or of species are not science because they are not testable" and Ken Miller, coauthor of the *Biology* textbook that the Dover teachers requested, puts it like this:

> One might say, for example, that the reason the Boston Red Sox were able to come back from three games down against the New York Yankees was because God was tired of George Steinbrenner and wanted to see the Red Sox win. In my part of the country, you'd be surprised how many people think that's a perfectly reasonable explanation for what happened last year. And you know what, it might be true, but it certainly is not science, it's not scientific, and it's certainly not something we can test.

John Haught, a theologian from Georgetown University, makes a similar argument:

> Suppose a teapot is boiling on your stove and someone comes into the room and says, explain to me why that's boiling. Well, one explanation would be it's boiling because the water molecules are moving around excitedly and the liquid state is being transformed into gas. But at the same time you could just as easily have answered that question by saying, it's boiling because my wife turned the gas on. Or you could also answer that same question by saying it's boiling because I want tea. All three answers are right, but they don't conflict with each other because they're working at different levels. Science works at one level of investigation, religion at another. . . . You can have a plurality of levels of explanation.

When it comes to the defense's turn, they don't have to disprove evolution; all they really have to do is prove that intelligent design is good science. But because it's not possible to use the natural to prove the existence of the supernatural, they can't do that, so they mostly resort to attacking the credibility of their opponents.

Forty days after the trial begins, it ends. Judge Jones produces an unequivocal 139-page opinion, ruling that intelligent design is simply a rebranding of biblical creationism and that to teach it in a public school science classroom is unconstitutional because it violates the separation of church and state.

"The citizens of the Dover area," he writes, "were poorly served by the members of the Board who voted for the ID [Intelligent Design] Policy. It is ironic that several of these individuals, who so staunchly and proudly touted their religious convictions in public, would time and again lie to cover their tracks and disguise the real purpose behind the ID Policy."

In the next school board election, all eight candidates who run opposing the addition of intelligent design to the science curriculum win.

If Only This Were the End

If this were the end, you and I could make a feel-good movie about all this, at the end of which the school board fundamentalists would shuffle off-screen, Judge Jones would fly-fish a pristine stream, the Dover High parents would hold a big racially inclusive backyard jamboree, and the ninth graders would grow up to save an endangered salamander, eradicate malaria, and discover a new solar system. In the final frames, a golden, reasonable light would cascade across the Republic, and our audience could head home thinking: *Gosh, remember that battle we had with ignorance and denialism back in 2005? Sure glad that's behind us.*

So, Um, Not the End?

In early 2018, a survey conducted by a number of Holocaust education nonprofits found that two-thirds of American millennials could not say what Auschwitz is. A couple of months later, the White House declared that American poverty "was largely over"—even as millions of Americans struggled to afford housing and health care. A few months after that, 53 percent of Americans said they believe—wrongly—that the flu shot could give them the flu.

A poll conducted at the end of 2018 by NBC and the *Wall Street Journal* found that only 15 percent of Americans who identified as Republican believe climate change is "serious" and "requires immediate action." (In 2007, that percentage was 16 percent.) Propagandists around the world continue to try to convince parents that it is dangerous to give their kids the measles vaccine, and almost four in ten American adults continue to believe that God created humans in their current form within the last ten thousand years.

Ironically, when a victory against denialism like *Kitzmiller v. Dover* occurs, it tends to feed a narrative denialists can use to fuel more denialism. See how they silence us? they say. We are the underdogs; we see the truth; it's all a conspiracy. "Central to denialism," writes the British sociologist Keith Kahn-Harris, "is an argument that 'the truth' has been suppressed by its enemies. To continue to exist is a heroic act, a victory for the forces of truth."

What seems almost quaint now, fourteen years after *Kitzmiller*, is that the school board and the Thomas More Law Center tried so hard to argue that intelligent design was "good science education, good liberal education." Like the authors of *Of Pandas and People*, they cloaked a religious agenda in the language of pseudoscience with the hope it would be accepted as mainstream.

Nowadays people don't bother to try as hard to be accepted as mainstream, because nowadays the mainstream has frayed into a thousand separate streams. Nowadays it's easier to manufacture whatever realities we please. "Just remember," the president of the United States told a group of veterans in July 2018, "that what you're seeing and what you're reading is not happening." And so poverty becomes a problem of the past, one-hundred-year storms become acts of God, climate change becomes a hoax, desperate migrants become dangerous invaders, and scientific consensus becomes a conspiracy.

Where to Go from Here?

Hey, we all refuse to believe things right in front of our eyes, particularly when the prospect of accepting those truths scares us. We are all denialists to some degree. I, for example, continue to believe, despite all evidence to the contrary, that Airborne effervescent drinks will keep me from getting colds, even though study after study has shown that the tablets do absolutely nothing more than give you a freakishly high dose of Vitamin C. I continue to believe that I will not become a corpse (corpses are what happen to other people), and I continue to believe that I care about climate change, even though I continue to drive a car, fly on airplanes, turn on heaters and air conditioners, use plastic every day, and participate in a system that is weaponizing our planet against my kids. And I continue to believe at least a thousand other things that my grandkids will likely find ludicrous. ("Grandpop thought his family photos would be preserved if he uploaded them to the 'cloud'!" "Grandpop used the word *America*!" "Grandpop thought aliens weren't real!")

I think we should all ask ourselves: Who's your villain? Is it the CEO of Monsanto? Rachel Maddow? Mitch McConnell? Vladimir Putin? The neo-Nazi in the newspaper, the immigrant down the street?

Remember Bill Buckingham, chair of the curriculum committee on the Dover school board? When I started this essay, Buckingham was my villain.

Then I started trying harder. Buckingham grew up seven miles from Dover in York, Pennsylvania. He joined the Marine Corps as a young man and returned home in 1969—a year of intense racial violence in York—to become a police officer. He went on to become a narcotics detective, during which time, according to the British journalist Matthew Chapman, he was shot at "and peppered once with pellets." When the strain of that job became too much, he became a supervisor at the York County Prison.

One day when Buckingham was in his thirties, he confronted two prisoners for passing a written note back and forth. The encounter became physical, and in the process of picking up one of the men and hauling him into a holding cell, Buckingham severely damaged his back. Over the coming months, he would undergo six spine surgeries. After the sixth, according to Chapman, Buckingham said, "When I woke up in the recovery room and they said, 'rate your pain from one to ten,' I begged them to kill me. . . . I told my wife, 'If I ever talk about back surgery again, you remind me of this, 'cause I'll die first.'"

During Buckingham's convalescence, no one from the Catholic church where he was a eucharistic minister visited him. But a pastor from Harmony Grove Community Church did; they struck up a friendship, and soon Buckingham was born again. Still, back pain hounded him. He started taking OxyContin in 1998 and became addicted. "I'd go out in a snowstorm with my pants and no shirt on and just breathe in cold air because I would get so hot," he said. "I was high all the time." Around this time he lost his dog, several relatives, and his parents.

Did Bill Buckingham truly believe that intelligent design was the theory that best explained the stupendous diversity of life on Earth? By 2005, he had been through addiction treatment twice, and it wasn't clear he even understood the debate. On the stand, he defined intelligent design as "a lot of scientists believe that back through time something, molecules, amoeba, whatever, evolved into the complexities of life we have now." That's a halfway decent definition of evolution, not intelligent design.

I think that, like all other humans, what Bill Buckingham really craved was community. As a Marine, detective, and corrections officer, he had served on intensely bonded teams of people, and when he became disabled and could no longer work, what did he have left to give his life meaning and purpose? His church. When he felt that one of his community's central beliefs was being threatened, in a public institution right down the street, Buckingham stepped up to defend it. Isn't that a value pretty much every person involved in *Kitzmiller*—and every person reading this book—can relate to?

On day sixteen of the trial, when Buckingham took the stand, a lawyer for the plaintiffs asked him to recount an interview he once gave to a Fox affiliate in which he said "creationism" when he meant to say "intelligent design":

BUCKINGHAM: And what happened was when I was walking from my car to the building, here's this lady and here's a cameraman, and I had on my mind all the newspaper articles saying we were talking about creationism, and I had it in my mind to make sure, make double sure nobody talks about creationism, we're talking intelligent design. I had it on my mind, I was like a deer in the headlights of a car, and I misspoke. Pure and simple, I made a human mistake.

Q: Freudian slip, right, Mr. Buckingham?

BUCKINGHAM: I won't say a Freudian slip. I'll say I made a human mistake.

Buckingham's behavior on the Dover school board was dogmatic and dangerous, but it wasn't impossible to understand. Before he was entry #43 in the *Encyclopedia of American Loon*s, before he was an addict or a fundamentalist or a creationist or a villain, he was a human, *Homo sapiens*, just like the rest of us, each of us 99.9 percent identical in genetic makeup to every other, each of us related to every other living thing on Earth by a trillion ancient and deeply beautiful threads.

The person you think you will never understand in a million years? The villain in the dark room? For every one thousand "letters" that make up one of your DNA sequences, he has 999 that are the exact same. Evolution has given us all the same tools; we all live in the same matrix of memory, fear, and perception; we all yearn to belong; we all use story and ritual to bind the world with meaning. And before each of us goes extinct, it would serve us all well to remember that.

SCHROER V. BILLINGTON (2008)

In 2004, the Library of Congress rescinded Diane Schroer's job offer on learning that she was in the process of transitioning from male to female. In *Schroer v. Billington*, the ACLU, acting as Schroer's counsel, urged the court to find that the library's actions violated Title VII, which prohibits employment discrimination on the basis of sex. Despite multiple appellate courts' prior refusals to find statutory protection for trans employees, the Court agreed with the ACLU, holding that the library's actions amounted to impermissible sex stereotyping, as well as a violation of the most literal reading of the text of Title VII. Schroer was awarded the maximum damages allowed, marking a significant personal victory and a deeper societal understanding of what it means to be protected from discrimination on the basis of sex.

You've Given Me a Lot to Think About

CHARLIE JANE ANDERS

Five days before Christmas 2004, Diane Schroer went to the Library of Congress to talk to her new boss. I picture it being one of those ugly DC winters, where the cold air from the Potomac stings your cheeks and gets inside your winter clothes. Schroer must have been doubly uncomfortable, because she was wearing men's clothing that no longer felt right. A twenty-five-year decorated veteran, Schroer had just been hired to work at the Congressional Research Service, and she was here to come out as a transgender woman.

Schroer was already midtransition but hadn't yet legally changed her name or gender marker, which is why she'd interviewed for the job under her assigned-at-birth name. And she already had facial feminization surgery scheduled before the job was supposed to begin. She explained all of this to the CRS's Charlotte Preece, who took in all this information and then just said, "You've given me a lot to think about."

Preece immediately set about the process of pulling the plug on Schroer's job offer, on the (probably bogus) theory that Schroer would need a whole new security clearance as "Diane" rather than keeping the security clearance she'd already obtained under her old name. Preece also felt that Schroer would be distracted by transitioning, plus both Schroer's old military contacts and Congress might not take her seriously as a transwoman.

Preece told Schroer, "You are putting me and CRS in an awkward position."

With the help of the ACLU, Schroer sued the CRS for job discrimination—and won, helping to reinforce that transpeople are protected under Title VII's prohibitions on sex discrimination. This was a big deal, because some other high-profile cases (like *Ulane v. Eastern Airlines*, 1984) had gone the opposite way, with judges insisting that Title VII applied only to people being discriminated against for their assigned-at-birth gender.

In *Schroer v. Billington*, Judge James Robertson dismissed all of the security concerns and other issues as "pretextual." And he held that discrimination against transpeople was "sex stereotyping," similar to the famous case of *Price Waterhouse v. Hopkins* (1989), where a female employee was discriminated against for being insufficiently feminine. He also held that discriminating against someone because that person is transitioning from one sex to another is necessarily sex discrimination prohibited by Title VII. (Robertson compares this situation to a recent convert from Christianity to Judaism facing religious discrimination.)

A few years after *Schroer*, in 2011, the ACLU won another major victory for transpeople, striking down a Wisconsin law, the Inmate Sex Change Prevention Act, which prohibited the use of any state funds to treat transprisoners with hormones or surgery. Wisconsin argued that because prisons were providing antidepressants and counseling to transprisoners, the law should stand. But an appeals court ruled that this would be similar to giving painkillers and therapy to cancer patients and calling it a day.

When I started to transition, I knew the law wasn't on my side. California hadn't yet passed a law protecting transpeople from discrimination, and the courts were spitting out rulings like *Ulane v. Eastern Airlines* all the time. If I wanted to rent an apartment, get a job, or even just walk on the street in peace, I had to depend on the enlightened goodwill of others. Even now, trans and nonbinary people (especially people of color) have much higher rates of unemployment and homelessness and have much worse access to health care and other services.

I was turned down for a couple of jobs explicitly for being trans. (In both cases, they had told me over the phone that I had the job, and then they met me in person, and suddenly I had given them a lot to think about.) I was turned down for health insurance too because being trans was a "preexisting condition."

So victories like *Schroer* matter a lot. It matters that employers and prisons will think twice before discriminating against transpeople—but also the reasons for these rulings matter. Judge Robertson's ruling in *Schroer* calls out other judges who had ruled that Title VII couldn't include transpeople for having too narrow a view of the statute's intent (quoting, of all people, Antonin Scalia, as propounding an expansive view of sex discrimination).

Back in the day, the ACLU was fighting just for people to appear in public in clothes that were at odds with their assigned gender—because even having a gender-nonconforming appearance was often illegal, under local "cross-dressing" ordinances. And according to ACLU attorney Chase Strangio, these cases were usually fought on the grounds of "free speech" and "due process" rather than sex discrimination.

For example, in 1985, the ACLU of Hawaii intervened on behalf of a group of LGBTQAI+ people who wanted to hold a Miss Gay Molokai pageant featuring contestants in drag. Some local churches objected, and Maui County mayor Hannibal Tavares decided to ban the pageant, calling it "unwholesome and inappropriate." But the ACLU fought Tavares in court and won. (The ACLU attorney in this case, Dan Foley, later won same-sex marriage rights in Hawaii and went on to become a judge.)

I can't imagine living in a world where I could be arrested just for being in a dress despite the label a doctor slapped on me when I was born. Or when a harmless drag show could be outlawed. (In the Miss Gay Molokai case, people expressed a concern that the mere existence of a drag performance on the island "might spread AIDS.")

But I also can't believe that in my lifetime, there was a moment when my identity as a transwoman could only have been defended as a free speech issue—as if I'm making some kind of a point or trying to express something. It's not enough for me to exist; I have to be saying something. And if my gender presentation is a form of speech, then I'm clearly giving people a lot to think about just by occupying physical space.

In the 1990s and early 2000s, the ACLU started taking on more cases involving people being disciplined at work for "being gender-nonconforming," says Strangio, plus more cases about student rights and employment discrimination. And the ACLU increased its already strong focus on the rights of transprisoners. But it wasn't until the past several years that the ACLU has been pursuing more sex discrimination cases involving trans-plaintiffs.

And now that the federal government is trying to erase transpeople in as many ways as possible—making it easier to deny us health care, keeping us from serving in the military, allowing discrimination based on religion, and even working to define gender as based on "biological sex"—these fights are even more important than before. And that's why I'm proud to be a supporter of the ACLU.

I'm not here to give you a lot to think about. My body is not a statement, or an inconvenience, or a threat to anyone's security. My gender isn't a mistake, or a disruption, or a rebellion against biology, and I don't need anybody's tolerance for my self-expression. Put simply, this is about bodies and personhood and transpeople's right to live our lives. When some bodies are illegal, when people are forced to choose either having basic rights or being their authentic selves, then everybody is diminished.

Trans and nonbinary people have only recently been recognized as having basic rights, and we'll have to fight to keep them. But when those battles come, at least we'll be standing on high ground thanks to the valiance and dedication of those who came before us.

ADOPTIVE COUPLE V. BABY GIRL (2013)

In the long history of the United States, there have been few victories for Native tribes. The US genocidal policy transitioned into less obvious means of ethnic cleansing, such as child theft, erasure of Native identity, and physical disruption of tribal communities. The Indian Child Welfare Act (1978) arose as a fitful response to this abuse. Congress heard reams of testimony on how the systematic kidnapping of Indian children caused severe emotional and mental trauma in those taken, and literally stole the future of tribal communities. The ICWA was passed as a direct attempt to end this epidemic of child theft.

While the ICWA was a victory for Native families, the case of *Adoptive Couple v. Baby Girl* illustrates how courts can undermine even social or legislative successes. The struggle continues to erect legal and regulatory safeguards for Native sovereignty. The ACLU stands with tribal authorities to contest the abuse and exploitation of Native persons.

Relative Sovereignty

A Brief History of Indigenous Family Separation in the United States

BRENDA J. CHILD

My son Thomas reported that you peoples tortured him like slave and went without eat for three days, punishment at hard labor just like he was in a penitentiary.

—Letter from the Omaha Agency to the Flandreau Indian School, 1917

She hasn't been home for 3 years and I am real anxious to have her here while we make maple sugar.

—Letter from the Leech Lake Reservation, Cass Lake, Minnesota, 1924

This makes my third letter to you in regard of my daughter Margaret. If you would only know how I feel longing to see her. Please take my word send her home to me for a few weeks you know it won't be long school start just to see her before she goes to school again you know she will be gone good four years.

—Letter from the Lac Courte Oreilles Reservation, Hayward, Wisconsin, 1925

It seems it would be much easier to get her out of prison than out of your school.

—Letter from the Red Lake Reservation, Redby, Minnesota, 1938

Hopefully, these regulations keep other Indian children, families and tribes from suffering the heartbreak that we experienced over the last 5 ½ years.

—Remarks of Dusten Brown, father in the case *Adoptive Couple v. Baby Girl*

Family Separation in US History

Four of the quotes are from letters written by American Indian parents in the Midwest whose children were forced to attend government boarding schools in the early twentieth century and illustrate the immense pain inherent in policies of family separation, which, according to the professed logics of American settler colonialism, was rationalized by American politicians and policymakers as the only way for American Indians to progress from *paganism* to *civilization*. For the children sent away, boarding school was not always a path to success, advancement, or steady employment. The metaphor American Indians—both parents and children—often used regarding the boarding school experience was that of incarceration.

Like other chapters of American Indian history, boarding school history is also a narrative about American settler-colonial desire for control over indigenous land and resources. Boarding schools were part of a plan to support the allotment of Indian reservations. Once they had been dispossessed of their lands, Indian people would need an education suitable to enter American society as lower-class workers. Reformers and politicians viewed the Indian community as obsolete, as one boarding school administrator commented in 1896: "The school is the only place for the Indian child to learn. He learns nothing of value at home; nobody there is competent to teach. He learns nothing from his neighbors; nobody with whom he associates does anything better than he finds in his own home." And so family separation became the means to compel Indigenous people to adopt values of individualism and become "US citizens." From Maine to California, it was a devastating assault on Indigenous families.

Adoptive Couple v. Baby Girl

The final quotation at the start of the essay is not from a letter but rather from a father involved in a US Supreme Court case. The speaker is Dusten Brown, a Cherokee citizen and the biological father in one of the most stunning cases of child removal in recent times, *Adoptive Couple v. Baby Girl* (2013). The case gained widespread media attention and went all the way to the Supreme Court, and in that sense it is remarkable, but there is a chilling ordinariness in the way it replicates patterns of Indian child removals throughout American history. A dual narrative about the powerful exploiting the powerless, first and foremost in the way it illustrates the tyrannical authority of the American government over the sovereignty of Indian nations, but also in the way in which it highlights adult authority in the face of children's vulnerability. Though it may appear to be less harsh and coercive than nineteenth-century policies, American settler colonialism continues to present itself in cases like this one.

The Indian Child Welfare Act

The boarding school period and plunder of reservation land ended in the late 1930s under the Roosevelt administration. Indigenous studies scholars and social workers refer to the 1940s as the beginning of the "adoption era" for American Indian children. Reservation hardships, primarily due to dispossession and the destruction of Indigenous economies, and urban poverty for those American Indians who had moved or been "relocated" to cities following World War II had placed a large burden on families. The largely European American employees of social service agencies sought solutions to complex problems, including mental illness, alcoholism, and family violence, by removing children not only from the troubled parents but from the Indian community itself—permanently. For one reservation in Minnesota, it has been estimated that 25 percent of White Earth children left the reservation for foster and adoptive homes in the postwar years. At the height of the crisis in Minnesota, the "ratio of Indian to non-Indian children in placement was five to one," while in Wisconsin, "Indian children were placed in either foster care or adoptive homes at a rate of 15 to 17 times higher than other children." Alarmingly high rates of child removal existed in South Dakota and other states with significant Indian populations as well.

In one extraordinarily successful political movement, women active in the urban community of Minneapolis–St. Paul paved the way for groundbreaking legislation in the continuing struggle against family separation in the form of the Indian Child Welfare Act (ICWA) of 1978. They systematically gathered testimony used to develop the legislation, though Senator James Abourezk of South Dakota introduced the act to the Senate Committee on Indian Affairs and is often given credit for the bill. The legislation was groundbreaking in the history of US and Indian relations. It gave some restitution to a troubled history of child removal and separation that Indians charged had been taking place for more than a century.

Rose Robinson was working on the Leech Lake Reservation at the time of the passage of the ICWA. She reminds people that it was an "unfunded mandate" that left administrators with few means to achieve its goals. She went to local counties in Minnesota to request financial support and entered into negotiations with the state to meet the requirements of the new law. With a growing résumé of child welfare experience, Robinson became director of a reservation-based child welfare program but acknowledged that the work of a child welfare agency is hard. Still, Robinson regards her long career in child welfare as "my life's work," and she passes on the skills to stand up against the state and county bureaucracies, in a configuration where "the system works against the tribes":

> We had a staff meeting today and I said, "You're all doing a great job. This is what we're here for. This is the tribe taking over this work. It's not the county saying to the community you've got to do it this way. It's the tribe. We're involved. It's about self-determination."

The ICWA recognized Indian political sovereignty in the self-determination era and protected the interests of Indian families and tribal nations "to establish standards for placement of Indian children in foster or adoptive homes, to prevent the break-up of Indian families," while promoting tribal jurisdiction over child custody proceedings. For the first time since the boarding school era and in a turning point for US-Indian relations, tribes regained sovereignty over their own families and children.

This federal law, which gives preference to American Indian families in foster care and adoption proceedings, had a profoundly stabilizing effect on Indian families. Rather than having children lost to the foster care system or being adopted out of the community, with the attendant loss of culture that entailed, children would be placed within the extended family or community. Foster care and adoption, with tribes in control, would allow Indian children to maintain their identity, as well as their religious practices and social life. Leaders and legal activists from tribal nations regard ICWA as one of the most significant pieces of legislation to come out of the self-determination era. In a unified message to the Supreme Court, 333 Indian tribes joined the coalition and filed amicus briefs in support of Dusten Brown, the Cherokee father who faced losing his daughter in *Adoptive Couple v. Baby Girl.*

Even with the legal support of ICWA for over forty years, American Indian tribal nations and their citizens still face struggles for authority over their own children, and the devastation wrought by policies of family separation has not abated. Local and state courts have at times disregarded the terms of the Indian Child Welfare Act, whether through ignorance of the federal law or in an effort to assert their own power and authority. An important case about modern child removal eventually landed at the US Supreme Court with *Adoptive Couple v. Baby Girl.*

To Prevent the Break-up of Indian Families

It would be difficult to argue that the plight of unwed fathers in Indian Country is generally a burning social issue for most Americans, and yet, in 2013, an ordinary case involving a Cherokee father became the source of tremendous public and media attention. Like most other stories involving young couples, babies, and adoption, there is a certain amount of heartbreak and anguish in the case. Dusten Brown, a citizen of the Cherokee Nation of Oklahoma and a soldier in the

US Army, was a few days away from being deployed to Iraq when he was informed that his infant daughter, Veronica, was being adopted. Brown was estranged from his former non-Indian fiancée, Veronica's birth mother, and she was the one who decided to put their baby up for adoption while she was pregnant. She never informed Brown of her plans. Soon after she was born, Veronica went to live with a white couple from South Carolina, who subsequently filed a petition for adoption. Brown, awaiting his deployment, was served with adoption papers when his daughter was four months old and already living in South Carolina. He previously believed that his daughter was with her mother and was unaware that the baby had been taken out of state.

A series of bureaucratic mishandlings and mishaps ensued. The birth mother had arranged for the private adoption, though she was aware that Veronica's father was a Cherokee citizen. Her attorney contacted the Cherokee Nation of Oklahoma to inquire if Brown's daughter was eligible for citizenship too, but misspelled Brown's name and gave an incorrect date of birth. These errors failed to produce the correct information about Brown's citizenship, who is one of the Cherokee Nation of Oklahoma's 355,000 citizens, and thus about his own children's eligibility for Cherokee citizenship. A second problem emerged when the Interstate Compact of Children form, processed because Veronica was born in Oklahoma, did not state that the child was an American Indian. If it had been filed correctly, the Cherokee Nation of Oklahoma would have been notified of the adoption proceedings and intervened, and Veronica would never have been illegally taken from Oklahoma. Furthermore, when Dusten Brown signed the papers prior to his deployment to Iraq, he believed he was relinquishing his parental rights to his daughter's mother, not to a couple from South Carolina who did not share his Cherokee identity.

Once Brown realized that Veronica's mother's plan was to have their daughter adopted by a non-Indian family in another state, he was faced with losing his child. The day after signing the papers, Brown realized his error and immediately consulted an attorney. As an active member of the military, he had no choice but to leave for Iraq, where he served in the US Army for the following year. In what must have been an agonizing departure, he left for Iraq without knowing his daughter's future.

As deeply troubling as this case was from the beginning, it got worse as it made its way to the US Supreme Court. When the non-Indian family took the baby to live permanently in South Carolina without informing Dusten Brown or the Cherokee Nation, there was a double sense of loss. Brown lost a fundamental right all parents possess, and the case also resonated for tribal people and their nations across the United States, who had struggled since the boarding school era against the removal of their children. Tribal nations had found support for their struggle within the legal grounds of the ICWA, but even that legislation was not sufficient to protect tribal jurisdiction over all of their relatives and kin, including the youngest and most vulnerable of their citizens.

What makes *Adoptive Couple v. Baby Girl* more than a custody dispute is the issue of sovereignty of tribal nations over their citizens. Indigenous sovereignty predates the formation of the United States but was virtually unrecognized and dismissed by US law until the self-determination era of the 1970s and laws such as the ICWA. Brown, supported by his tribal nation, went to court in South Carolina to assert his parental rights and explain that he and the Cherokee Nation were left out of the private adoption plans and to object to his daughter's removal from Oklahoma. The ACLU and the ACLU of South Carolina became early allies for Brown and the Cherokee Nation in this case, and stepped in to concur that the South Carolina Supreme Court properly applied ICWA when it ruled in favor of Dusten Brown.

The lower courts in South Carolina upheld the terms of the ICWA. They recognized that the law applied in this case to "children who are members of a federally-recognized tribe or eligible for membership and the biological child of a tribal member." They also recognized that Dusten Brown had not received proper notification according to the ICWA procedures, and there was no basis to terminate the Cherokee father's rights. It was clear that it was the mother, not the father, who had decided to put the child up for adoption. In addition, the Cherokee Tribe of Oklahoma was never notified of the potential adoption of a Cherokee descendent, one eligible for tribal enrollment, an ICWA requirement.

The case was complicated in ways that involved both race and gender. South Carolina, where Veronica resided with the white family who planned to adopt her, puts limits on the rights of unwed fathers. The petitioners argued that ICWA did not apply because the baby girl had never lived with an Indian family because her biological mother was non-Indian and "Hispanic." It bears reiterating that the biological father was deployed to Iraq for a year shortly after Veronica's birth, and under such circumstances knew that he could not be a full-time custodial parent until he returned to the United States. The courts ruled in favor of Brown and the Cherokee Nation, and in 2011, he assumed custody of his daughter, by then a two-year-old toddler. Veronica returned to her family and tribal nation in Oklahoma, where she remained for the next two years. But the case was not over.

When the adoptive couple, Matt and Melanie Capobianco, petitioned the case further, a disturbing decision emerged from the US Supreme Court regarding *Adoptive Couple v. Baby Girl*. In a stunning 5–4 decision, issued in June 2013 and at odds with the decades of federal legislation of the Indian Child Welfare Act, the Court held that a noncustodial father did not hold rights under ICWA, and the case returned to South Carolina because the adoption process was not fully complete. Once there, the courts reversed their earlier decision and eventually endorsed a determination that ICWA did not apply to the South Carolina case. Though Brown went to extraordinary lengths to keep his daughter, he had deployed to Iraq in the US military for over a year, and thus was not always present for the earliest parts of his child's life. From many angles, the decision to uphold the white South Carolina family's interests was shocking and distressing, especially to the Cherokee Nation of Oklahoma.

This ruling was a nightmare for Dusten Brown, an involved father and military veteran who demonstrated tremendous love and concern for his daughter. Furthermore, Veronica had been living with her father in Oklahoma for two years before the Supreme Court decision shattered their family life. Despite the legal intervention of his tribe, the courts finalized the adoption in South Carolina. The Oklahoma

Supreme Court almost immediately prohibited the decision because the child was residing with her father in Oklahoma. Nonetheless, in 2013, Matt and Melanie Capobianco assumed custody of the girl. Soon after her fourth birthday, they legally adopted her, despite her father's heart-rending objections and the deep legal opposition of the Cherokee Nation of Oklahoma. Later that year, the Capobiancos filed a lawsuit in Oklahoma against the military veteran father and his tribal nation totaling $1 million, as compensation for the expenses and legal fees they had accrued in their custody battle for Veronica. The Cherokee Nation responded appropriately, and their motion to dismiss the case, citing their sovereign immunity from suits without their consent, was granted.

As noted, the Indian Child Welfare Act was a landmark decision in the long quest of American Indian people and their tribal nations to protect their youngest citizens from being removed from their communities and cultures. It was also an important recognition of tribal sovereignty within tribes, as tribal courts and family service programs evolved to make the best decisions for the health and well-being of children in their communities. Off-reservation counties, courts, and adoption agencies were mandated to inform and collaborate with American Indian tribal nations in the work of Indian child welfare. This is critical considering that Indian children are more likely to be in the foster care system than the rest of the US population. Even for urban Indian children, tribal courts and programs back home on the reservation were increasingly involved in placement decisions regarding their youngest citizens.

ICWA has been a remarkably successful law and has been demonstrably good for tribal nations, children, and families and for the health and future of Indigenous community life. American Indian children were no longer set up to disappear completely into the child welfare system. In spite of the success of ICWA in placing children with Indian families and in culturally appropriate homes, its legal future has never been secure. Most troubling, at times the law has been dismissed by authorities at the state and local levels. Problems arise when county and state social workers, judges, and authorities violate the terms of ICWA and continue anachronistic and failed practices, which frequently result in placing American Indian children in non-Indian homes. States including South Dakota, the site of the Standing Rock resistance movement to oil pipelines (2016–2017), can be especially recalcitrant. South Dakota has nine tribal nations and governments within the state, and over half of the children in foster care in South Dakota are American Indians, though Indians comprise less than 9 percent of the state's population. Tribal nations have been forced to continuously defend the practice of maintaining sovereignty over their own citizens.

The ACLU has been a consistent ally to Indian Country, helping to ensure the proper implementation of the Indian Child Welfare Act. In a lawsuit filed in 2013 on behalf of the Oglala Sioux Tribe, the Rosebud Sioux Tribe, and three residents of Pennington County, the national American Civil Liberties Union, the ACLU of South Dakota, and a law firm in Rapid City, South Dakota, claimed that Indian children had been removed from their homes and families given only brief, inadequate hearings to determine whether they could get their children back. These hearings were fundamentally unfair. As the federal court noted, parents weren't given a copy of the charges against them, they were not allowed to offer any evidence on their behalf, they were not allowed to ask any questions of the social worker (who submitted a secret affidavit to the judge in all of these cases), they were denied counsel, and the judge made the decision based on the evidence submitted secretly.

In the aftermath, South Dakota made changes that allow for greater due process and rights under the terms of the Indian Child Welfare Act. For instance, parents now receive a copy of the petition and the affidavit filed against them by the ICWA worker and have the right to cross-examine the state's witnesses. They also have a right to counsel and the right to a decision by an impartial magistrate.

American Indian people, their tribal nations, and allies understand the necessity of the ICWA. The law is for the protection of Indian children and their families, so that Indian cultural and political formations persist in this country, even in the face of settler colonialism.

The case of *Adoptive Couple v. Baby Girl* illustrates that tribal nations must continue to struggle for sovereignty over their youngest citizens. In a contemporary story of Indian child removal, Dusten Brown knows what it is like to have a child permanently removed. He largely tried to avoid media attention as he pursued custody of his daughter under the terms of ICWA. Two years after the Supreme Court decision, he made just one short statement, and it came after the Cherokee Nation and the Bureau of Indian Affairs proposed new federal regulations to enforce the ICWA. Brown said simply, "Hopefully, these regulations keep other Indian children, families and tribes from suffering the heartbreak that we experienced over the last 5 ½ years."

UNITED STATES V. WINDSOR (2013)

United States v. Windsor is among the landmark legal cases in the recent history of the LGBT rights movement. At the heart of the contest was the constitutionality of the Defense of Marriage Act (DOMA), a 1996 law that had previously defined marriage for the purposes of the federal protections and benefits as the union of a man and a woman.

In conjunction with Paul, Weiss, Rifkind, Wharton and Garrison LLP, the ACLU represented widower Edith Windsor, who was forced to pay thousands of dollars in estate taxes upon the death of Thea Spyer, her wife and partner of forty years. Had Windsor been married to a man, she would have been exempt from these taxes under federal law. The couple had been married in Canada, and their union was recognized by New York State law; however, federal law, in accordance with DOMA, failed to recognize Windsor and Spyer as a married couple.

The Court's ruling found the Internal Revenue Service's interpretation of "marriage" and "spouse" in section 3 of DOMA in violation of the due process clause of the Fifth Amendment. The Court's opinions held that DOMA placed same-sex couples in the "unstable position of being a second-tier marriage," adding that such "differentiation demeans the couple, whose moral and sexual choices the Constitution protects."

The Court's decision in *Windsor* was also used as support in its reasoning for another landmark gay marriage case, *Obergefell v. Hodges* (2015), the decision for which was released on the second anniversary of the court's *Windsor* ruling. With *Windsor* and its legacy, an important aspect of full equality for people of all sexual orientations was achieved.

We Love You, Edie Windsor!

ANDREW SEAN GREER

I remember when the *Windsor* decision came out; I was overseas, in a country where gay marriage is not legal, and I awoke to the news with a sense of amazement and relief. I saw all my friends had taken to the streets in celebration; I was envious and felt far from home. I almost wished my middle-aged self could transport one message back to the nineteen-year-old Andy Greer marching across from the White House and tell him, "It's worth it; we won!" We all think of *Windsor* as the "gay marriage" case, but as with most other Supreme Court cases, it was supremely technical and unsentimental: in a truly American decision, it came down to taxes. The facts of the case hinged on Edie Windsor having to pay $363,053 in estate taxes after the death of her wife, Thea Clara Spyer, taxes a surviving spouse does not pay in the United States. Windsor and Spyer were legally married in Canada, but their marriage was not treated as a marriage by the federal government because of the 1996 Defense of Marriage Act (DOMA).

Despite the dry and technical elements of the case, I was not under the illusion that the core of this case had to do with taxes. Nobody was; Justice Antonin Scalia, in his dissenting opinion, wrote, "No one should be fooled; it is just a matter of listening and waiting for the other shoe. By formally declaring anyone opposed to same-sex marriage an enemy of human decency, the majority arms well every challenger to a state law restricting marriage to its traditional definition." Scalia was right: we were not fooled. We all knew what it meant: DOMA had just been ruled unconstitutional. It would be another two years before same-sex couples could legally marry in the United States, but by declaring DOMA unconstitutional, it was only a matter of time. A long, dark history of second-class citizenship was on the road to being abolished. I, reading the astonishing news from my room across the Atlantic, assumed, like many others, that full rights to all LGBT people would proceed from there. There was a sense, even among the most cynical, that the long, hard battle had been won. Forever.

Four years later, the Trump administration's Justice Department filed court papers in *Altitude Express v. Zarda Inc.* (2018), a case in which Don Zarda was fired from his job as a skydiving instructor because he was gay. "The sole question here is whether, as a matter of law, [federal civil rights law] reaches sexual orientation discrimination," the department wrote. "It does not, as has been settled for decades." The same day, Trump announced a ban on transgender people serving in the military. Less than a year later, the administration announced a "deploy or get out" policy in the US military; since service members living with HIV are nondeployable by current US military policy, that meant immediate discharge for those who were HIV positive. The Justice Department also argued to the Supreme Court that the Masterpiece Cakeshop should have a constitutional right to deny wedding cakes to gay couples. And so on.

I have written these paragraphs in as cool a legal manner as I can muster, and it's a handy thing that I am writing on a computer because if I had a pen in my hand it would be shaking with rage. Not at the Trump administration—it is no surprise they would wade in uninvited and urinate in the pool of freedom—but at myself. Not just myself a mere four years ago, when I breathed a sigh of relief, thinking I would no longer have to keep asking Amazon to delete one-star reviews that found my books "disgusting," or talk about my "wife" in small town diners, or butch it up in bars while waiting for a friend, just to keep from being beaten to a pulp. No, I'm enraged at myself right now—for still believing, despite all evidence, that the fairy-dust magic of marriage somehow dispels the smaller, pernicious evils of our country, when in fact, those evils are the only ones that count.

If we could tunnel back in time into a meeting of the LGBT Alliance at Brown University in 1990 and announce to the young people there (including my dear friends Angela, Kelli, and Ryan, and that nineteen-year-old Andy Greer, hair dyed blond) that gay marriage would be legal in twenty-five years, we would be met with laughing disdain. And why? Because of myriad battles we were fighting—for AIDS research, for women's rights, for bisexual rights, for transgender rights—not a single one of us was interested in marriage. Was it just because we were young? I don't think so. It's because we considered our lives to be in danger. Remember, we were watching our friends and fellow students die of AIDS in an unfeeling country, and lesbians harassed by police for dressing in masculine clothes, and women everywhere afraid to walk alone at night. We really were in it together: Angela, Kelli, Ryan, me, and all the others. We were, in a way, hold-overs from the seventies' gay rights movement, transformed in the eighties into one of rage and humor, but still with a single goal in mind: the sexual freedom of all people. Our slogan was, "We're here, we're queer, get used to it!" We did not want marriage and picket fences. We wanted to be something new and wild and queer. And we wanted equality with other citizens. Without having to dress or act like them. And more than that—we wanted to free heterosexuals as well, to break them out of their patterns, to open themselves to possibilities. If you had asked us then, I'm sure we would have said: "Marriage? Nobody should be married. But certainly not queers like us."

But even remembering the passionate disdain my friends and I felt for the idea of marriage, I don't blame us for celebrating *Windsor* two and a half decades later. Maybe we got older, and had partners and children of our own, and enjoyed a little normalcy. Maybe, like so many generations before us, we started out as rebels and mellowed into good neighbors. But really, I think we were so tired of fighting. It felt good, at last, to win and in some way hand over the fight to the next generation.

But the last few years have proven that we can't stop fighting. *Windsor* was a great moment in civil rights, but it wasn't ultimately what we were ever fighting for—and I know, from social media, that none of my old LGBTA friends have forgotten this. Because it is daily life that matters, and it is in daily life that the administration is waging its attack by telling us we are not protected by the law in anything except the abstraction of marriage; nothing flows from that single right. We are not fit to serve in the military (we've seen this one before). We are not fit to order the same cake or flowers as "normal" people. We are not fit to mention our lives in our workplace. We are being reminded that our lives depend not on federal protection but on the whims of our fellow citizens, whose hearts were not changed by the fact that the Supreme Court said we can now marry one another. And in this America, we are not human.

It was a beautiful day, the day that *United States v. Windsor* was decided. But I can think of days more beautiful still: the "kiss-in" we held in 1990 in the main quad of our campus, an act whose bravery seems hard to believe in these times, since it was just same-sex couples kissing (and since most of us were single and new to dating, as thrilling as a junior high dance). The 1991 antiwar march on Washington, protesting the Gulf War with ACT UP, in which a crowd of us crashed in my mom's living room and together took the Metro into the city with our outrageous signs for everyone to see. And the morning, years later in Montana, when a male friend came over to buff out the word FAG that had been keyed into the hood of my car, and I realized I had allies outside the gay community. And a reunion last year in Angela's house with Kelli and Ryan, all grown up and laughing at dinner because we had survived it all, were still totally queer, making queer art in the world. Those were beautiful days. And they were ordinary days when I did not feel afraid because I knew the people around me would protect me. And oh, because: love. You don't need to get married to join a fight for more days like that, for everyone.

ACLU V. UNITED STATES DEPARTMENT OF DEFENSE, ET AL. (2018)

Protests of the Dakota Access Pipeline (DAPL) at Standing Rock have come to symbolize the fight for climate justice. In May 2017, the watchdog group Intercept published leaked information indicating undue government scrutiny and surveillance of the Standing Rock environmental activists. Anticipating similar scrutiny by the government in response to planned protests of the Keystone XL Pipeline, the ACLU submitted a Freedom of Information request to the federal government to assess the character of the government's planned response to future pipeline protests. After many of the federal agencies withheld documents related to the government's activities, the ACLU brought a civil suit rooted in the agencies' refusal to release documents. The outcome of the litigation is pending at the time of writing.

Surveillance Capitalism Versus Indigenous-Led Protest

LOUISE ERDRICH

Cattle now graze the floodplain of the Cannonball and Missouri Rivers at Standing Rock, where the anti–Dakota Access Pipeline protest encampment once existed, but what happened there in 2016 reverberates. There is a powerful sense of unity and purpose among Indigenous people and environmental activists, but also an intensified collaboration between government law enforcement agencies and the private security firms hired by the corporate entities behind the large-scale fossil fuel pipelines. These groups are exchanging information about what worked to quell protest at Standing Rock. There, Indigenous-led peaceful prayer protesters faced water cannons used in freezing temperatures, attack dogs, beanbag cannons, tear gas grenades, tasers, rubber bullets, and long-range acoustic devices that beam concentrated sound intense enough to burst eardrums. If the Keystone XL pipeline, "game over for the planet" in the words of climate scientist James Hansen, wins court cases and crosses the Canadian border in Montana, these tactics and others will be the basis of a strategy of violent intimidation against protesters seeking not only to protect the water supply of Fort Peck reservation and surrounding communities, but to prevent the very worst effects of climate change.

In September 2018, the national American Civil Liberties Union and the ACLU of Montana sued federal agencies, including the Departments of Defense, Homeland Security, Interior, and Justice, over their refusal to release documents that detail antiprotest coordination between federal agencies and corporations. In advance of the civil action, the ACLU obtained, through right-to-know requests, the following information: The Montana Highway Department and US Department of Justice presented social networking and cyber awareness training in Circle, Montana. The Department of Justice hosted an "antiterrorism" training in Fort Harrison, Montana. The Bureau of Land Management hosted a "large incident planning meeting" in Miles City, Montana. The Federal Emergency Management Agency (FEMA) hosted "field force operations" training in Sidney and Glendive, Montana. And there are more. In addition to these sessions, the ACLU has documented government and corporate spying on and surveillance of Indigenous and environmental activists through social media and other venues.

"The First Amendment protects political speech from undue government scrutiny, and the extent of such scrutiny is currently unknown," wrote Jacob Hutt in an ACLU blog post. "If the government is planning to prevent or monitor Indigenous and environmental protests, the activists involved have a right to know about it."

Interior emails obtained by Intercept detail how the security firm TigerSwan operated without a license in North Dakota to monitor and infiltrate anti-DAPL protesters, as well as attempt to control public narrative. By labeling peaceful protesters "jihadists" and "terrorists," by calling the protest an "insurgency," the camp a "battlefield," and planting disinformation, TigerSwan fostered a good-versus-evil standoff that helped spread fear of protesters and justify the violent tactics that law enforcement used. There is no profit in depicting protesters as human, ordinary, or speaking for the public good. When government agencies get their information from profiteers of violence, it is tainted by business incentives that exploit paranoia and, increasingly, by extralegal information gathered via aerial surveillance and radio eavesdropping.

In addition, using the language of terrorism to describe citizen dissent makes it sound as though there is some form of national security at stake. In fact, quite the opposite is true. Climate change is already politically destabilizing the world as droughts cause mass migration and war. And what TransCanada and Energy Transfer Partners is doing has intensified climate change and will continue to do so. New pipelines will not make gas cheaper, and they do not have anything to do with ensuring a strategic supply of fuels for the United States. Since 9/11, our country has become energy self-sufficient. If we put our money in the right place, we could be clean energy self-sufficient. The Keystone XL pipeline is being built to ship the world's filthiest fuel, tar sands oil, which is obtained from stripping the boreal forest from Alberta, Canada. This heavy bituminous sludge would be pushed down to the Gulf of Mexico, and from there, refined and mostly exported.

In effect, the United States would pay an incalculable ecological cost in order to add billions to the Canadian economy. All along the way, this project has faced determined local and state opposition for good reason. All pipelines inevitably leak, and climate change is progressing more quickly and dangerously than anyone anticipated.

The Keystone XL tar sands pipeline would cross the Missouri River a quarter mile upriver from Fort Peck's southwestern border. The intake plant for the Assiniboine and Sioux rural water supply system lies seventy miles downstream. The tribe has treaty rights to the waters of the Missouri River, but years of tribal requests, courtroom testimony, public comments, letter after letter of protest, newspaper reports, and even personal letters to Justin Trudeau, Canada's prime minister, have gone unanswered. TransCanada's risk assessment study for the pipeline makes no mention of the water supply for the Assiniboine and Sioux, or for the surrounding non-Indian communities that depend on that water. Sandra White Eagle, program director of the water supply system, says that when a pipeline spill occurs, it would reach their water treatment plant in a couple of hours, and then "we're dead in the water." Fort Peck has already suffered the carcinogenic contamination of its northern aquifer by fracking. They know exactly what can happen.

"The government has a history of punishing those that fight for what is right," said Angeline Cheek, a Hunkpapa and Lakota activist, community organizer, and teacher from the Fort Peck reservation. "Now as people of different nations fight to defend their rights, land, water, identity and people, history is repeating itself. But the strength of our ancestors will remain within us. . . . We are the dream and vision of our ancestors. In prayers we are united—all my relations (*mitakuye oyasin*)."

Here in Minnesota, where I live, the ACLU is entering the fight for environmental justice. Another pipeline company, Enbridge, is pushing to build a thousand-mile tar sands pipeline, Line 3, which would cross tribal lands in northern Minnesota, endangering pristine lakes, wild rice beds, and the Great Lakes, which holds one-fifth of the world's freshwater. ACLU Minnesota's official comment to the Public Utilities Commission stated that the environmental impact statement regarding this pipeline was inadequate and that the pipeline was a form of environment racism. And again, this pipeline is not needed. The dirty oil is mainly for export. The Indigenous organization Honor the Earth has stated that Enbridge should clean up its old disintegrating pipeline and absolutely should not build a newer, larger, longer one, which would have disastrous consequences.

Law enforcement is already tracking Line 3 dissent, online and on the ground. The city of Duluth, over strenuous local objection, approved a proposal for $84,000 worth of riot gear to stop their neighbors from saving their water. And TigerSwan has reportedly initiated a nine-state dragnet to collect antipipeline activist information.

Antipipeline protesters are not using their First Amendment rights as a riotous social exercise, but are trying to save our place on this rapidly warming earth. Indigenous people know how quickly a world can end. It has happened to our cultures and our relatives many times. If fossil fuel interests are not checked, the resulting climate, blisteringly hot and with oceanic surges of water, will eliminate most of humanity. The so-called extremists opposing pipelines are acting on scientific fact. Energy Transfer Partners, TransCanada, and other giant pipeline corporations are operating out of an irrational and willful blindness that amounts to corporate terrorism. These companies seek to lock in fossil fuel infrastructure so that there is no clean energy alternative. In the face of such world-destroying greed, Standing Rock was an instance of collective sanity. Protest in Fort Peck, against Line 3 in Minnesota, or at other pipeline protests all over the world, is the triumph of hope over nihilism.

By defending the right to free assembly, the right to dissent, the right to know what the government is planning to quash Indigenous dissent and environmental activism, the ACLU is working toward a future place for us on this wildly beautiful, generous, living earth.

Acknowledgments

This book owes everything to Stacy Sullivan of the ACLU, who not only instigated it but shepherded it with such competence, confidence, and grace. James Esseks also was integral to its inception.

Thanks to Anthony Romero and David Cole for allowing us to celebrate the ACLU in this way.

Most special thanks to Tony Horwitz, whose editorial eye, remarkable reporting, and gorgeous prose will be missed so very much.

Thanks to the ACLU fact-checkers: Mark Carter, Nusrat Choudhury, David Cole, Jennifer Dalven, Zeke Edwards, James Esseks, Jonathan Hafetz, Omar Jadwat, Olivia Langley, Lenora Lapidus, Dan Mach, Susan Mizner, Stephen Pevar, Hina Shamsi, Chase Strangio, Betty Vine, Ben Wizner.

Thanks to Cecillia Wang and Laurie Hobart.

When we put the call out for help with writing the case introductions, professors Ian Haney Lopez and Laurel Fletcher of UC Berkeley Law School, and Jeannie Suk of Harvard Law School, sent students our way.

We must acknowledge the herculean efforts of Griffin Brunk, who wrote close to half of the case introductions, despite being enrolled both in law school and in a PhD program. Kyle Tramont also did more than his share. Thanks to Alexander Andresian, Brittany Arsiniega, Alexandra Avvocato, Tyler Bittner, Simeon Botwinick, Kathryn Combs, William Dobbs-Allsopp, Zachary Fuchs, Victoria Hall-Palerm, Shermila Kher, Minjae Kim, Monica Kwok, Nicole Lindahl, Alex Mabanta, Marissa Medansky, Priya Menon, Mohsin Mirza, Sanaz Payandeh, Daniel Parino, Kevin Ratana Patumwat, Mary Ross, Natalie Ritchie, Dru Spiller, Victoria Tang, Michael Zhang, and Ayyan Zubair.

Thanks to Michael Marshall Smith, John H. Bracey Jr., Christian Gregory, Edward R. Schmitt, and Caroline Rule.

Thanks to C-SPAN, Professor Murray Dry, Lauren Heaton, Don Herzog, Niquelle Orr, Jesse Rothman, Kayla Rothman-Zecher, Scott Sanders, Norman Slutsky, Nadine Strossen, and Ben Wizner.

Thanks also to professors Ronit Stahl, Dylan Penningroth, Mark Brilliant, and Christopher W. Schmidt.

We are grateful to our remarkable editor Jofie Ferrari-Adler, who supported this project wholeheartedly, and to the entire team at Simon & Schuster: Carolyn Reidy, Jonathan Karp, Meredith Vilarello, Ben Loehnen, Jordan Rodman, Alison Forner, Richard Ljoenes, Julianna Haubner, Carolyn Kelly, Allie Lawrence, Morgan Hoit, Brigid Black, Amanda Mulholland, Julie Ficks, Erich Hobbing, Kayley Hoffman, and Beverly Miller.

Special thanks to Daniel Kirschen, agent extraordinaire, and to ICM, which represented this book without renumeration.

Above all, the writers would like to express their gratitude to the ACLU for all that they do to keep our country sane and kind.

The Contributors

RABIH ALAMEDDINE is the author of the novels *Koolaids*; *I, the Divine*; *The Hakawati*; *An Unnecessary Woman*; the story collection, *The Perv*; and most recently, *The Angel of History*.

CHARLIE JANE ANDERS is the author of *The City in the Middle of the Night* and *All the Birds in the Sky*. She hosts the Writers with Drinks reading series in San Francisco and with Annalee Newitz cohosts a podcast, Our Opinions Are Correct.

BRIT BENNETT is the author of *The Mothers*. She earned her MFA in fiction at the University of Michigan, and her essays are featured in the *New Yorker*, the *New York Times Magazine*, the *Paris Review*, and *Jezebel*.

GERALDINE BROOKS is an Australian-born author and journalist who has written five novels, including the 2006 Pulitzer Prize winner, *March*. She was a *Wall Street Journal* correspondent for ten years, covering crises in the Middle East, Africa, and the Balkans. Her nonfiction work on Muslim women, *Nine Parts of Desire*, has been translated into more than twenty-five languages. She was awarded the Dayton Literary Peace Prize Lifetime Achievement Award in 2010 and in 2016 was named an Officer in the Order of Australia.

MICHAEL CHABON is the author of numerous novels, among them *Moonglow* and *The Amazing Adventures of Kavalier and Clay*, which was awarded the 2001 Pulitzer Prize for Fiction. He is the coeditor of *Kingdom of Olives and Ash: Writers Confront the Occupation*.

BRENDA J. CHILD is Northrop Professor of American Studies at the University of Minnesota. She is the author of several books on American Indian history, including *Boarding School Seasons: American Indian Families, 1900–1940* (1998); *Holding Our World Together: Ojibwe Women and the Survival of Community* (2012); *My Grandfather's Knocking Sticks: Ojibwe Family Life and Labor on the Reservation* (2014). Child was born on the Red Lake Ojibwe Reservation in northern Minnesota, where she is a member of a committee writing a new constitution for the 12,000-member nation.

DAVID COLE is national legal director of the ACLU.

MICHAEL CUNNINGHAM is the author of six novels, including *The Hours*, which won the 1999 Pulitzer Prize and PEN Faulkner Award. He is a senior lecturer in English at Yale University.

SERGIO DE LA PAVA is the author of three novels: *A Naked Singularity*, *Personae*, and *Lost Empress*. He is also a career-long public defender and legal director at New York County Defender Services in Manhattan, where he represents indigent criminal defendants and advocates for large-scale criminal justice reform. He has taught at Seton Hall Law School and presented on criminal justice issues for the *Guardian*, MoMA PS1, Harvard Law School, Public Radio International, UK Sky News, *New York Daily News*, and other venues.

ANTHONY DOERR lives with his family in Boise, Idaho. His most recent novel, *All the Light We Cannot See*, won the Pulitzer Prize for Fiction.

JENNIFER EGAN is the author of several novels, most recently *Manhattan Beach*.

TIMOTHY EGAN is a contributing op-ed columnist for the *New York Times*, where he shares a Pulitzer Prize for the series, "How Race Is Lived in America." He won the 2006 National Book Award for nonfiction and the Carnegie Medal for a nonfiction book. His most recent book of nonfiction, *The Immortal Irishman,* was called "one of the finest Irish American books ever written," and was a *New York Times* best seller.

DAVE EGGERS is the author or coeditor of many books, including *The Circle*; *The Parade*; *The Voice of Witness Reader: Ten Years of Amplifying Unheard Voices*; and *Surviving Justice: America's Wrongfully Convicted and Exonerated.*

LOUISE ERDRICH's most recent works include *The Round House* and *LaRose.* She owns a small independent bookstore in Minneapolis, Birchbark Books.

WILLIAM FINNEGAN is the author of five books, including *Barbarian Days: A Surfing Life,* winner of the 2016 Pulitzer Prize for autobiography. He has been a staff writer at *The New Yorker* since 1987.

NEIL GAIMAN is the Carnegie Medal, Newbery, Hugo, and Nebula award-winning author of *American Gods, The Graveyard Book, Neverwhere,* and *The Sandman.* Most recently he was showrunner for his adaptation for Amazon and the BBC of *Good Omens,* which he and Terry Pratchett wrote together. A passionate believer in the First Amendment, he is professor in the arts at Bard College and a United Nations Goodwill Ambassador for Refugees.

ANDREW SEAN GREER is the best-selling and Pulitzer Prize–winning author of *How It Was for Me, The Path of Minor Planets, The Confessions of Max Tivoli, The Story of a Marriage, The Impossible Lives of Greta Wells,* and *Less.* He lives in San Francisco.

LAUREN GROFF is the author of five books, including the National Book Award finalists *Fates and Furies,* a novel, and *Florida,* a story collection. She lives in Gainesville, Florida.

YAA GYASI was born in Mampong, Ghana, and raised in Huntsville, Alabama. Her first novel, *Homegoing*, won the PEN/Hemingway Award, the National Book Critic Circle's John Leonard Award, and an American Book Award. She was a National Book Foundation 5 Under 35 honoree and one of Granta's 2017 Best of Young American Novelists. She lives in New York.

DANIEL HANDLER is the author of seven novels, including *All The Dirty Parts* and *Bottle Grove* and, as Lemony Snicket, far too many books for children.

ALEKSANDAR HEMON is the author of *The Lazarus Project* and *This Does Not Belong to You/My Parents: An Introduction.* He has written for film and television, most recently for the Netflix show *Sense8.* He teaches at Princeton University.

MARLON JAMES is the winner of the 2015 Man Booker Prize. His most recent novel is *Black Leopard, Red Wolf.*

VICTOR LAVALLE is the author of seven works of fiction and a comic book. His most recent novel is *The Changeling.* He teaches writing at Columbia University and lives with his family in New York.

ADRIAN NICOLE LEBLANC is a journalist who lives in New York City. She is the author of *Random Family: Love, Drugs, Trouble, and Coming of Age in the Bronx*, and is finishing a book about stand-up comedy.

JONATHAN LETHEM is the author of *Dissident Gardens* and ten other novels. He lives in Los Angeles and Maine.

YIYUN LI is the author of seven books. Her most recent novel is *Where Reasons End.*

VIET THANH NGUYEN won the Pulitzer Prize in Fiction for his novel *The Sympathizer*. His other books include *Nothing Ever Dies:*

Vietnam and the Memory of War and *The Refugees*, a short story collection. He also edited *The Displaced: Refugee Writers on Refugee Lives* and is University Professor at the University of Southern California.

STEVEN OKAZAKI, an independent filmmaker, produced the 1986 Academy Award–nominated documentary *Unfinished Business: The Japanese American Internment Cases*, which told the stories of Min Yasui, Gordon Hirabayashi, and Fred Korematsu. He has produced numerous documentaries for HBO and PBS, including the Academy Award–winning *Days of Waiting* (1991), the Primetime Emmy–winning *White Light/Black Rain* (2007), and *Heroin: Cape Cod, USA* (2015).

MORGAN PARKER is the author of three poetry collections, most recently *Magical Negro*, and a young adult novel, *Who Put This Song On?*

ANN PATCHETT's latest novel is *The Dutch House*. She is the co-owner of Parnassus Books in Nashville, Tennessee.

MORIEL ROTHMAN-ZECHER is an Israeli-American novelist and poet. He is the recipient of the National Book Foundation's 5 Under 35 Honor. His first novel, *Sadness Is a White Bird*, won the Ohioana Book Award and was a finalist for the National Jewish Book Awards. His work has been published in the *New York Times*, the *Paris Review's Daily*, *ZYZZYVA*, and elsewhere. Moriel lives in Yellow Springs, Ohio, with his wife, Kayla, and their daughter, Nahar.

SALMAN RUSHDIE is the author of fourteen novels, a collection of short stories, and four works of nonfiction. He is a past president of PEN America.

GEORGE SAUNDERS is the author of ten books, including *Lincoln in the Bardo*, winner of the Man Booker Prize. He teaches in the Creative Writing Program at Syracuse University.

ELIZABETH STROUT is the author of seven works of fiction and the winner of the Pulitzer Prize for her 2008 novel, *Olive Kitteridge*. Her most recent work is *Anything Is Possible*, a pick of President Obama's best books for 2017.

MOSES SUMNEY is a performer and writer from Southern California by way of Accra, Ghana.

HECTOR TOBAR is the author of four books, including the novels *The Barbarian Nurseries* and *The Tattooed Soldier*. He is a native of Los Angeles and an associate professor at UC Irvine.

SCOTT TUROW is a writer and attorney. He is the author of eleven best-selling works of fiction and two nonfiction books about his experiences in the law, and his novels have been the basis of several films, including the movie *Presumed Innocent*. A former federal prosecutor, he served on a number of public bodies, including the Illinois Commission on Capital Punishment to recommend reforms to the Illinois death penalty system.

AYELET WALDMAN is the author of novels including *Love and Treasure*; works of nonfiction including *A Really Good Day*; and the coeditor of *Kingdom of Olives and Ash: Writers Confront the Occupation* and of *Inside This Place, Not of It: Narratives from Women's Prisons*.

JESMYN WARD is the author of the novels *Where the Line Bleeds*; *Salvage the Bones*, which won the 2011 National Book Award; and *Sing, Unburied, Sing*, which won the 2017 National Book Award. She is also the editor of the anthology *The Fire This Time* and the author of the memoir *Men We Reaped*, a finalist for the National Book Critics Circle Award. She has received the Strauss Living Award and a MacArthur grant. She lives in Mississippi with her family and is a professor of creative writing at Tulane University.

MEG WOLITZER is a novelist whose many books include *The Female Persuasion*, *The Interestings*, and *The Wife*. She was guest editor of *The Best American Short Stories 2017* and is a member of the MFA faculty at Stony Brook Southampton. She lives in New York City.

JACQUELINE WOODSON's books include *Brown Girl Dreaming*, *Another Brooklyn*, and *Red at the Bone*. She lives in Brooklyn, New York.

Copyright Credits

Copyright Credits

Copyright Credits